China in the Indian Ocean Region

India's Security Challenges

China in the Indian Ocean Region

India's Security Challenges

Prof. R. Sidda Goud

ALLIED PUBLISHERS PVT. LTD.

Noida • Mumbai • Kolkata • Chennai • Bangalore

ALLIED PUBLISHERS PRIVATE LIMITED

D-5, Sector-2, **Noida**–201 301
Ph. Nos.: 0120-4320295/2542557/4352866 • E-mail: delhi.books@alliedpublishers.com

17 Chittaranjan Avenue, **Kolkata**–700072
Ph.: 033-22129618 • E-mail: cal.books@alliedpublishers.com

15 J.N. Heredia Marg, Ballard Estate, **Mumbai**–400001
Ph.: 022-42126969 • E-mail: mumbai.books@alliedpublishers.com

No. 25/10, Commander-in-Chief Road, Ethiraj Lane (Next to Post Office)
Egmore, **Chennai**–600008
Ph.: 044-28223938 • E-mail: chennai.books@alliedpublishers.com

P.B. No. 9932, No. 15, 3rd Floor (Next to Vijaya Bank),
5th Cross, Gandhinagar, Karnataka, **Bangalore**–560009,
Ph.: 080-41530285 / 22386239 • E-mail: bngl.books@alliedpublishers.com

Website: www.alliedpublishers.com

First Reprint, 2024

ISBN: 978-93-90951-52-9

Published by Sunil Sachdev and printed by Ravi Sachdev at Allied Publishers Pvt. Ltd.,
D-5, Sector-2, Noida–201 301

Preface

The Indian Ocean, the third largest ocean in the world, surpasses the Atlantic and the Pacific Oceans in strategic significance as a trade corridor. The Indian Ocean Region (IOR), surrounded by Africa, Asia and Australia, serves as a maritime highway linking trans-continental human and economic relationships. Being the world's most populated region, one-third of the world's bulk cargo and two-thirds of the world oil shipments pass through it. The Strait of Malacca, located between Indonesia, Malaysia and Singapore, accounts for about 35 percent of global seaborne trade and is the shortest sea route between China, Japan, South Korea and Persian Gulf oil suppliers. If this Strait is choked for any reason, almost half of the world's fleet would need to rerouting, which could aggravate the oil and other transactional burdens for the importing countries. The Hormuz Strait, located between Iran and Oman, the world's most important 'oil chokepoint.' It has a daily oil flow accounting for about 40 percent of global seaborne trade and 90 percent of oil exported from Persian the Persian Gulf is destined for Asia.

China's interest in the Indian Ocean Region (IOR) can be traced back to the early 1960s when it began expressing solidarity with some of the beleaguered Afro-Asian states through economic and military aid. Since then, Beijing has increasingly deepened its presence in the Indian Ocean Region for a variety of reasons—oil, trade, security, etc. Currently, over thirty percent of China's seaborne trade, worth above $ 300 billion, transits across IOR. Sharing a quarter of the world's population, China faces an ever increasing demand for energy. According to a recent OPEC report, China consumed 12.79 million barrels of oil per day, which is about one-ninth of the world's total, while producing only 4.2 million barrels a day. In 2020, China used only half as much energy as the US. By 2009, it had surpassed the United States as the world's biggest energy user and later emerged as the number one oil importer. China has few choices but to look beyond its borders for its energy needs. About 77 percent of its oil imports are sourced from West Asia and Africa, transported through the Indian Ocean. Thus, China's dependence on the Indian Ocean continues to grow for energy imports from the Gulf, to import resources from Africa and for trade with Europe. China has been employing several soft power strategies, and in extreme cases, even force to satisfy its growing hunger for energy to fuel its economic growth.

Sea Lanes of Communications (SLOCs) in the Indian Ocean Region are not only vital for the world's economy, but for India too. According to K.M. Panikkar "while to other countries the Indian Ocean is the only one of the important oceanic areas, to India it is vital. Her lifelines are concentrated in that area, her freedom is dependent on the freedom of that water surface." India imports about 70 percent of its oil through the IOR to its various ports. As a consequence, China has been enhancing its strategic influence through the use of soft power, by becoming a major foreign investor in regional mining, oil, gas, and infrastructure projects. As the ability of China's navy to project power in the IOR grows, India is likely to feel even more vulnerable despite enjoying distinct geographical advantages in the region. China's growing naval presence around the Indian Ocean Region restricts India's freedom to manoeuvre. Of particular mention is what has been termed China's 'String of Pearls' strategy, which has significantly expanded China's strategic depth in India's backyard. China to protect its strategic sea lanes has a string of pearls strategy of bases and diplomatic ties that include the Gwadar port in Pakistan, naval and electronic intelligence-gathering facilities on the Burmese islands in the Bay of Bengal, port access and modernisation of Chittagong in Bangladesh, construction of Sri Lanka's harbor at Hambantota and serious plans for a canal construction across the Kra Isthmus in Thailand, also known as 'Kra canal', besides China initiating several corridors around India such as, CPEC, CMEC, BCIM, Polar Silk Road etc., part of China's Maritime Silk Road. These corridors may also facilitate encircling India in the long-run.

China's maritime presence in the Indian Ocean set to expand along with its economic interests, but the question for India is how to cope with this new geo-political reality. Indians are deeply apprehensive about the Chinese assertive and as well as aggressive attitude towards its neighbours and India. China has territorial disputes with all nations it shares border with and eight other nations also (Afghanistan, Bhutan, Burma, Brunei, Tajikistan, Cambodia, Indonesia, Taiwan, Kazakhstan, Laos, Kyrgyzstan, India, Malaysia, Mongolia, Nepal, Philippines, North Korea, Russia, Singapore, South Korea, Japan and Vietnam). Some of these countries do not belong to the Indian Ocean Region. India being a strong advocate of 'freedom of navigation in the sea' has made known its concern over China's aggressive postures in the South China Sea.

In the recent past, China announced $ 1.6 billion fund to advance its ambitious "Maritime Silk Road." This initiative aims to build ports and to improve maritime connectivity with Southeast Asia and Indian Ocean littoral countries, in support of infrastructure projects under the umbrella of the Silk Road plan. The MSR plan has become a key initiative of China's President after a high-profile trip to Southeast Asia in 2013. Hence, China is keen to set up free trade zones to link its coastal areas with countries in the Southeast Asia and the Indian Ocean, attempting to revive the ancient maritime Silk Road that connects China with the region. India, Sri Lanka, Malaysia, Singapore and Gulf countries have been sounded out about the initiative. The new Chinese plan focuses on infrastructure construction' in Pakistan, Sri Lanka and Bangladesh, where China is already involved in port projects. This clearly indicates China's intent to establish its footprints in the Indian Ocean Region.

In view of such Chinese assertive policies, India is compelled to carefully devise its own strategic responses. In the given circumstances one can't build a cordon against China's maritime presence nor does its growing influence in the Indian Ocean for free navigational rights to ensure energy security. However, many Indian strategists view Indian Ocean as India's 'rightful domain' and India has to play a mammoth role in ensuring prospects for peace and cooperation in the Indian Ocean Region. Therefore, in view of this fact, maritime friction is likely to increase between the countries of India and China, as the Indian Navy tries to expand its footprints in the South China Sea and the Western Pacific even as the Chinese Navy increases its presence in the Indian Ocean.

China and India are potential competitors for power and influence in the Indian Ocean Region, both countries share common interests in maintaining regional stability by combating the growing Islamic fundamentalist menace, exploiting economic opportunities, maintaining access to energy sources and markets and enhancing regional cooperation. On economic, environmental and cultural issues, both the countries have far more reason to build synergies. Improvement in China-India relationship will also depend upon Beijing's assessment of India's evolving political cohesion, economic growth, and military potential. China doesn't see India as a serious threat, but resulting change in India's stature as a rising power with its improved ties with USA is a new variable in the China's geo-political equations. Freedom of navigation is vital for China's and India's economic development as they both depend on the sea for trade and transportation. In view of the above, China and India's Indian Ocean strategies can mutually promote shared objectives amidst the tussle between India and China in the border since last May 2020, underpinning greater cooperation, rather than conflict or competition in the IOR.

Indo-Pacific has been widely used in recent years in global strategic and geo-political discourses. It was around 2010 that the Indo-Pacific gained importance in India, when New Delhi found promise in the idea in respect to its rationale and objectives to further India's national interests, international order in the seas, and freedom of navigation. But India seeks to develop a credible strategic deterrence against China. The Indo-Pacific idea provides India with a valuable opportunity to forge partnerships with the member countries of the Indo-Pacific by giving credence to the convergence of interests. The Indo-Pacific construct idea simply expands the conceptual region of Asia-Pacific to include India and the Indian Ocean. This strategic construct, besides including India and Japan is being bridged by Australia and supported by the US maritime dominance. The Quad translates this geopolitical understanding into strategy, envisaging the two oceans as a single strategic interest and security space.

The Biden administration sees the Quad grouping of the US, India, Japan and Australia as the fundamental foundation for establishing a substantial American policy in the strategically vital Indo-Pacific region. The US new dispensation of Biden declared recently that the Quad and the Indo-Pacific policies of the Trump Administration are one of the few policies that the Biden administration would like to continue to build on and strengthen is a welcome step from the Indian point of view, as these are useful to balance China's assertive efforts.

After Narendra Modi became the Prime Minister of India, his administration has constantly initiated several steps aimed at addressing China's influence in the Indian Ocean Region. To begin with, Modi has visited several small island countries in the IOR to improve relations. India has declared project 'Mousam' as an answer to Chinese Maritime Silk Road Plan. India is very active during the tenure of PM Modi in respect of multilateralism and multilateral forums in India's neighbourhood to mobilise opinion against China's increasing influence in the Indian Ocean Region. The grouping of 'Quad' and strengthening of it with Australia in the Malabar exercises is aimed to send signals to China amid India-China tensions in the border. China has implemented several initiatives and corridors under its Belt and Road initiative around India for the last one decade which may lead to encircle India, apart from its 'String of Pearl' strategy. Therefore, present dispensation in the New Delhi under PM Modi is taking all steps to face the challenges by China due to its "strengths as deemed to strategizing" to encirclement of India.

About the Book

This book is an outcome of the final report of the project sanctioned by the ICSSR, New Delhi under Senior Research Fellow for a period of two years, 2019–21 to carry out a study on 'China in the Indian Ocean Region: India's Security Challenges.'

Indian Ocean, the third largest Ocean in the world, surpasses the Atlantic and Pacific Oceans. Being world's most populated Region, one-third of the world's bulk cargo and two-thirds of world's oil ship tankers passes through the Indian Ocean. China's interests in the Indian Ocean Region can be traced and backed by early 60s. Ever since Beijing has been increasingly deepening its presence in the Indian Ocean Region for a variety of reasons, such as, oil, trade and security etc. Over 30 per cent of China's seaborne trade worth about $ 300 billion transits across Indian Ocean Region. Sharing a quarter of the world's population, China facing ever increasing demand for energy. China has little choice but to look beyond its borders for its energy requirements. Around 77 percent of its oil imports are sourced from West Asia and Africa and these are transporting through the Indian Ocean via Malacca Strait. Thus, China's dependency on Indian Ocean Region continues to grow for energy imports from gulf and to import resources from Africa and trade with Europe. With China steadily spreading its footprints in the IOR through increased military deployments and the rapid growth of its navy, equipped with warships, destroyers and nuclear submarines, it has pursued a strategy, known as the 'String of Pearls.' This strategy aims to establish a network of naval bases and facilities that could potentially encircle India at a convenient time in the near future. So, China has been emerging as the biggest threat for India by analyzing its actions in the Indian Ocean Region and along with India-China border from Easter Ladakh to Arunachal Pradesh as stand-off continues since June 2020. The Chief of the Indian Defence Staff, late Gen. Rawat also echoed the similar view recently in November 2021, stating that India faces biggest threat from China, much bigger than Pakistan.

To deal with Xi's China, the answer is through improving India's strength in all aspects, as there is a huge asymmetry between India and China. India will have to enhance its economic size over the coming years and quickly grow towards a minimum of $ 6–7 trillion economy to reduce the asymmetry and to face China on our own without depending much on Quad and Indo-Pacific grouping. Amid Russia's attack on Ukraine, India will need to keep a close watch on the annual exercises of the People's Liberation Army along the Line of Actual Control (LAC) and be prepared for any contingencies in the Indian Ocean Region. Additionally, China's pursuit of several infrastructural projects through the Belt and Road Initiative (BRI), aimed at serving its geopolitical interests, may pose security and economic implications for India. This book is particularly useful for students and scholars of international relations in the contemporary situation.

Acknowledgements

At the very outset I would like to thank sincerely the ICSSR, New Delhi for granting me this fellowship for the period of two years w.e.f. 1st March 2019 to 29th February 2021. This book is the outcome of the Fellowship sanctioned by the ICSSR, under Senior Research Fellow (SRF) category.

I would like to thank Osmania University authorities and officials of Non-UGC for their support and cooperation in providing office accommodation to me at Osmania University Centre for International Programmes. So, I wish to thank the Director of the OUCIP. I also thank the Head of the Department of Economics, Osmania University for support.

Further, I would like to thank few personalities who encouraged, guided and for their feedback through discussions during the tenure of the Fellowship and helped me in bringing out this book. First and foremost my gratitude to **Professor S.V. Seshagiri Rao,** Chancellor, Central University at Kasaragod of the Kerala state and Former Head, Department of Geophysics, Osmania University, Hyderabad for his valuable suggestions.

I also thank **Prof. P.V. Rao,** Emeritus Professor of Political Science (UGC & ICSSR) and former Director of Centre for Indian Ocean Studies, Osmania University, Hyderabad for his constant guidance. My thanks also goes to **Prof. G.V.C. Naidu,** Centre for Indo-Pacific Studies, School of International Studies, JNU New Delhi and to **Commodore Seshadri Vasan**, Indian Navy (Retd), Head, Strategy and Security Studies, Centre for Asian Studies, Chennai. Also, my thanks to **Lt. Col. Dr. Mohit Nayal, the** Strategic Analyst for his valuable suggestions.

My thanks are also owed to my former colleagues **Mrs. Maneesha Mukherjee** and **Dr. Sri Latha**, Associate Professors of the Center for Indian Ocean Studies, Osmania University for valuable suggestions. I also thank **Dr. B. Nagaraju**, Assistant Professor, Department of Economics & Development Studies, Mahatma Gandhi University—Nalgonda, Telangana, for his assistance and technical support.

Prof. R. Sidda Goud
Senior Research Fellow, ICSSR, New Delhi
Osmania University, Hyderabad, Telangana, India

Abbreviations

ASEAN	: Association of South East Asian Nations.
ANC	: Andaman Nicobar Command.
ARF	: ASEAN-Regional Forum.
ASBM	: Anti-Ship Ballistic Missiles.
ANI	: Andaman's & Nicobar Islands.
AIIB	: Asian Infrastructure Investment Bank.
ASI	: Archeological Survey of India.
AON	: Acceptance of Necessity.
AWACS	: Airborne Warning and Control Systems.
ADMM+8	: Asean Defence Ministers Meeting (its eight Dialogue Partners are namely, Australia, China, India, Japan, New Zealand, Republic of Korea (ROK), Russian Federation and the US).
BoB	: Bay of Bengal.
BJP	: Bharatiya Janata Party.
BIMSTEC	: Bay of Bengal Initiative for Multi-Sectoral Technical & Economic Cooperation.
BRICS	: Brazil, Russia India, China, South Africa.
BRF	: Belt & Road Forum.
BRO	: Border Roads Organization.
BIOT	: British Indian Ocean Territory.
BCIM-EC	: Bangladesh-China-India-Myanmar-Economic Corridor.
BRIN	: Bangladesh Russia India Nepal.
BRICS	: Bangladesh Russia India China South Africa.
BRI	: Belt & Road Initiative.
BBIN	: Bangladesh, Bhutan, India and Nepal.
bn	: Billion.
CPEC	: China Pakistan Economic Corridor.
CMEC	: China Myanmar Economic Corridor.
CTF	: Combined Task Force.
CBG	: Carrier Battle Group.
CDS	: Combined Defence Service.
CIOB	: Central Indian Ocean Basin.

CCP	: Chinese Communist Party.
DBO	: Daulat Beg Oldi.
EEZ	: Exclusive Economic Zone.
EAS	: East Asian Summit.
EU	: European Union.
FMS	: Foreign Military Sales.
FTA	: Free Trade Agreement.
FENC	: Far Eastern Naval Command.
FRANZ	: France, Australia and New Zealand (trilateral disaster relief arrangement).
GCC	: Gulf Cooperation Council.
G-7	: Group of Seven Nations.
GDP	: Gross Domestic Product.
HARD	: Humanitarian Assistance and Disaster Relief.
HRA	: High Risk Area.
HCQ	: Hydroxychloroquine.
IO	: Indian Ocean.
IOR	: Indian Ocean Region.
ICO	: International Liaison Officers.
IFC-IOR	: Information Fusion Centre for the Indian Ocean Region.
IOR-ARC	: Indian Ocean Rim Association for Regional Cooperation.
IUU	: Illegal Unregulated Unreported.
IAC	: Indigenous Air Craft.
IRTC	: International Recommended Transit Corridor.
IONS	: Indian Ocean Naval Symposium.
IORAG	: Indian Ocean Rim Academic Group.
IOMAC	: Indian Ocean Marine Affairs Cooperation.
IAF	: Indian Air Force.
INS	: Indian Navy Service.
IOR-ARC	: Indian Ocean Regional Association of Regional Co-operation.
IMB	: International Maritime Bureau.
ISPS	: International Ship & Port Security.
ICG	: Indian Coast Guard.
IT	: Information Technology.
IRTC	: International Recommended Transit Corridor.

IAC	:	Indigenous Air Craft.
IMR	:	Infant Mortality Rate.
ISC	:	Information Sharing Centre.
IBSA	:	India Brazil and South Africa.
IMSS	:	Indian Maritime Security Strategy.
ISBA	:	International Sea Bed Authority.
IMF	:	International Monetary Fund.
ICBM	:	Inter-Continental Ballistic Missile.
IMO	:	International Maritime Organization.
IDEAS	:	Indian Development Assistance Scheme.
J&K	:	Jammu & Kashmir.
JV	:	Joint Venture.
KKH	:	Karakoram Highway.
LIMO	:	Low Intensity Maritime Operations.
LAC	:	Line of Actual Control.
LEMOA	:	Logistic Exchange Memorandum of Agreement.
LNG	:	Liquefied Natural Gas
MGC	:	Mekong Ganga Cooperation.
MDA	:	Maritime Domain Awareness.
MILAN	:	Is a biannual Naval Exercise conducts since 1995 in the IOR.
MLSA	:	Mutual Logistics Support Agreement.
MSR	:	Maritime Silk Road.
MoU	:	Memorandum of Understanding.
MH-60r	:	Multi Mission Aircraft (was designed to support a variety of missions, including especial operations forces support).
NATO	:	North Atlantic Treaty Organization.
NLD	:	National League Democracy.
NIB	:	Nepal, India and Bangladesh.
NE	:	North-East.
NCE	:	Non-Combatant Evacuation.
NIB	:	Nepal, India and Bangladesh.
NBR	:	National Board of Revenue.
OBOR	:	One Belt One Road.
ORF	:	Organization Research Foundation.
OPEC	:	Organization of Petroleum Exporting Countries.

P-81	:	Is a long-range, multi-mission maritime patrol aircraft.
PNG	:	Papua New Guinea.
PoK	:	Pakistan occupied Kashmir.
PCMSP	:	Privately Contracted Maritime Security Professionals.
PLA	:	People's Liberation Army.
PRC	:	People's Republic China.
PM	:	Prime Minister.
PLAN	:	People's Liberation Army Navy.
PSR	:	Polar Silk Road.
QUAD	:	Quadrilateral Security Dialogue (QSD, also called as QUAD).
ReCAAP	:	Regional Cooperation Agreement on Combating Piracy and Armed Robbery.
RIC	:	Russia, India and China.
RSN	:	Republic of Singapore Navy.
SLOCs	:	Sea Lanes of Communications.
SCS	:	South China Sea.
SCO	:	Shanghai Cooperation Organization.
SAARC	:	South Asian Association of Regional Cooperation.
SOP	:	String of Pearls.
SIPRI	:	Stockholm International Peace Research Institute.
SAGAR	:	Security and Growth for All in the Region.
SIMBEX	:	Singapore India Maritime Bilateral Exercise.
SDG	:	Sustainable Development Goals.
Sq.km	:	Square Kilometers.
TPP	:	Trans Pacific Partnership.
TAR	:	Tibet Autonomous Region.
TMT	:	Trygg Matt Tracking.
TPSA	:	Tibetan Policy and Support Act.
TAA	:	Taiwan Assurance Act.
US	:	United States.
USA	:	United States of America.
USD	:	US Dollar.
UK	:	United Kingdom.
UAE	:	United Arab Emirates.
UNSC	:	United Nations Security Council.

UT	:	Union Territory.
UN	:	United Nations.
USSR	:	United Soviet Socialist Russia.
UPA	:	United Progressive Alliance (Congress led government).
UNCLOS	:	United Nations Convention on the Law of the Sea.
WHO	:	World Health Organisation.
WTC	:	Western Theater Command.
WTO	:	World Trade Organization.
UNESCO	:	United Nations Educational, Scientific and Cultural Organization.
ZTE Corporation	:	Zhongxing Telecommunication Equipment Corporation.
$	:	US Dollar.
5G	:	Fifth Generation.

Contents

List of Maps

List of Tables

CHAPTER I

Introduction

The Fall of the Cold War System and its impact on Asia carried serious geopolitical implications for India. India lost its close and dependable friend, the Soviet Union. India's relationship with the sole super power, the US was never warm, as were its relationship with the Asian powers like China, Japan and the ASEAN countries. Hence, India thoroughly revised its foreign policy objectives and strategic framework. India redefined foreign and strategic objectives aimed at moving closer to the USA and building equally closer relationship with the ASEAN countries, which India had neglected for a long time. A strategic partnership agreement was signed with the United States which led to build close bilateral, military, economic, technological and energy relationship between the two countries.

Similarly, India's 'Look East' Policy aimed at engaging closely with the Southeast and East Asian countries, as these countries represent Asian Dynamism. Assessing the outcome of the Look East policy, Prime Minister Narendra Modi upgraded it to the 'Act East' Policy, which is more dynamic and vibrant. India's strategic aspirations are to emerge as an Asian power and play an active role in the balance of power in Asia. A major objective of India's Asian strategy is to counter the growing power and the role of China in the Asian geo-politics and in the long run, in the Indian Ocean Region. Since the United States too is also concerned about the rise of China as an Asian and global giant, a strategic partnership exists between New Delhi and Washington. To bolster its strategic power, India is upgrading and building its military capabilities, and projecting power in Asia. India is adopting a dual strategy which aims at bolstering the hard military power and promoting close political, economic, energy and cultural synergies with Asian countries. A number of bilateral and multilateral agreements are signed with Asian countries, to the extent that there is hardly any Asian regional group in which India is not a member.

India's geographical location at the centre of east-west high-way across the Indian Ocean—linking Asia-Pacific with Europe, imposes greater security burdens on her. A large number of military, cargo and oil ships crisscross the sea lanes of Indian Ocean. Several regional and extra-regional powers that depend on the oil and resources of the Indian Ocean Region, have regular military presence in the Ocean. India has reason to be concerned about such military developments and regional conflicts, like the Iraq and Afghans wars.

India's primary concern is China's growing naval presence in the region, particularly in its neighborhood. India's defence preparedness is determined by the two-front threat to nation's security posed by Pakistan and China. Pakistan has historically been a close ally of both China and the US. These alliances have bolstered Pakistan's military strength and nuclear capabilities, making it a significant rival to India. After facing defeats in four wars with India, Pakistan has continuously fostered cross-border terrorism, especially in Punjab and Kashmir. Terrorism remains a major threat to India's national security. Additionally, India contends with cross-border military and criminal activities through Bangladesh, Nepal, and Sri Lanka, apart from Pakistan.

According to a survey conducted by the Australia, India Institute, University of Melbourne in May 2013, India perceives Pakistan and China as the biggest threats to the nation. The survey revealed that 84 percent of respondents believed threats from both countries are significant, with 60 percent identifying China and Pakistan as major threats. Additionally, 70% of the respondents agreed that, China aims to dominate Asia and 65% of people felt that, India should collaborate with other countries to limit China's influence[1]. Among those who identified China as a threat, over 80 percent cited reasons such as China's possession of nuclear weapons, its competition with India for resources in other countries, and its strengthening of relations with nations around India's periphery. Furthermore, 75 percent of respondents attributed the threat to China's strong military, its bigger economy, its military assistance to Pakistan, and its lack of because it doesn't show respect for India. As a result, managing the borders has become a major security task for the country. India's growing economy requires regular, uninterrupted oil supplies with 70 percent of energy needs being imported from Gulf countries. Ensuring adequate oil supplies should be a key goal of national security planning. In the overall interest of her growing security and economic interests, India must safeguard the Indian Ocean sea lanes, which China is attempting to bring under its influence.

India's growing economy requires regular, uninterrupted oil supplies, with about 70 percent of energy needs being imported from Gulf countries. Ensuring adequate oil supplies should be a key goal of national security planning. In light of its growing security and economic interests, India must safeguard the Indian Ocean Sea lanes, which China is attempting to bring under its influence.

The survey findings on Pakistan align with expectations, but include a significant counterintuitive element. While 94 percent of Indians believe that Pakistan poses a threat, 78 percent consider it is a major threat. Among those who identified Pakistan as a threat, over 90 per cent cited the possibility of terrorist attack from Pakistan, The Pakistan military's animosity to India, its possession of nuclear weapons; and its claims of sovereignty over Jammu and Kashmir as the primary reason for conflicts with India[2].

The findings of the Australia India Institute (AII) Melbourne were endorsed by Lt. Gen. Deependra Singh Honda (Retd.), a former northern Commander, and Happy Mon Jacob, Associate Professor of JNU, New Delhi. They recently co-founded the 'Council for Strategic and Defence Research', a New Delhi based think-tank. In an article published in 'The Hindu', on 29th December 2020, titled 'Dealing with India's Two-front Challenge—A politically guided doctrine and comprehensive military capability are needed to deal with the China-Pakistan collusion threat.

In the wake of the 'Balakot Strikes' and China's aggressive modernization of its armed forces, there were high expectations that the budget allocation for the three services—Indian Army, Navy, and Air Force—would be increased. Unfortunately, this did not happen. The allocation of Rs. 3.18 lakh crore, estimated at 1.6 percent of GDP, is the lowest since the 1962 war with China, according to experts. Notably, the allocation to navy from the defence budget declined to 13.5 percent in 2018 from 18 percent allocated during 2013–14, as reported by the Times of India on December 4, 2019. In stark contrast, China's defence budget has increased by 850 percent over 20 years, from $20 bn USD in 2002 to 224 bn USD in 2023[3], according to a Times of India report dated March 6, 2023. China possesses one of the largest militaries in the world and continues to enhance its capabilities. It has become increasingly proactive in the South China Sea and Africa, where it established its first overseas naval base in Djibouti in 2017[4] (Times of India, December 07, 2019).

China is well-known for trying to contain India's role and influence in the Indian Ocean through active bilateral and multilateral strategies. Its so-called 'String of Pearls' strategy and the OBOR (One Belt One Road) are hotly debated in the contemporary geopolitics. Additionally, Beijing has announced another strategy called the Maritime Silk Route (MSR). The objective of the MSR is to link China's east coast in the Pacific Ocean with the Indian Ocean via the South China Sea, Malacca Strait, Bay of Bengal, Central Indian Ocean, Africa, Red Sea and the Mediterranean Sea. This ambitious Maritime Scheme aims to connect almost all major littorals, with countries like the Maldives and Sri Lanka welcoming the MSR. India must be cautious about the implications of China's latest transoceanic doctrine. The potential impact on India needs to be seriously and continuously examined. The influence of the Maritime Silk Route can't be ignored by India, whose survival and destiny, by virtue of the Peninsula's critical location on the east-west maritime high way of the Indian Ocean, are heavily influenced by the geo-politics of the Indian Ocean.

The significance of the Indian Ocean Region (IOR) is loud and clear to the international community, especially in the recent times of globalization, where maritime trade, communications, and interactions are crucial. There are also some other new developments in the region, including the emerging power dynamics between the United States and a rising, resource-hungry China, as reflected in the Obama Administration's 'rebalance' strategy, and the idea of Indo-Pacific and Xi Jinping's 'Maritime Silk' road initiative, apart from non-traditional challenges such as piracy and natural disasters. China's actions, such as sending two submarines to Sri Lanka recently and deploying 7–8 warships in the Indian Ocean at any given time, are of particular concern to India. New Delhi faces several challenges in the region, but the government led by Modi has shown keen interest in addressing them. This is reflected in Prime Minister's visits to small island countries and commissioning of two naval vessels in his first hundred days of assuming office in June, 2014.

The traditional parameters of the Indian Ocean Region (IOR) remain the same, although fast changing due to the new actors and recent dynamics: (i) in terms of humanity, the Indian Ocean Region possessing of about 1/3rd of the world population, living in nearly 56 contiguous countries, including 1286 islands. These nations exhibit wide disparities in terms of territory, population, political systems, income levels, etc. (ii) geographically the Indian Ocean Region is about 74 mn sq.km in area and thus constitutes the third largest ocean in the world, after Pacific and Atlantic (iii) in terms of resources, the Indian Ocean Region is estimated to contain more than half of the global strategic resources and one-third of the world's gas resources. Huge deposits of uranium, gold, diamonds, coal, ore, iron, tea, jute and other resources are available in the countries of Indian Ocean Region. Hence, no rising or established power can afford to ignore these parameters. One-fifth of the global energy resources passes through the region and hence can be termed as a major strategic pass. Besides, several Asian manufacturing units also utilize the region for transporting goods to Europe and beyond and hence economically a major hub in the world[5]. As the Indian Ocean Region holds significant strategic raw minerals and gas reserves of the world, global dependence on such resources is expected to be intact long time to come in near future. The outward trade flow from the Indian Ocean Region constitutes nearly 80 percent and intra-Indian Ocean Region trade-a-mere 20 percent[6]. This underscores the IOR's critical role in global trade and resource supply chains.

Because of the narrow land outlets to other continents, the significance of the sea lines of communications and Choke points became prominent in this region. This character distinguishes the Indian Ocean Region from the Atlantic and Pacific Oceans. The Indian Ocean has nine major choke points, viz., the Strait of Malacca, Lombok and Sunda in eastern flank, while Hormuz, Red Sea Corridor, Suez Canal from the western flank, with Cape of Good Hope forming its South-Western flank. Of these, five routes are frequented by the energy resource-carrying ships—1/10th of the global trade oil is transported through the gulf of Aden, and about 40 percent of the global oil (15.5 mn barrel of oil) commerce passes through the Strait of Hormuz, compared to 11 million barrels through the Strait of Malacca[7]. Nearly 70,000 ships are passing through the Strait of Malacca every year. On an average, more than 80,000 ships pass through the Indian Ocean Region annually. Because of these narrow passes, their vulnerability has become a major security issue. During the cold war period, these choke points were kept under check partly due to super power rivalry and partly due to the presence of Western troops at Djibouti, Diego Garcia, Somalia and Comoros Islands and Soviets in Ethiopia and South Yemen[8]. Presently, as no single overarching security architecture prevails in the Indian Ocean Region, the situation breeds insecurities.

According to some estimates, the Indian Ocean Region constitutes about 70 percent of various forms of global disasters and hence from the point of view of security, this region is the global focus. With the above profile of the region, many powers have attempted to influence the region through unilateral, bilateral, or multilateral efforts. Foremost among these is the United States, which has a major base in the Indian Ocean Region with Diego Garcia, which has been used through the cold war and as recently as for global war on terrorism in Afghanistan and for Iraq operations. There is also a new idea coinciding with the rebalancing strategy—The Indo-Pacific region—to explain the new dynamics of the Indian Ocean Region. The US is the largest importer of energy from West Asia and Africa, besides over $ 1 trillion in trade transiting the Strait of Malacca every year. The US also needs to consider the interests of its allies' ships like Japan and South Korea. A number of US designated ships/tankers were also attacked by pirates for ransom affecting commerce.

China had been knocking at the doors of the Indian Ocean Region since the last two decades and had been contesting the US rebalance by selling its recent idea of Maritime Silk Road to its emerging allies and friends in the region through making bilateral and multilateral efforts. From around 2009, China had initiated a 'Two-Ocean Strategy' with Pacific and Indian Oceans as the focus. China's naval forces were deployed more than 14 times by 2013 for counter-piracy missions in the Gulf of Aden[9] and had sent rescue ships and aircraft for evacuation of thousands of Chinese citizens in Libya, Egypt and Syria. The context for China's new found enthusiasm in the Indian Ocean Region is domestic demands, apart from securing its burgeoning energy and raw material needs passing through the Indian Ocean Region. China has been active participant in the revival of the Asian Highway and Railway concepts and has made efforts to open up the country for expanding transportation corridors linking it with Southeast Asia, Central Asia and South Asia. China has been active only recently in expanding sea routes, as President XI Jinping announced Maritime Silk Road project in the Indonesian Senate in October 2013. Officials of Fujian province, one of the three key regions tasked with the MSR implementation, while setting up a fund of nearly $ 1.6 billion. This fund is to further the port development and other infrastructure projects in the Indian Ocean Region in future. To pursue these interests, China had been setting up dual use Maritime facilities in the Indian Ocean Region. One of the major project is the Gwadar port, a collaboration between China and Pakistan, is termed as a landmark in the bilateral relations similar to the Karakoram Highway project officially opened in 1978. Another project undertaken with active Chinese assistance is the Hambantota project in Sri Lanka which includes a port as well as an Airport. Originally offered to India, one phase of the port opened after cast escalation and "time overruns for international shipping" in 2012. China also offered to contract another port at Colombo with the assistance of China amounting to $ 50 bn.

In addition to expanding its interests in the South China Sea, China had also been making significant inroads in the region with implications for the Indian Ocean Region. China is reportedly planning to build an artificial island military base of five-square- kilometer with an airstrip and sea port at the Fiery Cross Reef with a cost of $ 5 billion. This is meant for forward power projection and enforcement of a proposed Air Defence Identification Zone in the region. In the long-term this is also meant to control the Strait of Malacca. China is also reclaiming areas at the Johnson South Reef, Gavin Reef and Calderon Reef contested by the Philippines. These projects are intended to support China's objectives in the Indian Ocean Region in the near future. As a major country in the Indian Ocean Region, with a vast coastline, vital national interests—commerce, energy imports, more than 4.2 million diaspora in the gulf countries and blue-water ambitions[10], India is an important factor in the Indian Ocean Region. India's parameters of security clearly extend beyond the confines of conventional geographical land borders. Given its size, location, trade-links and extensive Exclusive Economic Zone (EEZ), India's security environment extends from the Persian Gulf in the West to the Strait of Malacca in the east. Later in 2004 Indian Maritime Doctrine reiterated the sphere of interest, in addition to the Ministry of Defence annual report outlined in 2001, India's primary maritime interest is to ensure its national security.

This is not restricted to guarding the coastline and island territories, but also extends to safeguarding our interests in the EEZ as well as protecting our trade. This creates an environment that is conducive to rapid economic growth of the country. Further, in the 2007 "freedom to use the seas: India's maritime military strategy", the Indian navy had identified a few areas to implement, such as: (i) conflict with a state in our immediate neighborhood or clash of interest with an extra-regional power (ii) operations in the extended and/or strategic neighborhood in response to a request for assistance from a friendly nation (iii) Anti-terrorists operations—conducted multi-laterally or unilaterally (iv) actions to fulfill international bilateral strategic partnership obligations (v) ensure good order at sea, which includes Low Intensity Maritime Operations (LIMO), to combat asymmetric warfare, poaching, piracy and trafficking in arms/drugs (vi) actions to assist the Indian diaspora and Indian interests abroad (vii) ensuring safety and security of India's Sea Lanes through the Indian Ocean (viii) peacekeeping operations, under the aegis of the United Nations (UN), independently or as part of a multi-national force and Humanitarian Assistance and Disaster Relief (HADR) in our extended neighborhood or in response to a request for assistance from a friendly nation[11]. As a victim of the November 2008 Mumbai terror attacks through the Arabian Sea, India is at the forefront of tackling maritime security issues. There have been several attempts by the Indian Coast Guard and the Indian navy to combat such activities unilaterally, bilaterally and multilaterally. To curb maritime security issues in the coastal regions, India planned to commission 204 interceptor boats, 73 coastal security police stations, 97 check-posts and 58 outposts; however, progress in this regard has been slow.[12]

India has joined several bilateral/multilateral efforts in countering piracy and is one of the 16 members of the Regional Cooperation Agreement on Combating Piracy and Armed Robbery against Ships in Asia (ReCAAP). India hosted the first Indian Ocean Naval Symposium (IONS)—a conclave of naval chiefs from more than 30 Indian Ocean States, on February 18–19, 2008, in New Delhi. This is broad-based multilateral organization includes all major regional navies, while the US, UK and Japan have applied for "observer status"[13]. In 2006 India and the US agreed to the Indo-US framework for maritime security cooperation. 8500 naval staff from India and the US participated in a week-long maritime exercise "Malabar" in the Arabian Gulf. These exercises, which enhance interoperability between the two naval forces, have been conducted for over two decades. By July 2019, 23 such engagements had taken place, during which Japan was also invited to the Malabar exercise. Subsequently, Japan became a member of the Malabar exercises. Later, Australia also showed interest and became a member, making the Malabar exercises quadrilateral. India considered inviting Australia to the forthcoming 'Malabar' exercises, which were held in the Bay of Bengal in November 2020.

Apart from the above efforts made by the US, China and India, there are also multilateral initiatives to address emerging issues in the Indian Ocean Region. Among these, the non-security related multilateral grouping Indian Ocean Rim Association for Regional Cooperation (IOR-ARC), formed in 1997 in Mauritius, is notable[14]. Other initiatives include BIMST-EC, IORBF, IORAG, IOMAC, etc. However, the mandates of these institutions are focused more on expanding economic cooperation rather than tackling pirates. A Regional Cooperation Agreement on Combating Piracy and Armed Robbery against ships in Asia (ReCAAP) was concluded in 2004 by 16 countries of Asia mainly to resolve issues piracy in the Strait of Malacca. Given this backdrop, it is well known that India's Maritime interests are vast and expansive and defending them require considerable sea power. Besides a long coastline of about 7,600 km and numerous major and minor ports, nearly 96 percent of India's trade is sea-borne, including the bulk of its energy imports. Additionally, the two archipelagos of Andaman and Nicobar in the Bay of Bengal and Lakshadweep in the Arabian Sea, numbering around 400 islands, are situated far away from mainland but astride some of the most important sea trade routes in the Indian Ocean. India has also acquired an area of 2.2 million sq km of Ocean space as its Exclusive Economic Zone (EEZ).

Concomitantly, the Indian Navy's force structure is undergoing a fundamental shift. It has been receiving lot more attention both in terms of funding and political support, since the mid-2000s. It is on a course that would make it a blue-water-capable force if ambitious plans it has set were to be realized. According to former Naval Chief Adm. Nirmal Verma Former Naval Chief, by 2027 the Indian Navy will wear a brand new look with approximately 150 principal combatant ships and an additional fleet of around 500-aircraft. The share of the navy from the defence budget has also been steadily increasing, rising from 12.7 percent in 1990–91, to about 19 percent by 2012–13,[15] excluding allocations for the Coast Guard. But unfortunately, the share of navy has fallen again to 13.5 percent in 2018–19.

Along with a new force structure, an entirely new maritime strategy is taking shape. The earlier defensive and basically centered on coastal protection, is being replaced by a strategy under which the navy would be also able to undertake 'out of area operations'. Contrary to the past practice, between 2009 and 2012, the Indian navy has produced several documents on maritime doctrine (Indian maritime doctrine 2004 and a revised one in 2009) and strategy, known as freedom to use the seas; India's maritime military strategy, 2007. The Maritime Doctrine and strategy papers clearly delineate the region's primary and secondary interests in the Indian Ocean and beyond. The force modernization and the new strategies clearly suggest that India is aiming to emerge as the predominant power in the Indian Ocean. There is no question that China's potential role in the Indian Ocean figures in India's strategic calculations. It would be imprudent to take an unrealistic view of the threat it may pose, while keeping a watchful eye on China's emergence as a maritime power, its navy evolving into blue-water capability, and its activities in the Indian Ocean. Many concerns that India harboured during the Cold War have dissipated; however, a variety of new challenges have surfaced. New Delhi would certainly be wary of China's presence in the Indian Ocean, although it is a different issue to what extent China has the capabilities to make such forays by way of military bases. China certainly is involved in building several port facilities in countries around India and is actively courting island states such as the Maldives, Seychelles, Mauritius and Sri Lanka etc. with generous aid. In order to consolidate its position in the Indian Ocean, India has begun to qualitatively increase its engagement with its neighbours and the island states in the Indian Ocean, particularly after Narendra Modi took over charge as Prime Minister of India since 2014, through bilateral and multi-lateral cooperation. Secondly, India is also trying to enhance its political, economic and strategic leverage over the Maldives, Sri Lanka, Seychelles, Mauritius, Madagascar and Comoros etc. so that they do not undertake actions that might undermine Indian interests.

In any case, managing security in the Indian Ocean will be problematic since there are no mechanisms, military or non-military, track-I or track-II, or tangible regimes. The only multi-lateral institution that exists, the Indian Ocean Regional Association (IORA) is moribund and ineffectual, although security issues have been included in its agenda. India certainly harbours the ambition of emerging as a predominant power, but it cannot ignore the reality that they are many security challenges that need concerted multilateral efforts, as demonstrated in the counter-piracy operations in the Gulf of Aden. As India emerges as a net security provider by ensuring the security of sea lines of communication, China will have to depend on India to safeguard its trade in much of the Indian Ocean in the foreseeable future.

Yet, given the growing stakes of great powers in the region, they would strive to be present in one form or other. The US has a huge military presence in Diego Garcia, and China too may, in the long run, like to explore ways to protect its interests. Even Japan has opened its first overseas military base in Djibouti in 2001[16]. Given the Indian Ocean's growing security complexity, there is an urgent need to create certain maritime regimes and promote maritime dialogues, as well as confidence building measures and greater maritime cooperation, in an inclusive fashion so that any misunderstandings that may arise, are addressed and common interests are protected.

The Indian Ocean Region (IOR)

From a formal point of view, the Indian Ocean Region has been defined as comprising those states that border directly on the Indian Ocean. From a functional point of view the Indian Ocean Region comprises 19 states that belong to the Indian Ocean Region—(IOR-ARC). In the case of latter criterion, it includes, states associated with the tributary waters of the Indian Ocean as well as those land-locked states for which transit to and from the sea is primarily oriented towards the Indian Ocean. Using the broadest regional definition, the Indian Ocean consists of a total of 51 states, 28 of which are Indian Ocean Rim States, plus a further 10 that are coastal states of the Red Sea and the Persian Gulf, together with an additional 13 Indian Ocean land-lacked states.

Table 1.1: The 51 States of the Indian Ocean Region[17]

Sl No.	*Indian Ocean Rim States*	*Other Coastal States of the Red Sea and the Persian Gulf*	*Indian Ocean Land-lacked States*
1.	Australia	Bahrain	Afghanistan
2.	Bangladesh	Egypt	Bhutan
3.	Burma (Myanmar)	Eritrea	Botswana
4.	Comoros	Iraq	Burudi
5.	Djibouti	Israel	Ethiopia
6.	France *	Jordon	Lesotho
7.	Kenya	Kuwait	Malavi
8.	India	Saudi Arabia	Nepal
9.	Indonesia	Sudan	Rwanda
10.	Iran	Qatar	Swaziland
11.	Madagascar		Uganda
12.	Malaysia		Zambia
13.	Maldives		Zimbabwe
14.	Mauritius		
15.	Mozambique		
16.	Oman		
17.	Pakistan		
18.	Seychelles		
19.	Singapore		
20.	Somalia		
21.	South Africa		
22.	Sri Lanka		
23.	Tanzania		
24.	Thailand		
25.	Timor-Leste		
26.	United Arab Emirates		
27.	United Kingdom*		
28.	Yemen		

*For France and United Kingdom, because of their island territories.

Source: Indian Ocean Digest, a biannual Publication by Centre for Indian Ocean Studies, Osmania University, Hyderabad. Issue 54, January–June 2014, Vil. 33 No. 1.

One view of a preferred regional security construction is that, it will be built around the Indian Ocean Region. This view argues that strategic reassessments of the Indian Ocean Region and associated security challenges are contributing to the development of a new collective Indian Ocean security paradigm built on maritime regionalism. This paradigm is primarily designed to facilitate confidence building and to deal effectively with a wide range of so-called 'non-traditional' security challenges.

The Indian Ocean Region is potentially an arena for geostrategic rivalry among great powers, reinforced by the 'great base race' around the region. The result is an 'Indian-Oceanic arc of militarization' stretching from Egypt to Indonesia and Australia[18]. In 2010, the Indian Ocean Region included two of the world's top military spenders, Saudi Arabia and India, with 2.8 percent and 2.5 percent of global expenditure on arms respectively[19]. Attempts to objectively measure security and precisely define security threats are fraught with difficulty, unlike the number of piracy attacks. Threat assessment, at best, is an imprecise science, and depending on its policy impact, runs the risk of exacerbating insecurity between states. However, since World War II, most conflicts have occurred within, rather than between states.

Map 1.1: Indian Ocean Region

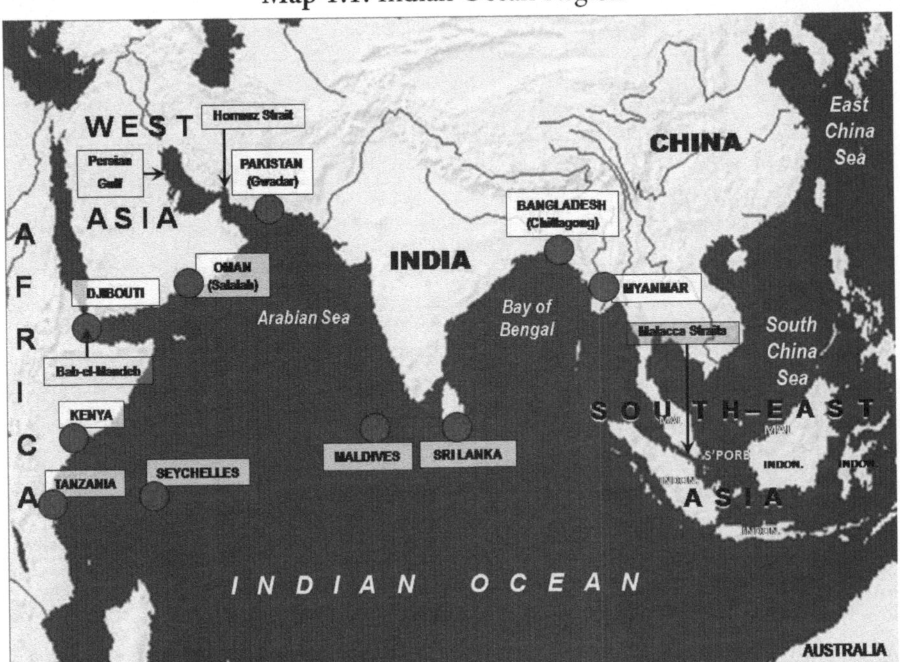

Source: www.googlemaps.com

Almost half of the Indian Ocean States have armed forces exceeding personnel 1,00,000 and/or military expenditure levels in excesses of three percent of GDP. Six states have armed forces in excess of 4,00,000 personnel—India, Pakistan, Vietnam, Iran, Burma and Egypt. The size of armed forces is not a good indicator of the degree of state militarization. Furthermore, five other Indian Ocean states have militarization levels above one percent—Brunei, Singapore, Oman, Bahrain, Djibouti. Of these 11 states, six have military expenditure exceeding 3 percent of GDP—Pakistan, Brunei, Singapore, Oman, Bahrain and Djibouti. Additionally,, four other regional states have similar military expenditure priorities—Saudi Arabia, Burundi, Sudan, and Kuwait. In short, by one measure, or another, approximately, one-third of all Indian Ocean States place a relatively high, and in some cases increasing expenditure priority on traditional military security.

Andaman and Nicobar Islands

The Andaman & Nicobar Islands, a Union Territory of India comprising 572 islands of which 37 are inhabited, are a group of islands at the junction of the Bay of Bengal and the Andaman Sea. The territory is about 159 km north of Aceh in Indonesia and is separated from Thailand and Myanmar by the Andaman Sea. It comprises two island groups, the Andaman Islands (partly) and the Nicobar Islands, separated by the 150 km wide Ten Degree Channel, with the Andamans to the north of this latitude, and the Nicobar to the South. The Andaman Sea lies to the east and the Bay of Bengal to the west.

The territory's capital is the city of Port Blair. The total land area of the Islands is approximately 8249 sq.km. The territory is divided into three districts: Nicobar district with Nicobar as its capital, South Andaman district with Port Blair as its capital, and North and Middle Andaman District with Mayabunder as its capital. The islands host the Andaman and Nicobar Command, the only tri-service geographical command of the Indian Armed Forces.

The Nicobar Islands are an archipelagic chain in the eastern Indian Ocean. They are located in Southeast Asia, 150 km north of Aceh on Sumatra, and separated from Thailand to the east by the Indian Sub-Continent, across the Bay of Bengal. They form part of the Union Territory of Andaman & Nicobar Islands, India. The archipelago, 1,000–1,400 km away from the mainland, is nearer to the South East Asian countries of Myanmar, Thailand and Indonesia. The southern tip of Great Nicobar, Indira Point, is only 145 km (six Degree Channel or Great Channel) from the Indonesian Island of

Sumatra. Great Nicobar is 450 km from Phuket, Thailand. North Andaman is 280 km Southwest of Cape Negrais and Middle Andaman is 520 km west of Mergui, Myanmar.

The Coco islands, a group of seven small islands, 30 km away from north Andaman, have an area of 20.5 sq.km. Though geographically part of Andaman Archipelago, they belong to Myanmar (In 1882, the Coco Islands were detached from India and placed under Burma by the British. In 1937, Burma was separated from India and was directly ruled from London as a Crown Colony until it became Independent in 1948). India should not be exclusively viewed as a South Asian nation. By virtue of the location of the Andaman & Nicobar Islands, it is also part of South East Asia.

The length of the Andaman Arc is 457 km, and of the Nicobar 259 km. The two archipelagos are separated by the Ten Degree Channel, which is 122 km wide. Out of the 520 islands, reefs, cays and banks of the archipelago, only 38 are inhabited: 26 in Andamans and 13 in Nicobar. The archipelago has an area of 8249 sq.km and the Nicobars have an area of 1841 sq.km. It has a coastline of 1962 km, 24.5 per cent of the coastline of India. One-third of India's Exclusive Economic Zone is due to the Andaman & Nicobar Archipelago.

The Andamans consist of six main Island—North Andaman (81 km long), Middle Andaman (71 km long), Baratang (28 km long), South Andaman (84 km long), Rutland (19 km long), and Little Andaman (43 km long). This main chain is flanked on the west by Interview Island (24 km long) and on the east by the Ritchie Archipelago. Among the principal outlining islands, mention may be made of the isolated mountain, the extinct Volcano of the Narcondam, rising 713 meters high, located 130 km to the North-east of Port Blair, and the North Sentinel Island, about 37 km to the west of South Andaman.

There are several straits separating these Islands: Austin (between North and Middle Andaman), Homfray's (between Middle and South Andaman), Macpherson (between south Andaman and Rutland), Amitla Boisha (between Baratang and south Andaman). The Diligent Strait separates South Andaman and Ritchie Archipelago. Rutland and Little Andaman are separated by the 50 km wide Duncan passage, which serves as the main commercial highway between the Andaman and the East Coast of the mainland.

The Nicobar Arc consists of five main Islands: Car Nicobar, Camorta, Katchell, Little Nicobar, and Great Nicobar. The Revello Channel separates Camorta and Katchell; Sombrero Channel separates Katchell and Little

Nicobar and St. George's Channel separates Little Nicobar and Great Nicobar. Trinket is a natural harbour. Great Nicobar, the largest, is 49 km long, and has an area of 1045 sq.km.

Map 1.2: Andaman and Nicobar Islands

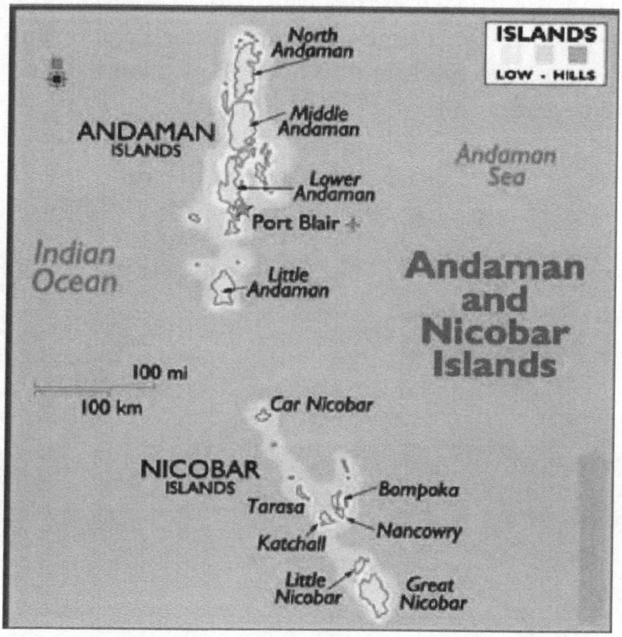

Source: www.googlemaps.com

Andaman Sea

The Andaman Sea, the eastern periphery of Indian Ocean, is flanked by Andaman and Nicobar Islands on the west, and by Myanmar, Thailand and Indonesia on the other three sides. It covers an area of 798,000 sq.km and is connected to the South China Sea through the Malacca Strait. India's Exclusive Economic Zone has spread into a large part of Andaman Sea. Ships traversing from the Suez, Gulf, South Asia, and North East Africa to Singapore Pass through the Great Channel (six Degree Channel) of the Andaman Sea. The Great Channel is the gateway to the Malacca Strait. Shipping through the Malacca Strait constitutes about 25 per cent of the world trade.

Lakshadweep Islands

The Lakshadweep Archipelago, located between 71–74 degree East Longitude and 8–12 degree north Latitude off the Coast of Kerala in the Arabian Sea, consists of 35 Islands. The total area of Lakshadweep is 32 sq.km and is close to the Maldives than to the West Coast. The nearest Island of Lakshadweep is at 200 km and the farthest is at 440 km from the Coast of Kerala.

The Muslim-majority Lakshadweep archipelago became a part of India at the time of Independence in1947, as they were part of the Madras Presidency. On the orders of the then Dy. Prime Minister Sardar Patel, a ship of the Royal Indian Navy was sent to the Island to hoist the Indian flag and to ensure the archipelago's integration into the Union of India.

Map 1.3: Lakshadweep Islands

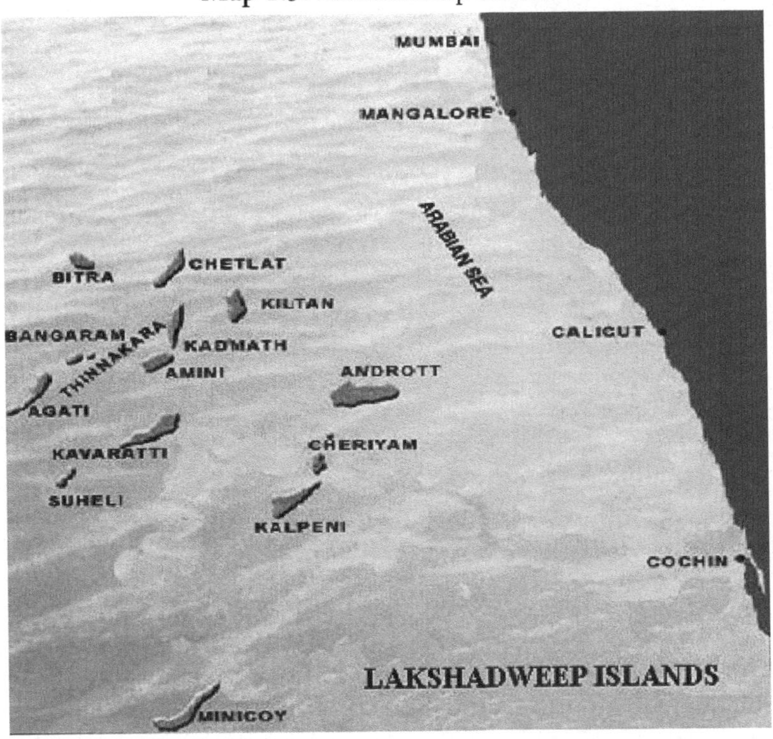

Source: www.googlemaps.com

Kavaratti is the Capital of this union Territory. There is an airport on the neighbouring Agatti island. All air transportation to and from the mainland operates from Agatti, which is known as the gateway to the Lakshadweep. Bangaram Island, close to Agatti, is a major tourist attraction. Androth Island, the biggest of the group, has an area of 4.9 sq.km.

The importance of the Lakshadweep manifests in many aspects. Its lagoon covers about 4,200 sq.km, territorial Sea 20,000 sq.km and Exclusive

Economic Zone 4,00,000 sq.km. The Lakshadweep, Maldives, Chagos, Mauritius and Seychelles archipelagos constitute a chain of dotted islands that connect India and Africa. These islands, spreading on either side of the equator, looks like glittering diamonds studded in the Indian Ocean.

Maldives

The Maldives is a tropical archipelago of 1,190 coral islands, scattered over an 800 km long stretch, close to India's southern tip. Minicoy island of Lakshadweep and Ihavandhippolhu Atoll of the Maldives are separated by the 60 km wide Eight Degree Channel. The Capital Male is a tiny three- mile island. The importance of this country does not lie in its area of 300 sq km and population of 4,00,000, but in its strategic location situated in the North-West Indian Ocean. The Maldives has a coastline of 640 km and an Exclusive Economic Zone of 923,000 sq.km. It was a protectorate under the Dutch in the 17th Century and then came under the British rule. The Maldives became Independent in 1965.

Chagos Archipelago

The Chagos archipelago is a group of seven coral atolls comprising more than 60 individual tropical islands in the Indian Ocean. Located at 71–74 degrees East Longitude and 8–12 degrees North Latitude, it is about 500 km south of the Maldives archipelago. This chain of islands is the southernmost archipelago of the Chagos-Laccadive Ridge, a long submarine mountain range in the Indian Ocean. Diego Garcia is the largest of the Chagos possessing 32.5 sq.km. The other major atolls are Peros, Eagle, Banhos, Boddam and Egmont. Its total area is 56.13 sq.km, but the lagoon is more than 15000 sq.km and the Exclusive Economic Zone has an area of 639,611 sq.km.

It was under the British rule till 1967 and in 1973 UK evicted locals to allow the US to build a military base on Diego Garcia. Since 1971, only Diego Garcia atoll has been inhabited. The sovereignty of British over Chagos disputed by Mauritius. The British separated Chagos from Mauritius before granting independence to the latter in 1965.

Mauritius

Mauritius is an Indian Ocean archipelago state south of the equator, about 2000 km off the south east coast of Africa. The groups of islands in the archipelago are Agalela, Carajos Shols, Rodrigues, and Mauritius. It has an area of 2040 sq.km and a population of 1.3 million (2011). Since it is just north of the Tropic of Capricorn, the climate is very similar to peninsular India. Port Louis is the Capital. The French occupied Mauritius in 1715, set up a naval base and started sugarcane plantations. The British captured it in 1810. Mauritius gained independence from Britain in 1965. The Exclusive Economic Zone of Mauritius extends over an area of about 2.3 million sq.km making Mauritius one of the countries with the largest EEZs in the 20th Century world. There are additional claims of 123,000 sq.km and 180.000 sq.km near Rodrigues and the Chagos archipelago, respectively under application.

Seychelles

The Seychelles is an archipelago of 115 small islands, located 1500 km from the east African coast in Western Indian Ocean. It is the nearest African country to the southern coast of India. The population is less than a lakh and consists mostly of African descent, known as the Creoles. The Capital Victoria is located at the biggest Island. It is home to numerous beaches, coral reefs, nature reserves as well as rare species. It also has mountain rain forests. The land mass of Seychelles is only 459 sq.km, but its EEZ is spread over 1,374,000 sq.km.

The French took control of these islands in 1756 and named them after Jean Moreau de Seychelles, a minister of Louis XV. Within a few years, it came under British domination. Seychelles became independent on 29th June, 1976. It is prosperous and has the highest per capita GDP in Africa.

Choke-Points of Indian Ocean Region

Malacca Strait: Malacca is a narrow 890 km long stretch of Andaman Sea, bounded by Malay Peninsula and Sumatra of Indonesia. It is the main shipping channel between the Indian and Pacific Oceans. Over 70,000 vessels pass through the strait each year, making it the busiest strait in the world and carrying about 30 per cent of the world's traded goods. About a quarter of the oil transported by the sea passes through the strait, mainly from the Persian Gulf to Asian markets. In addition, it is one of the world's most congested shipping choke points because it narrows to only 2.8 km wide near the southern end of Singapore. The strait's minimum depth is 82 feet, which is not enough for large ships. Such ships take a detour and traverse through Lombok strait.

Map 1.4: Choke Points

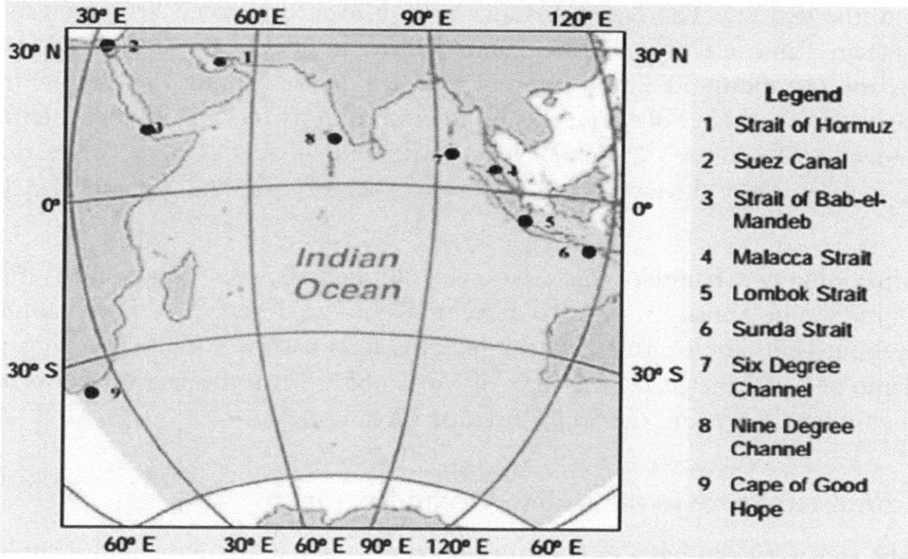

Source: www.googlemaps.com

Lombok Strait: Lombok strait connects the Java Sea to the Indian Ocean, and is located between the Islands of Bali and Lombok in Indonesia. Its narrow point is at its southern opening, with a width of 20 km. It is much deeper than Malacca Strait. This strait is entirely an integral part of Indonesian territorial waters.

Sunda Strait: Sunda is the strait between the Indonesian islands of Sumatra and Java. It also connects the Java Sea to the Indian Ocean. It stretches roughly north-east to south-west, with a minimum width of 24 km at its north-eastern end. The strait's narrowness and shallowness make it unsuitable for large ships.

Harmuz Strait: Harmuz Strait connects the Persian Gulf and the Gulf of Oman. It provides the only sea passage from the Persian Gulf to the Indian Ocean. It is one of the world's most strategically important choke points. About 20 per cent of the world's petroleum tankers pass through the strait. On the north coast lies Iran, and on the south coast are the UAE and Musandam, an enclave of Oman. At it's narrowest, the strait has a width of 54 km.

The Harmuz Strait is almost closed by the territorial waters of Iran (22 km) and Oman (22 km). In 1993, Iran enacted a law on maritime areas, several provisions of which conflict with the UN Law of Sea, to which Iran was also signatory.

Bab el-Mandeb Strait: It is the narrow passage that links the Indian Ocean with the Red Sea. The Bab el-Mandeb strait is located between Yemen on the Arabian Peninsula, and Djibouti and Eritrea in the Horn of Africa. The distance is about 30 km from Ras Menheli in Yemen to Ras Siyyan in Djibouti. The Island of Perim divides the strait into two channels: the eastern, known as Alexander's Strait, is 3 km wide and 30 meters deep, while the western, or Dact el-Mayun, has a width of about 25 km and a depth of 310 meters.

Mozambique Channel: This Channel is located between Madagascar and Mozambique-South Latitude 10 degrees 28' and 26 degrees 53'. The channel is about 1600 km length and 419 km across at its narrowest point, reaching a depth of 3,292 meters off the coast of Mozambique. It is the gateway between the Indian Ocean and the South Atlantic Ocean.

Contested Space in the Indian Ocean Region

The Indian Ocean has a long history of extra-regional influence, and it could be argued that some of the many remaining legacies of this, evident around the region, are potential sources of stability. Apart from Indian Ocean States, all major industrial powers and energy suppliers have an innate interest in Indian Ocean security and stability.[20] An important aspect in this respect is the extent to which any extra-regional security presence, while aiming to guarantee regional as well as its own security interests, is also perceived by other states as a source of insecurity. From this perspective, regional and extra-regional states are seen as competing for influence and resources.[21] It should be recognized and accepted that the United States and China, as well as other extra-regional states, have legitimate regional security interests. If we consider the Indian Ocean Region as an overall arena of competing influence, then it is instructive to note the significant presence of the United States and China, along with the regional presence of India. This creates an interesting geographical distribution of Chinese 'pearls', USA 'diamonds' and Indian 'nuggets'[22], principally reflecting concerns over energy security and securing access to SLOCs.

China has some presence in northern Indian Ocean rim locations—Chittagong, Gwadar, Hambantota in Sri Lanka and Sittwe in Myanmar. According to the US Department of Defence Base Structure Report[23], the USA has some presence in 12 Indian Ocean locations—Diego Garcia, Bahrain, Kuwait, Oman, Qatar and UAE (Persian Gulf region), three in Africa—Egypt, Djibouti and Kenya and a three in the eastern rim—Australia,

Indonesia and Singapore. If we add to these, India's presence in the Andaman islands, Mauritius and Maldives, we are left with a number of what might be called 'contested spaces', that is, they remain competitive arenas which have yet to be incorporated into the influence of powerful external states. These include the failed states of Somalia and Yemen and much of Oceanic Africa.

Maritime security problems and jurisdictional issues in the Indian Ocean Region offer considerable regional security challenges, especially in the areas of the limits of maritime jurisdictions, unresolved boundaries, maritime boundary disputes, sea lanes of communication (SLOCs), non-traditional maritime security threats as well as the uses of the Ocean floor, and the long-term management of seabed resources. However, there appears to be no commonly accepted definition of what constitutes maritime security that might be used as a basis for regional cooperation.[24] Till date, the collective maritime security environment has tended to be conceptualized as a composite sea power, the naval arms build-up, island and maritime boundary issues, navigational regimes, activities in the Exclusive Economic Zones (EEZ), competition over resources and the maintenance of law and order at sea, including protection of SLOCs.[25] To these essential elements can also be added others associated, primarily with the stability and integrity of Ocean littoral states, the insecure role of non-state actors and the maritime environmental insecurity.

The security of SLOCs is vital to the functioning of the global economy. About 80 percent of world trade by value and 90 percent by volume are in the form of sea trade and this involves 1.2 million sea fares, 46,000 vessels and 4000 ports.[26] Maximizing the economic security of sea trade thus necessitates the maximization of security within all five essential elements in the maritime trading process. Any understanding of the security of SLOCs can't be fully appreciated in isolation from the overall maritime security environment.

In terms of international trade, the Indian Ocean is clearly the world's most important energy route. Half of the global daily oil production is transported by tankers on fixed maritime routes.[27] Approximately, 40 percent of the world's oil imports come from the Middle East, making secure interregional oil shipments through the Indian Ocean vital to world prosperity. Oil import security is especially important for Japan (80%), China (40%), Europe (21%) and the USA (16%). Further, more than 80 percent of the world's seaborne trade in oil passed through only three Indian Ocean choke points.

In recent years, a significant proportion of maritime piracy attacks have occurred on energy vessels, with the vast majority against oil tankers.[28] In the last decade in the Indian Ocean, the largest proportion of attacks on energy vessels has been in Indonesia and the Strait of Malacca. However, in the last couple of years, the capacity of pirates in Somalia to operate at significant distance from shore, together with continued attacks off the coast of Nigeria, mean that there has been an important shift in the geography of maritime piracy from Asia to Africa.

The international community responded via the United Nations and through collective state action. In 2008, the UN Security Council (UNSC) adopted resolution 1816 which, with the consent of the Somalia government authorized foreign military vessels to enter Somalian territorial waters to combat piracy for a period of six months. On 24th August 2008, 14 states reportedly committed naval vessels to patrol Somalia waters and a 'security corridor' was established to offer merchant vessels safe transit. While the corridor has since remained virtually free from attacks, piracy has actually increased outside the corridor boundaries.[29]

The hijack of the supertanker MV Sirius Star and its international crew of 25 on 15 November 2008 raised new concern about maritime energy security and the effectiveness of any joint naval response in the Gulf of Aden. Not only was this the largest energy vessel ever hijacked, but it was carrying two million barrels of crude oil, representing about 25 percent of Saudi Arabia's daily output and about the equivalent of France's daily consumption—the attack also indicated an escalation in the goals of the pirates since they would have had to travel up to four days out to sea to intercept the vessel.

Until recently, much of the maritime security debate has concentrated almost exclusively on its military definition. Thus, states have been framed only with the use of 'hard power' and the development of maritime strategies and military security policies that ignore a wide range of non-military considerations. Modern maritime security involves air, sea and land forces operating jointly to influence events in the littoral. Along with traditional blue water maritime concepts of sea denial and sea control.[30]

It has been argued that, while most strategic thinking in Australia is locked into hard power, the Oceanic region offers us great potential to apply soft power and creative diplomacy.[31] Soft power essentially derives from the ability to shape or change the preference of others through an appeal to the sense of attraction or duty shared values and goals. The emergence of US President Obama's 'new engagement' associated with the likely realization of a broader conception of power and its use, especially the notion of smart power is significant, not only in dealing with maritime energy security threats in the Indian Ocean.

There is a compelling need to develop maritime security cooperation in the Indian Ocean Region as current structures are both fragmentary and incomplete[32]. The current maritime energy security policy in the Indian Ocean represents a fragmented collection of regional and extra-regional cooperative arrangements and individual regional and extra-regional state initiatives.

The 16 -state Regional Cooperation Agreement on combating piracy and Armed Robbery against ships in Asia (ReCAAP) initiative, which came into force in 2006, has its Information Sharing Centre (ISC) based in Singapore and aims to assist in the processes of facilitating cooperation, collaboration and preparation of relevant data and supporting regional capacity building. In October 2008, eight EU states led by France declared plans to create an EU maritime security force to combat piracy in Somalia. Furthermore, NATO has also become involved in anti-piracy duties off Somalia.[33]

Individual state action has involved several states from both the region and beyond. Extra-regional states, of course, have declared their interest in maritime security in the Indian Ocean. In March 2009, the imminent dispatch of two Japanese maritime self-defence destroyers to the Gulf of Aden to guard Japanese vessels off Somalia, under the maritime police action, under the provisions of the self-defence forces law, was announced.[34] The adoption by the International Maritime Organization (IMO) of a comprehensive maritime security approach in 2002, provided security assessment guidelines and risk management strategies for some of the basic elements in the maritime trading process—seafarers, vessels, cargoes, and ports. A more comprehensive approach is needed, especially in relation to the security of energy flows through the Indian Ocean. It should not only deal with the effects of insecurity but also begin to systematically address its causes. A key cooperative policy initiative has been the creation of the Indian Ocean Naval Symposium (IONS) under India's leadership. The central vision of IONS is to bring 'regional navies together for the greater collective good', to enhance safety and security, share knowledge, and support disaster relief and humanitarian assistance'.[35]

Review of Literature

Since the 1990s, China has been looking towards the sea as a strategic arena vital for its economic growth and development. In fact China's economic growth depends on maritime access and security of maritime space. China has been a net energy importer before the 1990s and China's energy needs and volume of trade continues to expand.

Chinese expansion towards the Indian Ocean had two aspects: economic and military. In the recent years China has steadily spreading its wings in the Indian Ocean Region with its rapidly growing and well-equipped navy, supported by logistics. China has established several access ports through various arrangements for refuelling, replenishment, crew rest and low level maintenance facilities. By doing so, China is mainly trying to ensure the protection of its sea lanes for critical energy needs. To realise these objectives beyond its natural geographical and historical maritime boundaries—China began setting up a series of bases to project its power in Sri Lanka, Myanmar, Pakistan, Bangladesh, Djibouti and also in the Maldives. With secured land borders, China built a strong navy and increasingly concentrated on South China Sea and in the Indian Ocean Region.

Chinese naval presence, though not substantially threatening, has increased into the Indian Ocean Region in the recent past, at any given point of time 5–7 ships are deploying in the region by China without any requirement. It clearly shows that China's aim is to build a strong navy capable of projecting power across the greater Indo-Pacific Region.

The rise of China as a sea power is one of the biggest developments since the end of Cold War. Dominance in the South China Sea and East Sea makes China a great regional power, but its presence in the Indian Ocean makes it a great naval power. As a state from outside the region, it is difficult for China to deploy its naval forces permanently in the Indian Ocean. To overcome this problem, China has made Pakistan, Myanmar, Bangladesh, Maldives, Sri Lanka and other littoral countries and Islands in the region its allies, forming what is known as the 'String of Pearls' approach. Furthermore, the strategy of the Maritime Silk Road proposed by China has put Indian authorities in a state of threat, which impinges on Indian security and sovereignty through its various initiatives, including of OBOR and corridors. Indian strategists apprehended that, the MSR/OBOR/BRI may further strengthen the China in the Indian Ocean. Despite the security issues arising from China's strategies, India has so far received a lukewarm attention from the government. Hence, academics and expert organisations are cautioning the Indian government to enhance its security measures by increasing the defence budget to modernise India's naval capabilities in order to counter China. Some of the reviewed literature highlights this as follows:

- S.V. Seshagiri Rao (2018), "India's Ocean Neighbourhood—Narendra Modi's Strategic Initiatives", thoroughly analysed about the India's maritime policy in the Indian Ocean during the Congress government rule. The author felt that until Modi became Prime Minister of India in

2014, the Indian Ocean did receive its due importance, it is only after 2014 under Modi rule only a substantial amount of interest has been shown. To begin with, he has started visiting neighbouring countries and small Island nations in the Indian Ocean to maintain good relations, especially those situated in the Central and Western Indian Ocean. In his book the author emphasized the strategic assets in the Indian Ocean Region, such as Andaman & Nicobar Islands and the Lakshadweep Islands in terms of their importance from a security perspective. He elaborated on the usefulness of these islands in containing China at the Strait of Malacca through the Great Channel which is located in the Andaman Sea. The Six Degree Channel, or great channel, facilitates China's entire trade flow through Strait of Malacca. Hence, the author underlined in his book that India can checkmate China in the Six Degree Channel, if China creates problems for India along the LAC. The author further explained the importance of choke-points existing in the Indian Ocean. This book is useful to this study, as the author has also discussed thoroughly about the significance of Indian Ocean and its SLOCs in the book. The author further stated that, since ancient times how China has encroached into the Indian Ocean and expanded its presence through the practice of the 'encirclement of the Indian Ocean' policy, known as the String of Pearls strategy.

- Jayachandra Reddy's (Ed.) book, published in 2007, titled "India's Multilateral Engagements: Opportunities and Challenges", is an outcome of an International conference. Many authors in this book expressed and emphasized the importance and usefulness of multilateral engagements, especially in light of the China's aggressive behaviour towards neighbouring countries. The message of the book is very clear from a foreign policy point perspective. It is useful to my study, as many scholars advise collaboration with like-minded countries to address common challenges. The growing recognition and significance of multilateralism, though bi-lateralism still survives and remains a channel for achieving national goals. In this present world, where global economic and political system is inter-related in character, no nation can remain alone and for India also there is no exception. Therefore, India's interest in multilateralism dates back to the pre-colonial period when an Indian delegation participated in the Bretton Woods Conference in 1944. Thereafter, India embraced multilateralism very actively and enthusiastically associated itself with the formation and promotion of multilateralism organisations.

Many authors stated in this book that multilateralism not only helps enhance India's image and role in the international arena of politics but also serves to advance its economic and security interests significantly. At the same time, few authors felt that multilateral diplomacy also becomes imperative to project India's views and protect its interests in the negotiations on global issues, such as, climate change and terrorism. The multilateralism also seeks to demonstrate India's military prowess by participating in multilateral military exercises, as seen in the case of 'QUAD'.

Since the post-Cold-War period, India began to evince interest in multilaterals and actively participating with multilateral institutions such as ASEAN, ARF, EAS, MGC, BRIN, RIC, BRICS, BIMSTEC and IBSA. Exhibiting its growing interest in multilateralism mechanism, India joined as a full member of SCO, the China dominated security grouping. In this edited book, an attempt has been made to offer insights into the dynamics of India's multilateral engagement and its prospects in this fast-changing global, political socio-economic and security scenario. Many authors discussed scholarly various dimensions of India's multilateral engagement. So this book is important to this study, as many suggested taking help from other countries in the Indian Ocean Region to counter China, as this is possible only through multilateralism.

- Pankaj K. Jha's book, "India and the Oceania: Exploring Vistas for Cooperation," published in 2016 by the Indian Council of World Affairs in New Delhi, is very much applicable to the present study. China in Indian Ocean Region; some security issues. As India neglected relations with littoral countries of the IOR, but also neglected with Small Island nations in the region those are strategically significant for influence. In the Indian foreign policy and strategic discourse, island nations have found a special reference. China today, aspiring for super power status in the world, has made it possible for the country to establish relationship with small island nations in the Indian Ocean Region by adopting Aid diplomacy, following trade relations and investing funds in the poor and under-developed countries. China has even reached the Oceania Region, which comprises 21 nations and 19 dependencies. China has developed relations with some of the small island nations for want of energy, minerals and for military purposes.

  Oceania is one of the regions where Indian's approach is dependent on the information from the larger neighbours, such as Australia and New Zealand. The relatively less expertise about the region is because of limited data related to economic development and emerging challenges of these nations, creating constraints in studying the region. One of the severe limitations has been the lack of diplomatic missions and commercial liaison offices in many of the Oceania countries, excluding larger countries like Australia, Fiji, New Zealand, and Papua New Guinea (PNG). So, the mindset in Delhi needs to change as any island nation can be a strategic asset both in terms of monitoring and using that island as a refuelling base or transit point, as felt by the author in this book. It has been stated in this book how the Oceania Region has been neglected since the late 1980s, with the collapse of USSR. For India, the problem of selecting new partners has somewhat stymied the flow of knowledge and intellectual capital to these nations from India. As a result, these nations of Oceania Region have increasingly gravitated towards other emerging powers, such as Japan and China.

From the Indian point of view, according to the author, there are a number of areas that need to be studied in this region to help shape India's policy towards Oceania. These include creating awareness about India's nuclear policy, climate change negotiations, India's stand on WTO agreements, food security and its role as a globally accepted player. Furthermore, among the major players in the region, India needs to devise a strategy to engage these nations. One possible option could be a larger participation in the Pacific Island Forum, for the comprehensive study of the capacities and capabilities and building sustainable development modules in order to engage these nations under India's developing nations programme. Overall, this book addresses the emerging challenges and the historical backdrop of the region with special reference to India. In view of this, the book is very helpful for India's foreign policy perspective towards Small Island Nations, in the contemporary situation, as China increases its presence not only in the Indo-Pacific but also in the Oceania Region.

For India to be a global player, becoming a permanent member in the UN Security Council, the votes from these island nations would matter as this Oceania Region has a large number of UN members. India's low cost education, particularly in distance education, health care, and agriculture equipment exports to this region, would create positive influence in the region, as per the views of the author of this book.

- Amitabh Matto, 2013 (ed.), "The Indian Ocean Region: Security, Stability, and sustainability in the 21st Century", an edited book from Australia India Institute, Melbourne, discusses in detail the geopolitics of the Indian Ocean Region, its changing significance, various perspectives of regional states and the Indian Ocean Region's relationships with other regions for an analysis of security issues and security challenges of India Ocean Region, including major non-traditional security issues in comparative analysis in respect of differences and similarities in Indian and Australian perspectives. So, this book is applicable to my study. Further, in this book, a thorough discussion has taken place with respect to SLOCs and security along Indo-Pacific littorals. Also, the author analysed the roles of Indian and Australian perspectives on their future roles in the Indo-pacific security.

The editor in this book elaborated on creating freedom from fear in the Indian Ocean Region, which requires all regional states to commit themselves to implement a new security consensus based on the recognition that threats are interlinked, with development, security and human rights being interdependent. So, no nation can protect itself by acting entirely alone and all states need an equitable security to address threats ranging from international war and weapons of mass destruction to terrorism, state collapse, civil conflicts, deadly infectious diseases like Covid-19, extreme poverty and environmental destruction. On the whole, this book supports my study, wherein increasing interdependence between nations is recognised in view of the globalisation, implying greater inter-state cooperation.

P.V. Rao, (ed.) 2001, "Regional Cooperation in Indian Ocean: Trends and Perspectives", was an edited book discussing Regionalism and Regional cooperation in the Indian Ocean Region for the growth and development of all littoral countries of the region. As per the author, Indian Ocean Region is an elusive system that defies a precise description as either a region, a security system, or an economic area. It is characterized by dissimilarities and heterogeneity. Hence, the book is useful for my study. A region with huge natural resources, but these very sources serve as source of conflict, both globally and locally. The book it states that all layers of development and overlapping layers are found in the Indian Ocean region's economic structure. The editor of the book emphasises the significance of the IOR countries, representing 3/4th of the underdeveloped world, trying to reconcile themself to seemingly contradictory processes—globalisation and economic regionalism. This book is aptly useful to my topic, as many scholars suggest multilateralism to counter China in the Indian Ocean Region. Long back ago in 2001, this book advocated the importance of regional cooperation to overcome several problems, such as economic, trade, political, piracy and security threats.

- Srikanth Kondapally, 2015, in his article published, "New Dynamics of Indian Ocean Region and Indian Role", aptly analysed the changes in the IOR and argued India's role in it. The emerging trends in the Indian

Ocean Region indicate that there are long-term consequences for the international and the IOR orders—ensuring sustainable energy supplies, counter-terrorism, protection to the shipping & communications, working for pro-actively for natural disasters relief, and crafting a favourable maritime and security environment in the Indian Ocean Region—are all major tasks for a resident and rising state like India. In this article, the author argued that India needs to protect its interests and factor in the emerging context between the US and China in the IOR, as China is making concerted efforts to enter and sustain operations in the Indian Ocean Region through naval modernisation and power projection. India has made several efforts to strengthen the maritime security environment in the IOR, and is working with several multilateral institutions in this regard, according to the author.

- Sidda Goud & Maneesha Mukerjee (ed.), 2015, elaborately presented that China is constantly trying to encircle India. The editors suggested that India take appropriate measures to protect itself from China in the Indian Ocean and along the China-India 3488 km border from Eastern Ladakh to Arunachal Pradesh, due to China's muscle power vested in its huge economy with a 13 trillion GDP. Many writers expressed in their papers at the conference on China in Indian Ocean Region that India should take the help of neighbouring countries, including small island nations, to face China's challenges. China is implementing several initiatives like maritime silk road, One Belt One Road/Belt and Road Initiative (BRI), and a few corridors, such as BCIM, CPEC, CMEC, Kra Canal Project through Indian territory, which may hurt India's security & sovereignty. That is why India is not a party to the Chinese projects. A couple of papers addressed China's String of Pearls strategy around India in the Indian Ocean Region by constructing ports in India's neighbouring countries like in Sri Lanka, Myanmar, Bangladesh, Pakistan, Djibouti and even in the Maldives, clearly understanding China's strategy to encircle India This is a cause of concern for India. So, the edited book is applicable to my study.
- GVC Naidu, 2015, in his published article "India, China and the Indian Ocean", discussed in detail the importance of the Indian Ocean for India. The Indian Ocean is not merely India's backyard but is also the main link to the rest of the world for more than 2500 years. India's destiny is inexorably tied to this Ocean. The author further summarised that amazingly the discourse in India on the Indian Ocean and the developments in the Rim region are limited. Sadly, very little serious research output is coming out, as observed by the author.

Day by day, the maritime domain in the Indian Ocean region is under intense focus for several reasons, according to the author. The Indo-Pacific Region, that has immensely benefitted from growing trade, is a case in point. This region has also witnessed momentous changes in the maritime sector. The writer felt that the Indian Ocean is home to numerous territorial and maritime boundary disputes, which remained dormant but have now become a major source of tension and instability.

The author is seriously concerned in his paper that the challenges India harboured during the Cold War have dissipated; however, new challenges have surfaced. In this paper, the author further stated that New Delhi would certainly be wary of China's presence in the Indian Ocean. China is involved in building several ports facilitates in the countries around India and is actively courting Island States, such as, Maldives, Seychelles and Mauritius, with generous to consolidate its position in the Indian Ocean. India has to begin qualitatively increasing its engagements with its neighbours and the Island states.

- Kouser J. Azam (ed.) 2019, "Indian Ocean; The New Frontier", is an edited book of conference proceedings. Focus has been given to draw the attention of scholars and policymakers to the ever- widening relevance of Indian Ocean in India's external relations in the light of the fresh initiatives announced by Modi after he became Prime Minister of India. Several contributors in the volume identified the recent upsurge in Indian Ocean Studies as a part of a new phenomenon, with Delhi focusing on studies of Indian Ocean Region a lot after 2014 onwards. The author of this volume stated that it is obvious that Indian Ocean studies have moved beyond their traditional 'marginal' status to a global discourse involving social sciences, sciences, and humanities. A growing body of multi-disciplinary studies has expanded its traditional scope and has brought within its fold fascinating new areas of lives and societies within the Indian Ocean Region. This new knowledge is going to influence both in policy and practice in the entire region in the years ahead. This book is relevant to my topic.

  Several contributors in this book focus on increasing concerns for environment, Climate Change, Natural calamities, Biodiversity and Historical sites, indicating a shift towards oceanic studies across disciplines. This book is useful in the contemporary situation regarding the growing importance of the Indian Ocean Region.

- P.V. Rao (ed.), 2008, "India and The ASEAN, Partner's at Summit", focuses on India's relationship with 10-nation ASEAN group in the 1990s. ASEAN is a regional intergovernmental organisation comprising ten countries in Southeast Asia, promoting inter-governmental cooperation and facilitates economic, political, security, military, educational, and socio-cultural integration among its members and other countries in Asia. India and ASEAN began to forge a formal relationship at that time, keeping future requirements in mind, as many changes occurred in East Asia, prompting ASEAN to reach out to Southeast Asian countries from which it had been estranged. At the same time, India opened up and liberalised its economy, adopting its Look East Policy driven by economic & strategic imperatives.

Most papers in this book emphasise, address and analyse the situation for mutual advantage and the dynamics between the nations. It is worth mentioning that a couple of papers discuss India's relationship with ASEAN group, focusing largely on security issues in the Region. A substantial part of the book is devoted to the China factor, making, it valuable for my study, as the strong relationship between India and the ASEAN bloc will protect these nations' security from the expansionist China.

- Jayachandra Reddy G. (ed.) 2017, "South China Sea Emerging Scenario", most of the papers in this edited book deal with the importance of the South China Sea, which is one of the world's most important waterways, carrying half of the global merchant fleet. Its Sea Lanes of Communication carry most of the energy supplies to Japan, South Korea, Taiwan, as well as a large portion of China's trade. The editor states that the South China Sea connects two of the fastest growing regions of the world—India and China.

Through this, global trade route, more than $ 5 trillion worth of goods are transported each year. The South China Sea is critical for China as it is the only major outlet to the open seas that it can access with fewer constrained compared to the East China Sea. India and Australia are interested in the SCS, both economically and geographically. The US is also interested in upholding the rule- based order in the region. This book also analyses Australia conducting its own Surveillance in the South China Sea and the Indian Ocean since 1980s for security purposes. India's interest in the SCS is significant because 55 per cent of its trade passes through the SCS. Therefore, India also emphasizes free and open trade and navigation in the South China Sea. Despite the International Tribunal order, China claims 90 per cent of the waters of the SCS as its own on historical bases. Many authors in this book state that freedom of navigation is the need of the hour in the SCS and that the rule of law should be followed as per the UNCLOs. Hence, this volume is useful to the present study.

- Sidda Goud R. and Maneesha Mukherjee (ed.), 2013, India-Sri Lanka Relations; Strengthening SAARC", Most of the articles in this volume are allocated to analyzing the concept of Regionalism and security concerns, focusing on the commonalities between India and Sri Lanka and diluting differences to emerge as a strong block in the South to realise its Objectives, such as economic, social, cultural and environmental issues. Several papers in this book deal with trade relations and economic cooperation between India and Sri Lanka.

  The concept of regional cooperation in South Asia is epitomized in the establishment of SAARC, which is based on the principles of sovereignty, equality, territorial integrity, political independence, non-interference in the internal affairs of other member states, and cooperation for mutual benefit. Myriad issues such as micro-finance, health insurance, ethnicity, plurality, governance, human rights, media and information technology and communication in the e-Governance, urban development and regional planning are also discussed in this book. Therefore, this volume is important for my study.
- Feldt Lutz, P. Roell and R. Thiele (2013) in the article *"Maritime Security—Perspectives for a Comprehensive Approach"*, discuss the emerging challenges and draw attention to non-traditional maritime security threats. These threats include piracy, armed robbery and maritime terrorism. According to the authors, nautical protection involves defensive and reactive designed to defend oceanic territory. In the wake of increasing non-conventional threats, the lack of operational necessities in the state of India makes it vulnerable to threats arising in the Indian Ocean region.
- Rahul Roy Choudhury (2015) in the book *India's Maritime Security* argues that India lacks a comprehensive maritime policy. The author highlights the need for a holistic approach to the various elements of maritime power. Drawing attention to the Chinese activities in the Indian Ocean region, the author contends China is actively involved in developing economic, political and military alliances with the several states in the Indian Ocean, thereby encircling India's neighbouring countries.
- Jaimie Hatcher (2013) in the book *China's Growing Indian Ocean Maritime Interests: Sowing the Seed of Conflict,* recognises the increasing requirement of energy and resources as the major driver of potential contestation over maritime interests in the Indian ocean between India and China.
- Jonathan Holslag (2009) in the article *The Persistent Military Security Dilemma between China and India* evaluates the extent to which the improving Sino-Indian relations correlate with a reduction in military

threat perceptions. By reviewing the demilitarisation of the border, its military strategies with respect to the Indian Ocean and nuclear arms programmes, the author observes that the two countries remain locked in a military security dilemma. Distrust also results in military balancing, which has led to a complex and multi-level military balance of power that, while not bringing about peace, enhances stability.

- Pragya Pandey (2014) in one of his paper, "*Emerging Maritime Security Environment in the Indian Ocean Region: Challenges and Responses,*" describes the Indian Ocean as the world's strategic and economic centre of gravity because of its geostrategic location. The region is witnessing sweeping changes in the geopolitics and geo-strategy of the world due to the presence of strategic resources, strategically important shipping routes, the rise of India, the involvement of the USA and the entry of China. The present situation suggests that peace and security will be a challenge in the coming future.
- Sarabjeet Singh Parmar (2013) discussed in a seminar, *"The Growing Chinese Maritime Influence: Implications for Regional Security"* that China's maritime strategy has been influenced not only by Mahan but also by the Ideas of Corbett. Maritime strategy is important for China in three ways: a departure from coastal defence tradition, consolidation of immediate areas in the wake of threats from the US and japan, and the entry into the high seas. To expand its influence, China has resolved to achieve sea denial tactics and sea control through submarines and Anti-Ship Ballistic Missiles (ASBM) and to gain establishment of working control and control in disputes. China has also emphasized the necessity of naval operations for trade protection outside the first and second island chains and the strategy of overseas bases being undertaken by China in Myanmar, the Maldives, Sri Lanka, and East Africa.
- Adam P. MacDonald, observes in a paper, *"China's Maritime Strategy: A Prolonged Period of Formulation,"* that China is continuing to build itself into a maritime power with wide-ranging priorities, including the expansion of its maritime power, aspirations for growing political influence in the maritime domain, and continued use of seaborne trade. He explains that having many areas of contestation with other maritime countries, it can't be assumed that China is a benign actor.
- Wang Lirong states in his paper, *"The Indian Ocean and the Chinese Strategy for Maritime Security"*, his observations about China and its security parameters in relation to the Indian Ocean. He explains that the Indian Ocean, being the third largest water body on the face of earth, is of vital importance for China because it acts as a trade lane, resource lane

and strategic lane, all crucial for China's security. He observes that China faces various kinds of threats on these strategic lanes in the Indian Ocean, so there is a need for China to establish a comprehensive maritime security concept. This will be possible if China develops friendly relationship with the neighbouring countries, makes efforts for the promotion of multilateral cooperation around the Indian Ocean Region, establishes enduring institutions for the safety of the sea lanes, and strengthens its naval force structure.

- Daniel M. Hartnett and Frederic Vellucci in a study titled *"Toward a Maritime Security Strategy: An Analysis of Chinese Views since the Early 1990s"* analyzed the trends that are likely to emerge as components of a future Chinese maritime strategy. They argue that as the Chinese economy becomes increasingly dependent on maritime resources, overseas trade and energy, its security strategy will increasingly focus on the maritime direction. Safeguarding these maritime interests requires developing China's maritime capabilities, including economic, military, diplomatic, scientific, and cultural capabilities.
- Sithara Fernando (2012) in his study, *"China's Post-1978 Maritime Relations with South Asia: Towards Greater Cooperation"* states that China's most important maritime concerns in its relationship with South Asia are oceanic trade transit points for Western China and the sea lanes connecting the Strait of Hormuz and the Strait of Malacca, which carry its energy imports.
- Prem Mahadevan (2014) in his study, *"China in the Indian Ocean: Part of a Larger PLAN"* argues that by investing in sea power, China has found a sustainable means for combining economic and military power to reshape the international system. The fact that the Indian Ocean is a vital transit corridor for the country provides it with strong grounds to establish a permanent presence there. Many IOR states see Chinese investment infrastructure as a matter of pride, showcasing domestically bright economic prospects. They also see it as an opportunity to make a point to the West that deficiencies in governance need not be hyped to a degree where they become a hindrance to business. This weakens the prospect of an international consensus forming against Beijing, if and when a requirement arises to use military force.
- Christian Bedford (2009) in an article, *"The View from the West: String of Pearls: China's Maritime Strategy in India's Backyard"* argues that China's emergence as a global power has meant an increase in Chinese involvement in the Indian Ocean basin. From the Persian Gulf to the

Bay of Bengal to the South China Sea, Beijing has increased its strategic footprint along the routes that carry the majority of its oil imports. Through infrastructure improvements, diplomatic agreements and military installations, China is seeking to create a 'String of Pearls' (SOP) to protect and monitor its vitally important sea lines of communication (SLOC).

- David Scott in the article "*China's Maritime Strategy for the Indian Ocean*" details the increasing Chinese naval operations under the proposed 'Far Sea Defence plan. The expanding footprint involves the announcement and initiation of Maritime Silk Route, sailing of submarines and carrying out live missile drills in the Eastern and Western quadrants of the Indian Ocean. He has provided ample examples of China's plans for increasing involvement in the future and asserts that China will not reverse this trend. This posturing of China towards the Indian Ocean has alarmed India and has invited countervailing responses from the Indian side.
- J. Garver (2000) in his book *Protracted Contest: Sino-Indian Rivalry in the Twentieth Century* draws attention to the critical role that the Indian Ocean has in the future stability of South Asia. The search for increasing influence or hegemony over the Indian Ocean among India and China will shape the security environment of the region in the coming century. He suggests determining the relationship between India and China through the scenarios where either China accepts India's emergence as a regional power in South Asia—in other words, the dominance of the Indian Ocean by India—or India accepts China's economic emergence and influential role in the region.
- C. Raja Mohan (2013) in his book *Samudra Manthan: Sino-Indian Rivalry in Indo-Pacific* mentions that the two vast bordering civilisation states, having unresolved territorial frontiers and seeking power and influence, as they compete and cooperate, contain and engage each other, could run into a continuing rivalry. Their maintenance of high growth rates would depend on their critical approach to and transportation of mineral resources from the rest of Asia, Africa, and immensely extended seaborne vocation capacities on Sea Lanes of Communications (SLOCs) across the Indian Ocean and Pacific Oceans.
- Robert D. Kaplan (2010) in his book *Monsoon: The Indian Ocean and Future of American Power,* argues that the Indian Ocean region's emergence at the centre stage of international politics is due to the transformation in the post-Cold War period. The region is also experiencing conflicting cultural trends, such as the spread of Islam in the littoral states and their interaction with each other. In this context,

Kaplan implies the vertical expansion of China's power and horizontal spread of India's influence. The vertical expansion of China's power is guided by the search for an alternative to the Strait of Malacca through the Indian Ocean. The development of ports in Bangladesh (Chittagong), Myanmar (Kyaukphyu) and Sri Lanka (Hambantota) ensures the transportation of oil and natural gas to mainland China avoiding dependence on the Strait of Malacca. This results in moving beyond the traditional area of influence, consequently resulting in a clash of interests between these two states. It will create strong undercurrents of competition and conflict between the two Asian giants. On land as well as on water, China certainly represents and threatens as a major long-term competitor and even primary security challenges to India.

Objectives of the Study

1. To study the significance of Indian Ocean Region.
2. To analyse India's Security policies in the region.
3. To examine China's strategic interests in the Indian Ocean Region.
4. To study India's Security collaboration with like-minded countries in the Region and to analyse India's security policy limitations in the Indian Ocean Region.

Hypothesis

1. India hold's strategic position in the Indian Ocean Region.
2. India has a weak security policy in the Indian Ocean Region.
3. China is a serious threat to India in the Indian Ocean.
4. India, being in a strategic position in the Region, needs to enhance security policies to counter China's increasing presence in the Indian Ocean Region.

Research Methodology

To test the objectives and hypothesis of the study given method has been adopted, since the problem of the research theme is purely of the theoretical in nature but not of empirical in regard to geo-strategic area.

The study based on secondary sources of information and data, which include books, journals, periodicals, national and international daily newspapers, and participation in conferences related to the subject, as well as interaction with the subject experts. The data and information collected from various sources have been analysed with a simple explanation and analysis.

Secondary Data: The relevant data is collected from government policy documents, Books, Newspapers, Journals, all authentic internet websites, and other published and unpublished documents.

Chapter-Scheme

1. Introduction
2. ***Indian Ocean Region:*** Prime Minister Narendra Modi Strategic Approach.
3. ***China's 21st Century Maritime Silk Road:*** Encirclement of India?
4. China in the Indian Ocean Region: Impinge on India's Security and Sovereignty.
5. India's Maritime Security Strategy in the Indian Ocean Region.
6. Suggestions and Policy Recommendations.
7. Executive Summary and Conclusions.

Conclusion

From the above, the emerging trends in the Indian Ocean Region indicate that there are long-term implications for both the international community and the Indian Ocean Region. Ensuring sustainable energy supplies, counter terrorism, protection of shipping and communications, proactive preparation for natural disaster relief, and shaping a favourable maritime and security environment in the Indian Ocean Region are all major tasks for a resident and rising state like India. Clearly, India, apart from protecting its interests, has to factor in the emerging contest between the US and China in the Indian Ocean Region. China has been making concerted efforts to enter and sustain operations in the Indian Ocean Region. This is to be realized by China, through its navel modernization, String of Pearls strategy and power projection in the medium to long-term, even as it makes clear moves in the short term. While India has made several efforts to strengthen the maritime security environment in the Indian Ocean Region, it is also working with several multilateral institutions in this regard. India has also recently concluded a trilateral maritime cooperation agreement with the Maldives and Sri Lanka.

India, of course, will have to keep in mind the China factor. One should remember that China strongly objected to the India-US Malabar exercises in the Bay of Bengal in 2007 when it was expanded to include Japan, Australia and Singapore as well, firm in its belief that a multilateral naval construct was emerging to "counter and contain" China in the region. Prime Minister Modi invited Australia to participate in the 24th Malabar Exercise, which was held in the Bay of Bengal in November 2020 and Australia readily accepted the invitation and participated in the Malabar Exercises.

As China's continuing muscle flexing in SCS, India is hosting top-tier Malabar naval exercise with the other Quad countries in the Bay of Bengal shortly in October 2024. The 28th edition of the Malabar exercise, with a major focus on advanced anti-Submarine Warfare will be conducted on India's seaboard to further enhance military interoperability among the Quad countries.

An aggressive China figures high on the radar screens of most countries. With the World's largest navy with 355 warships and Submarines, Beijing has been strong- arming its neighbors in SCS, with expansionist claims while also building artificial islands and expanding strategic Footprints in the Indian Ocean Region. Similar Chinese "grey zone" and salami-slicing tactics are evident along the land borders with India. Malabar is all about with the strong ties, shared values and collective ability of the Quad nations to ensure a free, open and inclusive Indo-Pacific, which China is trying to disturb.

References

[1] Amitabh Mattoo and Rory Medcalf, India, Indian's, and the world: Public opinion and foreign policy, Australia India Institute, University of Melbourne, May, 2013.

[2] Ibid.

[3] Times of India report, dt. 7-12-2019.

[4] Ibid.

[5] Robert, D. Kaplan, Monsoon: The Indian Ocean and the Future of American Power, Random House, 2010.

[6] Lehr, Peter, The Challenges of Security in the Indian Ocean in the 21st century: plus ca change….? Working paper No. 13, November 2012, Heidelberg papers in South Asian and Comparative Politics University of Heidelberg.

[7] The rate of increase of oil flows through the Strait of Malacca's is estimated to be above 3 percent annually till 2025.

[8] Harrison, Selig's et. at Super Power Rivalry in Indian Ocean, Oxford University Press 1989.

[9] Ji, You and Kia, Lim Chee, "China's Naval Deployment to Somalia and its Implications" EAI background brief no. 454 May 29, 2009.

[10] According to David Scott, while the Nehruvian focus was largely continental, recent Indian focus is on expanding its blue water capability and protect interest in the Indian Ocean Region and beyond, *Asia-Pacific Review*, Vol. 13, No. 2, 2006, pp. 97–129.

[11] Integrated Head Quarters Ministry of Defence (navy), Freedom to Use the Seas: India's maritime Military Strategy New Delhi, 2007 (p. 61).

[12] Verma, B.K., "Coastal Security: Where are we headed?" February 16, 2009 at http://www.maritimeindia.org/modules

[13] "Navies from Indian Ocean Region to chalk out anti-piracy plan" The Times of India, May 7, 2010.

[14] Wilson, Brain, "Indo-US Maritime partnering: Time for next step" January 23, 2009 at http://www.maritimeindia.org/modules

[15] Naidu, G.V.C., India, China and the Indian Ocean, Seminar paper, November 13–14, 2014, Osmania University.

[16] Martin, Alex, First overseas military base since WWII to open in Djibouti, Japan, Times, July 2, 2011, http://www.japantimes.co.jp/news/2011/07/djibouti#2jART wlvA

[17] Bouchard, C. and Crumphin, W. (2010). 'Neglected no longer: the Indian Ocean at the forefront of world geopolitics and geostrategy; *Journal of the Indian Ocean region*, Vol. 6(1), p. 35.

[18] Chaturvedi, S. (2009). 'Indian Ocean', in R. Kitchin and N. Thrift, eds., *International Encyclopedia of Human Geography*, Vol. 5, Oxford: Elsevier, p. 46.

[19] Stockholm International Peace Research Institute (SIPRI) 2011, website at: http://www.sipri.org/research/armaments/milex

[20] Rumly, D. and Chaturvedi, S., eds. (2005). Energy security and the Indian Ocean Region, New Delhi: South Asian Publishers.

[21] Brewster, D. (2010a). An Indian Sphere of influence in the Indian Ocean? Security Challenges, Vol. 6(b) spring, pp. 1–22.

[22] Brewster, 2009; Kostecka 2011; US department of defence 2010.

[23] Paink, J.H. (2005). Maritime Security in East Asia; major issues and regional resources; *Journal of International and Aren Studies*, Vol. 12(2), pp. 15–29.

[24] Harrald, J.R. (2005). Sea trade and security; An assessment of the post – 9/11 reaction, *Journal of International Affairs*, Vol. 59 (1), pp. 157–178.

[25] EIA (2009). Country Analysis Briefs: World Oil Transit Checkpoints, p. 1, available at the US Energy Information; website at http://www.eia.doe.gov

[26] Nincic, D.J. (2009). Maritime piracy: implications for maritime energy security, journal of energy security, 19 February at www.ensec.org

[27] Ibid.

[28] Australian Government (2009). Defunding Australia in the Asia-Pacific century: Force 2030.Defence White paper, Canberra department of Defence, p. 8.

[29] Bateman, S. and Bergin, A. (2009). Sea Challenges: Advancing Australia's Ocean Interest, A Strategy paper Canberra: Australian Strategic Policy Institute (ASPI), March, p. 4.

[30] Cordner, L. (2011). Progressing maritime security cooperation in the Indian Ocean naval War College Review, Vol. 64(4), Autumn, pp. 68–88.

[31] IISS (2009). The Military Balance 2009, London.

[32] Hongo, J. (2009). 'MSDF Somalia dispatch slammed by opponents at rally' Japan Times, 6 March, p. 2.

[33] Cordner, L. (2011). "Progressing Maritime Security Corporation in the Indian Ocean Naval War College Review, Vol. 64(4), Autumn, p. 69.

[34] Future Directions International (FDI) (2011). 'Strategic Objectives of United States in the Indian Ocean Region, 'Workshop Report, 29, September.

[35] Medcalf, R. and Gill, A. (2009). Unconventional Partners; Australia-India Co-operation in Reducing Nuclear Dangers; Lowy Institute Policy Brief, October.

CHAPTER II

Indian Ocean Region—Prime Minister Narendra Modi's Strategic Approach

Despite the significance of the Indian Ocean in global geopolitics and the world economy, India did not pay due attention to it even after independence. It was only through the efforts of Sardar Patel that India was able to save the strategic Lakshadweep Archipelago in 1947 by sending the Royal Indian Navy to hoist the National Flag. Though a tiny island, it possesses a huge Exclusive Economic Zone (EEZ) and has a strategic location in the Arabian Sea, despite the fact that it was an integral part of the Madras Presidency. As the Strait of Malacca becomes a lifeline for China for its energy imports. Every Chinese ships has to pass through Malacca, Sunda and Lambok Straits and is supposed to cross the Lakshadweep and Andaman Sea Lanes. 80 percent of Chinese energy imports pass through the Six Degree Channel. Recently, seven Chinese navy warships have been operating in and around the Indian Ocean Region, including over 27,000 tonne amphibious vessels, which have been tracked by the Indian Navy using its P-81 anti-submarine warfare spy planes and other surveillance assets. Considering the requirements, the deployments seem to be more than needed. The aim of the Chinese People's Liberation Army Navy (PLAN) appears to be power projection in the Indian Ocean Region, as they want to spread their influence in the area, which is a matter of concern for India's security. India can block Chinese transportation at Strait of Malacca in the Indian Ocean Region if necessary. So, China should be mindful of sending nuclear-powered submarines to the Indian Ocean repeatedly without any necessity under the guise of security its SLOC, even though the rate of piracy cases has been decreasing since 2003 at Somalia and the Gulf of Aden However, piracy attacks have risen in 2018, according to the IMB report.

The Indian Ocean, the third largest in the world, surpasses the Atlantic and Pacific Oceans as the world's largest and most significant trade corridor. The Indian Ocean Region (IOR), which is surrounded by Africa, Asia and Australia, serves as a maritime highway linking trans-continental human and economic relationships. Being the world's most populated region, one-third of the world's bulk cargo and around two-third of the world's oil shipmates pass through it. The Strait of Hormuz, located between Iran and Oman, is the world's most important Choke point with a daily oil flow accounting for about 40% of global seaborne trade. 90% of the oil exported from the Persian Gulf is destined for Asia, Western Europe and the United States. The 'Strait of Malacca', located between Indonesia, Malaysia and Singapore, accounts for 40% of global Seaborne trade, and is the shortest sea route between China, Japan, South Korea and the Persian Gulf. If this strait is choked for any reason, almost half of the world's fleet would need to reroute, thus, aggravating the oil and other transactional burdens for the importing countries.

One-fifth of the global energy resources pass-through the region, making it a major strategic passage. Additionally, several Asian manufacturing units utilize the region for transporting goods to Europe and beyond, establishing it as a major economic and commercial hub in the world.[1] Also, for fuelling their industrial rise, energy consumption is expected to increase in future. Since the IOR holds significant strategic raw minerals and gas reserves, global dependence on these resources is expected to remain strong for a long time, as the intensification of globalization further enhances the dependence of several countries in the Indian Ocean Region on maritime trade.[2] However, compared to the Pacific and Atlantic Oceans, the outward trade flows from the Indian Ocean Region constitute about 80 percent, while intra-Indian Ocean Region trade accounts for a mere 20 percent.

It has been estimated that 15.5 million barrels of oil pass through the Strait of Hormuz compared to 11 million barrels through the Strait of Malacca.[3] Nearly 20,000 ships navigate the Gulf of Aden passing through the Suez Canal, while 33,000 ships navigate Horn of Africa every year, and 70,000 ships pass through the Strait of Malacca.[4] 1/10th of global crude oil is transported through the Gulf of Aden, while over $ 200 bn worth of oil makes its way through the Strait of Hormuz.[5] Because of these narrow passes, their vulnerability has become a major security issue, during the period of cold war they were kept under check partly due to super power rivalry and partly due to the presence of western troops at Djibouti, Diego Garcia, Somalia and Comoros Islands and Soviets in Ethiopia and South Yemen. The absence of a single overarching security architecture in the IOR leads to insecurities.

In view of the above profile of the IOR, many countries have attempted to influence the region through unilateral, bilateral and multilateral efforts. Foremost among these is the United States which has a major base in the IOR at Diego Gracia. This base has been used during the Cold War and as recently as the global war on terrorism in Afghanistan and for operations in Iraq. There is also a new idea coinciding with the rebalance strategy—the Indo-Pacific region—explain the new dynamics of the Indian Ocean Region.

The US is the largest importer of energy resources from West Asia and Africa, with over $ 1 trillion in trade transiting the Strait of Malacca every year. The US also needs to consider the interests of its allies like Japan and South Korea. Attacks on US and allied ships were wake-up calls. The US fifth fleet established the Combined Task Force (CTF) 151 in 2009. Other task forces include CTF 152, with an operational focus on the Central and South Gulf Region; CTF 150 for the Southern Red Sea, the Gulf of Aden, Gulf of Oman, North Western IOR and CTF 158 for the protection of Iraq's oil platforms. Naval ships from 20 countries, including the US, Germany, Australia, Italy, Japan, South Korea, Netherlands, Pakistan are involved. Additionally, the US helped enforce the Maritime Security Patrol Area in the Gulf of Aden from August 2008.[6]

China has been an active participant in the revival of the Asian Highways and the Railways concepts and has made efforts to open up the country for expanding transportation corridors linking it with Southeast Asia, Central Asia and South Asia. Recently, China has also been expanding its sea routes.[7] In May 2014, officials in Fujian province—one of the three key regions tasked with MSR initiative—announced the setting up of a fund of nearly $ 1.6 bn, to be channeled from the China Development Bank and the China-Africa Development Fund.[8] This fund is intended to further port developments and other infrastructure projects in the IOR in the near future.

To fulfill these interests, China has been setting up dual use Maritime facilities in the IOR. One of the major projects is the Gwadar port, a collaboration between China and Pakistan, which is considered a landmark in bilateral relations. The Gwadar naval port, located on the western Makran coast of Pakistan, was built with Chinese assistance by China Harbor Engineering Company, a subsidiary of China communications construction. The first phase of project, conceived in 1964 but started only in 2002, saw China spending $ 198 million against Pakistan's share of about $ 50 million in a project estimated at over $ 1 bn, and it was completed by 2006. In 2003, Pakistan transferred the port to Chinese Overseas Port Holding Ltd.

Another project undertaken with active Chinese assistance is the Hambantota project in Sri Lanka, which includes a port as well as an airport. Originally, this project was offered to India One phase of this port was opened for internal shipping in June 2012, after cost escalation and time overruns, with an estimated additional cost of $40 million out of a total of $ 400 million. China has also offered to construct another port at Colombo, with reports of possible investments from China amounting to $ 50 million.

The Indian Ocean on littoral comprises 29 states and six island republics in its waters.[9] It includes the largest and perhaps the most heterogeneous combination of countries, with states as large as India and Australia and small economies like the Maldives and Comoros. These countries have income per capita levels ranging from very high, like those of Singapore, Australia or the United Arab Emirates (UAE), to very low, like those of Mozambique, Tanzania, Somalia and Bangladesh. Despite this tremendous socio-economic, ethnic, cultural and religious heterogeneity, the ocean has bond them together through the ages, influencing their historical developments. The diversity and variations in geography, social organization, culture, economy, historical experience, political development and structure not withstanding all its littoral and island states are dependent on the ocean, making the IOR a fascinating world for study and investigation.

The Indian Ocean includes the Andaman Sea, Arabian Sea, Bay of Bengal, Flores Sea, Great Australian Bight, Gulf of Aden, Gulf of Omen, Java Sea, Mozambique Channel, Red Sea, Savu Sea, Strait of Malacca, Timor Sea and other tributary water bodies. These subwater areas within the Indian Ocean have attracted numerous scholars to investigate them independently as well as in relation to the wider ocean realm and their correlation. Its monsoon cycle and tropical cyclones have been studied for their impact on agriculture and economies of the littoral states.

Before the Second World War, the Indian Ocean was considered a 'British lake'—encircled by the Britishers to kept a strict vigil on strategic supplies such as Persian oil, Malayan rubber, Indian tea, Australian & New Zealand food stuffs. British supremacy in the Indian Ocean ended after Second World War and gradually Britain gave up most of its possessions in the region. Finally, the British withdrew their focus from east of Suez in 1971.[10] The Indian Ocean was not considered to be of any political and strategic significance until the mid-1960s and had largely escaped the attention of academics, scholars, and political and military strategists.

In the 1960s, the super powers of that time, the United States and the Soviet Union, emerged on the horizons of the Indian Ocean, justifying their presence to fill the so-called vacuum, led by Britain's exit and to pursue their political, economic and strategic interests. Their continued and expanding naval presence turned into a rivalry aimed at political and economic advantage and the quest for markets for vast quantities of military and consumer goods. This increased presence converted the region into an era of turbulence and tension. Concerned with this growing rivalry, the states of Indian Ocean Region came together to oppose the super power naval build up. In 1971, on a Sri Lankan proposal, the UN General Assembly declared the Indian Ocean as a 'Zone of Peace' and took practical measures by establishing the Ad Hoc

Committee on the Indian Ocean to consult the great powers and persuade them to abstain from further military expansion in the Indian Ocean.[11]

Living resource are the most significant assets of the Indian Ocean. About 14.6 percent of the world's fish catch comes from its waters, and it also represents a large share of farmed fish, shell-fish and other aquatic animals. The Indian Ocean has oil and gas fields, sand and gravel aggregates and deposits of manganese and poly-metallic nodules beneath its waters. India has been pursuing research in seabed exploration since the early 1980s. In 1987, India was accorded the pioneer inventor's status by the International Seabed Authority (ISBA), giving it exclusive rights for exploring poly-metallic nodules for mineral resources like copper, cobalt and manganese among others, in the Central Indian Ocean Basin (CIOB). As the competition in field grows, in 2011, China also obtained approval from ISBA to explore a 10,000 sq.km area poly-metallic sulphide ore deposits in the international seabed region of the South West Indian Ocean.

This approval marks an important Chinese inroad into the Indian Ocean. There is a galaxy of scholars who are devoting considerable space to study the quantum and nature of Ocean bed resources possibility of their commercial exploration and its ecological cost. Maritime security and security- related issues in the Indian Ocean, both at sea and in littoral states, is another field of study and research. Robert D. Kaplan described the region as the 'Center Stage for the 21st Century' and emphasized the growing importance of the Indian Ocean, which has long been neglected in the study of international politics.[13] He also explained the civilization and political connections of disparate Asian, African and Middle Eastern players in the Indian Ocean. Kaplan also examined the Sino-Indian competition in the Indian Ocean and US interests in the region.

Regional Cooperation and Conflict in Indian Ocean Region/ Multilateral Initiatives

To promote multi-dimensional regional cooperation, the countries of Indian Ocean formed the Indian Ocean Rim Initiative and Indian Ocean Rim Association for Regional Cooperation (IOR-ARC) in 1977. Renamed as the Indian Ocean Rim Association (IORA) in Mauritius, it is a regional forum of coastal states bordering the Indian Ocean. The Association brings together the representatives of government, business and academia to promote cooperation and closer interaction among them. It also aims at strengthening Economic cooperation, particularly in trade facilitation and investment promotion, as well as social development in the region.[14] Similar organizations include the Bay of Bengal Initiative for Multi-Sectoral Technical and Economic Cooperation (BIMSTEC), which comprises Bangladesh, India, Myanmar, Sri Lanka, and Thailand..." The Indian Ocean Rim Business Forum, Indian Ocean Rim Academic Group (IORAG) and the Indian Ocean Marine Affairs Cooperation (IOMAC), established in 1980s with 35 member states. However, the mandates of these institutions (organizations) focus more on expanding economic cooperation rather than combating piracy. A regional cooperation agreement on combating piracy and armed robbery against ships in Asia (ReCAAP) was concluded in November 2004 by 16 Asian countries, mainly to address issues of piracy in the Straits of Malacca.

India and Indian Ocean

India is a gift of the Indian Ocean, by virtue of its location. India has close neighbors not only with Indonesia, Malaysia, Thailand, Burma, Bangladesh, Sri Lanka, Maldives and obviously Pakistan, but it is also central to the entire Indian Ocean. The African continent and Arabian Peninsula to its west and South-West and Southeast Asia to its east, impart a unique centrality to India in the Indian Ocean. Until the advent of Europeans in the 16th century, the life and history of India was entirely with north-bond.

The Europeans brought about a qualitative change in the life of Indian subcontinent. The experience and legacy of colonialism and imperialism have notable contributed to the country's consciousness of the Indian Ocean. The second world war changed India's perspective of the Indian Ocean drastically. The importance of the Indian Ocean was realized in the wake of the Japanese penetration of South Asia. Noted historian K.M. Panikkar emphasized that India should set up its bases in Singapore, Mauritius, Aden and Socotra as outposts of the country's defence so that India must remain truly Indian.[15]

In contrast to the India's strategy, after the end of the Cold War, China has increased its presence in the Indian Ocean Region and has established its 'nodes of influence', called the 'String of Pearls', under which China has strengthened economic and strategic ties with Bangladesh, Myanmar, Pakistan, Sri Lanka, Maldives. These ties include joint port constructions such as building Chittagong port in Bangladesh, establishing close relations with the Maldives with possible future development of Marao Island, setting up surveillance systems in the Coco islands of Myanmar, developing Hambantota port in Sri Lanka and leasing the Gwadar port of Pakistan. To feed China's industry, China is increasingly dependent on Middle East for energy supply and needs markets to sell its excesses capacity of goods. These are readily available on the Asian and African littorals of the Indian Ocean.

To secure the supply lines, China needs to protect the sea lanes of communication and is compelled to venture into the waters of the Indian Ocean. China's presence in the Indian Ocean poses a serious challenges to the Indian Navy and includes reports of Chinese submarines, including nuclear ones, docking in the Indian Ocean under the pretext of protecting its ships from piracy. The strategy or theory of string of pearls has become one of the most widely debated subjects in the contemporary strategic studies of the Indian Ocean region.

Indian Quest to Dominate the Indian Ocean Region

Indian Ocean Region is widely regarded as the hub of global economic and strategic activities for several reasons. It provides a predominant outlet for oil from the Persian Gulf to various destinations across the globe. It is important to remember that more than 80% of global oil trade passes through the Indian Ocean Region. India has long held the desire to dominate the region through the presence of its naval forces and by attempting to exert greater control over its related economic activities. Alfred Mahan once declared that whoever controls the Indian Ocean, has prospects of ruling the world. Perhaps it is this theory which best describes India's quest to dominate the Indian Ocean Region. In the last few years, the region has once again gained significant importance by becoming a hub of strategic competition among regional and extra-regional rivals. India's interests in the region are challenged by the emerging global powers like China.

To secure its strategic influence, India initiated an unprecedented naval buildup under its vision to turn the Indian Ocean into India's Ocean. As a result, India is allocating more and more funds in the budget to its naval war fighting capability, including both its conventional and strategic forces. Additionally, India's growing economic interests have heightened the Indian Ocean Region's strategic significance. India wants to secure sea-lanes of communication to the Middle East, comprising vital oil and energy supply chains. In this connection, India is not only strengthening its naval capabilities but also seeking to strengthen relationship with smaller states within the Indian Ocean Region. These include Sri Lanka, the Maldives, Myanmar, Thailand, Bhutan, Bangladesh, Mauritius and Seychelles.

This is further evident in PM Modi's emphasis on greater engagement with the littoral states of the Indian Ocean. After securing a landmark victory in 2019 general elections, PM Modi chose the Maldives and Sri Lanka as his first official visit abroad this term to consolidate India's position in the Indian Ocean. This choice clearly shows India's foreign policy priority in the

Indian Ocean Region. Moreover, Mr. Modi has adopted an agenda led by trade and investments to achieve greater power status while benefiting the economy at the same time. A reflection of Indian Ocean outreach is thus reiterated in the 2019–20 budge, which aims at maintaining such hegemonic influence.

India not only economically assists these smaller states in terms of trade and economic development but also attempts to build a lasting military relationship with them. This plays a significant role in its blue water strategy.. This is evident in India's plan to build up its naval and air bases in the Andaman and Nicobar Islands. Sardar Vallabhbhai Patel specifically directed the Royal Indian Navy to hoist the national flag in Lakshadweep on August 15, 1947, to ensure the archipelago's integration into the Indian Union, despite the fact that it was an integral part of Madras presidency. His apprehensions were not unfounded; hours after the arrival of the Indian naval ship, vessels of the Royal Pakistan Navy were seen near the island. After observing the tricolor and the Indian naval presence, they retreated. The initiative had saved Lakshadweep. Sardar Patel knew the strategic importance of this archipelago, as it was not merely a tiny territory but spread over a vast area in the southern Arabian Sea.

After the passing away of Sardar Patel in 1950, such strategic thinking and initiatives receded and a different mindset took root. No importance was given to the study of geography in general and the Indian Ocean in particular. Even under Nehru, maritime strategy was not given enough prominence. Until 1958, the Indian navy was headed by British officers, so one can imagine the policy pursuits in the Indian Ocean. During this era, the vision of the navy was just confined to coastal waters. The South Block never paid any attention to the strategic advantages due to the country's long coasts protruding into the Indian Ocean, including Lakshadweep, and the Andaman & Nicobar Islands. Even the advantage of the UN Law of the Sea enacted in 1982 and the vast Exclusive Economic Zone did not mean anything to the Government of India at that time.

The Indian Ocean today is heavily infested with nuclear submarines, particularly those of belligerent China. Nuclear submarines are not only equipped with the delivery platforms, but also have the capacity to be loaded with nuclear warheads, unlike land and air missiles delivery systems, since submarines can operate thousands of kilometers away from their base. For over a decade, China has been making concerted attempts to gain strategic foot-hold in the Indian Ocean Region.

Only a navy would believe that these are exclusively commercial ventures, but China declared recently that it is planning to explore the possibility of more foreign outposts in Africa, West Asia and other areas.[16] China has almost succeeded in pushing India into a corner in the Maldives. The grand plan of 'strategy for force buildup', with a 160 ship navy and 90 frontline combat platforms by 2022, along with the imperative diplomatic initiatives for achieving the goal of the 'Maritime Strategy of 2027', remained only on paper until the Narendra Modi government took it seriously.

In 2015, Prime Minister Modi unveiled a ten year $ 1.5 billion infrastructure package for the Andamans, including a commitment to double the number of naval patrol aircraft and Israeli-origin unmanned drones through the Andaman Nicobar Command (ANC) in March 2016.The ANC received new landing craft and interceptor boats from the Coast Guard. In April 2016, a guided missile corvette, the INS Karmuk, was dispatched to the Andamans. India's security concerns should be effectively addressed, as suggested by experts, by having three Aircraft Carriers and at least five nuclear submarines available in the Andamans.

During Prime Minister Narendra Modi's visit to Mauritius, India signed an MOU for the improvement of sea and air transportation facilities at Agalega. This step will enhance the capabilities of the Mauritius Defence Forces in safeguarding their interests in oil and gas-rich Agalega. In a significant shift in strategic approach, Narendra Modi convinced Seychelles to allow India to establish a naval base on Assumption Island during his visit to Seychelles in March 2015. Also in the same year (2015), India and Mozambique agreed to broaden defence training beyond the navy and to resurrect a joint-defence working group. As a result, India has begun providing training and equipment to Mozambique's intelligence service.

In May 2016, India signed twelve (12) MOUs with Iran and Afghanistan to allow Indian goods to reach Afghanistan through Iran. India entered into the Quadrilateral Security Dialogue (Quad) with the US, Japan and Australia in Manila on 11th November 2017, which enables patrolling and exerting influence on waterways from the Indian Ocean to the Pacific, including the East and South China Sea. The 'Quad' assures a free and open region, with respect for international law and a rule- based order in the Indo-Pacific.

In an another move in 2017, India and Singapore signed a bilateral agreement that will facilitate logistical support to Indian navy ships, including refueling at Singapore's Changi Naval Base located in the South China Sea. In February 2018, a logistical agreement was signed with Oman, facilitating the use of Port Duqmby the Indian navy and Omani air bases by the Indian Air Force.

India and France also entered into a logistical support agreement in March 2018, seeking to extend logistical support through reciprocal access to respective facilities for the Indian and French armed forces. It also aims to enhance both Indian and French ability to respond to common challenges. France has naval bases at Reunion Island, South west of Mauritius in the Western Indian Ocean and at Heron in Djibouti at the mouth of the Red Sea.

From the above narration, it is understood that, the strategic importance of the Andaman and Nicobar islands and the Lakshadweep Islands, particularly the 'Great Channel', enables India to not only defend its Himalayas but also safeguard its borders by solving all boarder disputes with expansionist China by threatening a blockade of the Great Channel of the Andaman Sea. Strong presence of the Indian Navy in the Andaman & Nicobar islands and Lakshadweep would be the biggest deterrent to restrain China from any future adventures. Every Chinese ship that passes through the Straits of Malacca, Sunda and Lombok has to cross the Lakshadweep and Andaman sea lanes.

The Malacca Strait: A Strategic SLOC

The Strait of Malacca is located between the east coast of Sumatra and the west coast of Peninsular Malaysia, stretching for about 250 miles. The Strait of Singapore, about 100 miles long, is located south of the island of Singapore, between the South Eastern tip of Peninsular Malaysia and North of the Indonesian Riau Islands. Using the Strait of Malacca instead of Indonesia's Lombok Straits can save up to 1600 km or roughly three days of sailing time, as this is the shortest trade route from the Indian Ocean to the South China Sea, making it one of the most important shipping lanes in the world. Thus, the Strait of Malacca is a critical and strategic waterway in the global trading system, with more than 70,000 vessels transiting through its waters every year, carrying more than a quarter of the world trade and almost all oil imports for Japan and China through the South China Sea. Threats to shipping in the Malacca Strait primarily emanate from piracy, transnational crime and maritime terrorism. Any disruption to the flow of maritime traffic through the Strait of Malacca would seriously affect the global economy. Therefore, the security of Malacca Strait is an important concern to both the littoral as well as international community.

Over 40% of India's rapidly growing trade passes through the Strait of Malacca. Ensuring its security would, therefore, also be in India's national interest. The mercantile traffic transiting the Malacca Strait passes close to the Indian area of maritime interest and therefore any unforeseen contingency in the Malacca Strait has security implication for India. Hence, India has a stake in maintaining the safety and security of the Strait of Malacca and the Government of India should aggressively pursue a strategy by contributing to the region's efforts to keep the Strait safe and free from any kind of threats.

Indian naval strategy in the 21st century demands more submarines, a strong mine-laying and mine-clearing capability and naval air reconnaissance capabilities. India is following an important strategic maritime goal in a period of interdependence between the world's geo-economic regions and is establishing an overall maritime presence in its sea area of strategic interests. This strategy includes India's desire to project its prowess beyond its borders. Therefore, India is working under PM Modi's leadership towards building a navy that can counter multiple sea challenges to the mainland. India is also emphasizing its claim as a leading maritime power through a strong forward presence in each of its major island territories. Port Blair is of special maritime importance because of its closeness to the Burmese Coco-island, used by China as a 'land-bridge' to the Indian Ocean, the strategically important sea lanes of communication and the strategic chock point, the Strait of Malacca.[17]

Map 2.1: Strait of Malacca

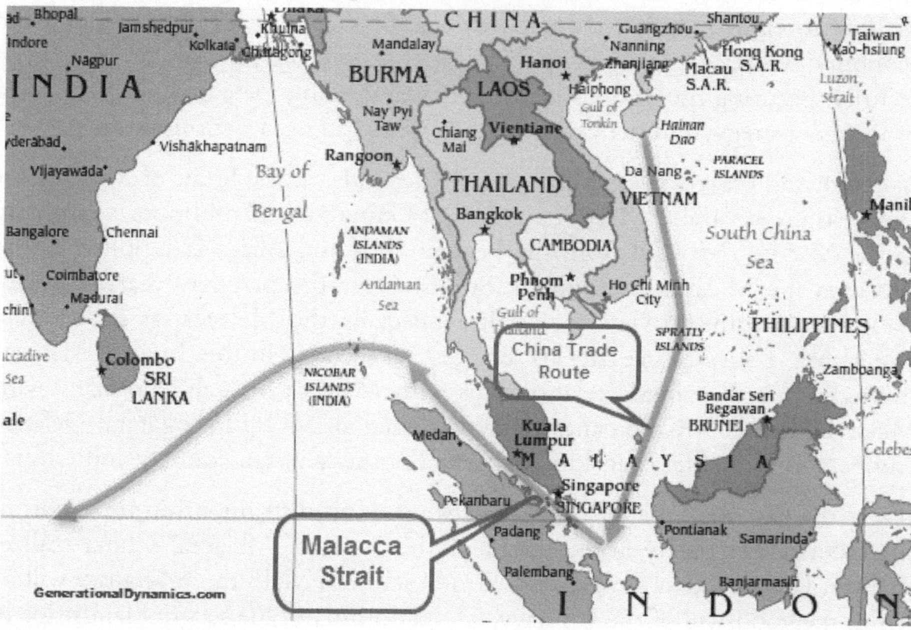

Source: www.googlemaps.com

India's strategic interest is also strongly illustrated by an Indian security analyst, who argues that the limits of the Malacca Strait should be redefined to reflect the contemporary situation to ensure effective security management. According to Rajeev Sawhney, only a composite system of maritime security is needed, with the eastern limits defined by the Singapore Straits at one end and the 'six degree channel' at the other end. Since Indira point is separated by the six degree channel, and is only 165 km from Sumatra, such proximity makes India as much a part of South East Asia. Therefore, comprehensive security could be ensured only by the inclusion of both India and Thailand as bona fide littorals of a redefined Malacca Strait system.[18]

China, as a maritime power, has very long shore lines, numerous islands, vast sea areas and abundant ocean resources. Its sea area is the nation's main artery of foreign trade and its maritime economy is projected to move across the great oceans by 2020. China's maritime commerce is expected to exceed $ 1 trillion, which could force the country to import three quarters of its oil from overseas. Beijing's major political concerns are regime survival, territorial integrity and domestic stability, which are primarily linked to its growing economy. Hence, China's great strength, as well as its vulnerability, is its economy. To sustain its economic growth, China must increasingly rely on external sources of energy and raw materials, which makes the SLOCs vitally important as most of China's foreign trade is conducted by sea. Since energy is the lifeline of the economy, China's economic policy depends on the success of its energy security. Securing the SLOCs is the principal guiding force behind the 'String of Pearls' strategy, and hence it relates to China's grand national strategy.

As a growing great power, China heavily depends on the Strait of Malacca for energy transportation. More than 60% of China's crude oil imports originate in the Middle East. Oil from the Persian Gulf and Africa is supplied to the PRC via the Malacca or Lombok Straits. Over the past few years, Chinese leaders have come to view the straits, especially the Malacca, as strategically vulnerable. Thus, China tries to seek SLOC security in the Strait of Malacca through close diplomatic relationships with Malacca littorals, especially with Malaysia. In 2005, China and Malaysia signed an MOU for bilateral Defence Cooperation, the first of its kind between Southeast Asian country and China.

It was the first time that China publicly announced its intention to be part of the security and safety arrangement of the Strait of Malacca. China realizes that if it fails to actively engage the littoral states of Malacca, its security will be left to the good-will of the US navy, which dominates the security landscape in the region.[2] Chinese security analysts believe that the US and Japan are exaggerating the threat of terrorism to expand their naval presence in the Malacca Strait. China is no less concerned about India's enhanced presence in the region, especially, the Indian modernization of military facilities on the

Andaman and Nicobar islands. Similarly, US-Indonesia military cooperation, which highlights maritime cooperation in the Strait of Malacca, also worries China.

Thus, the Malacca Strait becomes critical to China in light of the US military presence in the region, as well as the expanding naval presence of the US and Japan due to growing terrorism in the region. The US-Indonesia military cooperation, Indo-Indonesia Defence Co-operation and military agreement and Indonesia's agreement to India's request to establish a naval base at Sabang Island are causes for concern to China regarding its freedom of navigation, safety & security in the Strait of Malacca. Hence, due to this vulnerability, which affects China's energy supply and trade practices, China has been building a corridor as an alternative route, called the China- Pakistan Economic Corridor (CPEC), in collaboration with Pakistan, through the Pakistan Occupied Kashmir (POK), connecting China with Gwadar Port.

The keen efforts by India and China reflect the strategic importance of the Strait of Malacca's safety and security, assisting the littoral states to enhance their capacity to ensure freedom of navigation in the Straits. However, the littoral states are watching carefully on the rising interest of these nations in the Malacca Strait. Singapore's defence minister, Teo Chee Heun, remarked earlier that over the next few decades, the Asia-Pacific would be the region where big powers like China, Japan and India actively emerge for power and influence. The emergence of these maritime powers is a concern for the littoral states. China and India are expected to emerge as powerful maritime nations by 2025; both nations would concentrate on a maritime economic buildup, which will lead to high military spending and efforts to secure the SLOCs. Both nations will build naval forces with significant strategic reach and power projection.

Six Degree Channel (Great Channel) of Andaman Sea

A large number of ships traversing Strait of Malacca have to pass through either the Great Channel or the Ten Degree Channel. The 122 km wide Ten Degree Channel which separates the Andaman's and Nicobar wholly lies within India's sovereign waters. The 166 km wide Great Channel (Six Degree Channel) separates the Southern tip of Great Nicobar (Indira point) and Sumatra in Indonesia.

Presently, China is a rising power in the Asia and has been emerging into a global super power, with whom India has long standing, unresolved border disputes. About 42,645 sq.km of Ladakh have been under illegal Chinese occupation since 1957. Another 5,130 sq.km of Kashmir territory were given (gifted) to Pakistan by China after the former usurped it. Therefore, directly or indirectly connected to the Tibetan question, it is all the more important to understand, analyze and integrate these strategically important issues into our defence strategic approach.

Map 2.2: Six Degree Channel/Great Channel of Andaman Sea

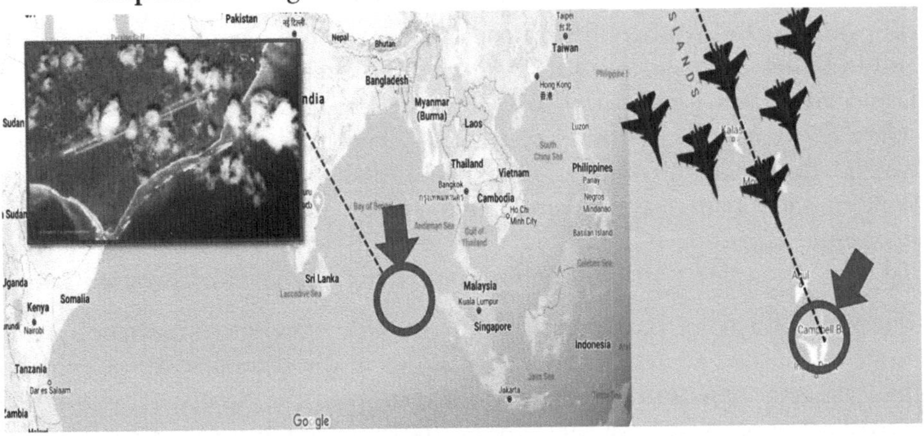

Source: www.googlemaps.com

About 40 percent of world trade passes through the Andaman Sea, via the Six Degree Channel, which is one of the vital sea lanes on the globe, situated at the mouth of the Malacca Strait. China depends on this Six Degree Channel for 80 percent of its oil imports and for most of its international trade. China's energy supply is vulnerable at this Choke point. Any attempt by China to repeat the events of 1962 can be checkmated by blocking the Six Degree Channel in the Andaman Sea. Even the scattered uninhabited islands of the Andaman & Nicobar archipelago are vital for strategic networks, useful for setting up surveillance posts, radars and anti-aircraft artillery. China has been developing even the submersible banks and reefs of the Spratly Islands for setting up its military bases to monitor the South China Sea route.

India Needs Strong Indian Navy

To fulfill the contemporary military requirements, the Indian navy will seek an increase in its share of the budget, which has decreased over the years, according to Navy Vice-Chief Admiral Ashok Kumar, who spoke to the press on September 17, 2019, in Delhi. The Indian navy will seek a larger budget to face the challenges and meet its growing aspirations within the defence services budget, which has dropped in the last 6–7 years. Recently, in early September 2019, seven Chinese navy warships operated in and around the

Indian Ocean Region, in the waters of Sri Lanka, including an over 27,000 ton amphibious vessel, which was tracked by the Indian Navy using P-81 anti-submarine warfare spy planes and other surveillance assets. Their presence in the Southern Indian Ocean Region is a matter of great concern for India's security. The share of the navy was 18% of the Defence budget in 2012–13, but today it has fallen to about 13.66%. According to Ashok Kumar, the navy's aim is to convince the authorities to enhance its share of the Defence budget.

According to the Stockholm International Peace Research Institute (SIPRI), the 4.6 lakh crore military expenditure figure for India includes defence pensions, which amount to of the total. Of the remaining amount, two-third one-fourth goes for day-to-day running costs, salaries and maintaining the almost 1 lakh-strong armed forces. Therefore, overall, this leaves only about one-fourth of the 4.6 lakh crores for military modernization and new weapon systems. Despite India being the world fourth largest spender, displacing even Russia, its armed forces continue to suffer from critical shortages on several fronts. On the other hand, China has increased its defence budget for 24th consecutive year. Keeping this scenario in view, the Indian Navy wants to increase its share of defence budget, which has recently gone down over the years.

Towards the objective, India is set to go ahead with a $ 3.1 billion deal with the US to acquire maritime aircraft for the navy, which will add to its surveillance capabilities in the Indian Ocean Region. The procurement of 10 Boeing P-81 Maritime Patrol Aircraft is likely to be cleared at a key acquisition meeting soon, with the contract to be processed under the Foreign Military Sales (FMS) route.[21] The Maritime Patrol Aircraft, which specialize in tracking and hunting down enemy submarines with lightweight torpedoes and depth charges, are also operated by the US and Australia. India uses them to keep track of ship movements. The P-81 aircraft have been a source of pride for the Indian navy, which depends on the fleet for various operations, from tracking submarines to search and rescue and even reconnaissance over land. Interestingly, the aircraft provided valuable data to the defence forces during the Doklam standoff with China after they were deployed to carry out a reconnaissance mission in the high-altitude location in 2017.

With China setting a furious pace in the construction of new air craft carriers, India is in the danger of losing its combat and power projection edge in the Indian Ocean Region. Therefore, the Indian Navy now plans to take up afresh its long pending case for a third air- craft carrier with the government to showcase how a multi-dimensional Carrier Battle Group (CBG), which can move around 500 nautical miles (900 kms) in a day, is formidably powerful and extremely flexible in providing a wide range of tailored responses across the entire spectrum of warfare, but it presence, surveillance, deterrence, coercion, intervention, or war fighting.

The Indian Navy has long advocated the requirement of three carriers to ensure at least two are available at any given time, one each for the eastern and western seaboards, which the third is undergoing its maintenance and refit cycle. China already has six to seven warships deployed in the Indian Ocean Region at any given time. The permanent presence of a Chinese CBG in the Indian Ocean Region in the near future will create power imbalances in the region. Therefore, India must plan for the future. The Indian Ocean Region's frangible maritime domain, along with the collusion threat from China and Pakistan, necessitates a strong Indian Navy to meet future challenges. Multi-dimensional Carrier Battle Groups (CBGs) provide much more operational flexibility and lethality than shore-based airfields (Times of India, dt. October 1, 2019). To maintain this, India needs to allocate at least 20–25 percent of the defence budget to the Indian Navy consistently over a long period, keeping in view the strength and allocation towards military of China and its defence sector.

Indian navy currently operates 10 submarines including two nuclear power underwater boats. In comparison, the people's Liberation Army Navy has a fleet of more than 60 submarines, both nuclear and conventional. The Scorpene-class submarine has superior features such as advanced acoustic silencing techniques, low radiated noise levels, a hydro-dynamically optimized shape and the ability to launch a crippling attack on the enemy.

The Indian naval fleet has reached the size of 140 warships and the planned induction of 56 more warships and 6 submarines is underway. Emphasizing the importance of the Indian navy's submarine programme, the Indian navy Chief Sunil Lanba noted that after successful induction of the first Scorpene-class submarine, INS Kalavari. In December 2017, several trials have been conducted by India on its second Scorpene-class attack submarine, INS Khanderi, which is ready for commissioning. The ambition of the Indian Naval Chief is to increase the number of warships to 200and aircraft to 500 in the Indian Naval force. Besides increasing its naval capabilities at sea, the Indian navy is expanding its resources and firepower to achieve control over the seas, in addition to following the military doctrine of enemy denial. India aims to safeguard its merchant ships, ensuring they can easily navigate the waters for business and commercial purposes.

A significant development occurred when India and Saudi Arabia planned to conducted a joint naval exercise in December 2019 – January 2020, notwithstanding tensions in and around the Persian Gulf. India and Saudi Arabia agreed on the bilateral engagements to ensure security and safety of waters of Indian Ocean & Gulf regions from the threats that may affect the interests of two countries. To this effect, a memorandum of understanding (MoU) was signed on Wednesday, October 28, 2019 to set up a strategic partnership council. The proposed Indo-Saudi engagement in the Indian Ocean Region, as a part of New Delhi's Indo-Pacific vision, is key to stability and order amid China's growing influence in the region. With almost 1/3rd of the worlds liquefied natural gas and about 25% of total global oil consumption passing through the narrow Strait of Harmuz is highly important strategic route for international trade (The Hindu, dt 1/11/2019).

It took nearly four and a half decades to move away from the Nehruvian thinking of ignoring the ocean neighborhood, which had deeply penetrated deep into New Delhi's defence and diplomatic mindset. Despite the committed academics in India and the West, more and more analysts and strategic thinkers are voicing the geo-strategic importance of India's Islands and the navy's role in the Indian Ocean. Air marshal Dhiraj Kukreja (Retd.) felt that India needs to grow out of earlier thinking and develop the islands as a hub or spring- board for power projection in the region, without referring to the Andaman & Nicobar Islands. Admiral Raja Menon argues that China's strength is the huge logistical network they have built up in Tibet, but their weakness (Chinese) lies in the Indian Ocean.

David Scott's article, published in the Journal of Strategic Studies (7-2-2013), expressed that, in the case of the Malacca Strait, India has the ability to easily block Chinese access to the Indian Ocean. Similar views were also expressed by Ajay Shukla, an eminent defence journalist, who stated that the Indian Navy can shut down the Indian Ocean shipping lanes whenever it chooses. According to a retired fleet commander, a couple of submarines and a fighter squadron at Car Nicobar could easily enforce a blockade if declared. Jeff M. Smith, Director of South Asia Programmes and Kraemer Strategic Fellow, described the Andaman Nicobar Islands (ANI) as India's strategic outpost. With all its capabilities more fully developed, the ANI could help India monitor military and commercial traffic passing between the Indian Ocean and East Asia. This forward position would serve India's growing economic, political and military interests in East Asia and further position India to act as the gatekeeper of the Indian Ocean, especially at a time when the PLAN is increasingly active in the region.

Piracy and its Implications in Indian Ocean Region

Due to the chaos and violence in Somalia after 1991, rising economic deprivation, and an uncertain future, many coastal people of Somalia were pushed into piracy to feed themselves and their families. These pirates became predators as they had no mission other than acquiring money. Piracy off the Somalia coast gradually began to threaten international shipping after the early 1990s. International maritime organizations, the World Food Organization and Navy Trading Countries in the Indian Ocean felt concerned over the rise of piracy. It contributed to increased shipping costs, higher shipping insurance premiums, and delays in the delivery of Food Aid Shipments ates.

The seriousness of the issue of piracy in the Indian Ocean Region is reflected in the fact that more than US $ 330 million was paid in ransoms to pirates between 2009 and 2012. According to a World Bank report in 2013, maritime piracy by Somali pirates costs US $ 18 billion a year. Out of the total 264 piracy cases reported in 2013, as stated by the International Maritime Bureau, 189 incidents took place in the Indian Ocean Region. The most vulnerable regions for piracy in the Indian Ocean Region are along the Horn of Africa, off the Somali Coast, the Gulf of Aden and the region near Indonesia in Southeast Asia. Singapore is the country most affected by the Maritime Piracy in the Indian Ocean Region. 39 of its ships were attacked in 2013 alone. Malaysia and Hong Kong have also been adversely affected by Maritime Piracy, with 20 Malaysian ships attacked by pirates.. In Hong Kong, the number of attacks was 10 in the same year. In 2013, 304 crew members were taken hostage, 54 of whom were from Malaysia and 34 from Indonesia. According to Wayne Bowen (2014), Somalia is not alone in its inability to prevent piracy from its coasts; Yemen, Pakistan, Burma and Tanzania have also failed to prevent pirates from launching from their territory.

According to the International Maritime Bureau (IMB), the Piracy Reporting Centre recorded 201 incidents of Maritime piracy and armed robbery in 2018, up from 180 incidents reported in 2017. The peak years of the Somali piracy crisis were during the period from 2007 to 2012. Piracy made a strong comeback in Somalia in 2017, according to Abdi Latif Dahir (May 24, 2018). After years of decline, piracy of the Somali coast occurred in the Gulf of Aden again. Consequently, the piracy attacks were on the rise again in 2018. Global maritime piracy may see its first significant increase by the end of 2019, since the height of Somali piracy incidents reported in 2010.

To tackle this problem, more than 20 nations contributed to maintaining an international naval force in the Gulf of Aden, ensuring that 17 naval ships are on patrol there on any given day. They have created an internationally recognized transit corridor that provides security to about 30,000 cargo ships that transit the corridor every year.

To deal with the issue of maritime piracy, the US and its allies operate through the Combined Task Force (CTF-150), a coalition 25 nations, based in Bahrain. China and India are not a part of the CTF-150. However, Russian, Chinese and Indian anti-piracy operations do exist in the Indian Ocean Region. However, the constraints faced are primarily due to the vastness of the Indian Ocean.

In 2008, a multinational coalition task force called as Combined Task Force-150 was formed to tackle and to fight Somalian Piracy by establishing a Maritime Security Patrol Area (MSPA) within Gulf of Aden. The United Nations Security Council adopted a resolution in 1838, calling on nations with vessels in the area to use military force to repress the acts of piracy. In December 2008, the UN Security Council again l deplored all acts of piracy and urged the states and regional organizations to fight against piracy and armed robbery at sea off the coast of Somalia and enter its territorial waters to repress acts of piracy. The pirates have continued expanding their area of operation into the Indian Ocean, in some cases more than 1850 km off the coast of Somalia, and have attacked ships close to Seychelles. Rising piracy has threatened to reduce world trade through the Suez Canal by about one-third. It also has economic implications, as some shipping companies have decided to re-route vulnerable vessels around the Cape of Good Hope.[22]

India's efforts to bring more nations into coastal radar network system is a good sign. As part of efforts to further expand the coastal radar chain network to enable real-time monitoring of the high seas for threats and expand India's assistance for capacity building to Indian Ocean littoral states, efforts are in advanced stages to set up coastal radar stations in the Maldives, Myanmar and Bangladesh, according to defence sources.

Mauritius, Seychelles and Sri Lanka have already been integrated into the country's coastal radar chain network. Similar plans are in the pipeline with Maldives and Myanmar and discussions are ongoing with Bangladesh and Thailand. Two of the coastal radar stations in the Maldives were functional as of last year and works was underway on the third station. The Indian navy's Information Management and Analysis Centre (IMAC), located in Gurugram, and set up after the 26/11 Mumbai terror attacks, is the nodal agency for maritime data fusion.

As part of an information exchange regarding traffic on the high seas, the navy has been authorised by the government to conclude white shipping agreements with 36 countries and three multinational constructs. So far, agreements have been concluded with 22 countries and one multi-lateral construct. Of these, 17 agreements and the one multi-lateral construct have been operationalized. At the navy's Information Fusion Centre for the Indian Ocean Region (IFC-IOR), which is meant to promote Maritime domain Awareness, three more International Liaison Officers (ILOs) are expected to join soon. The ILOs from France, Japan and the US have joined the centre.

Under phase I of the coastal radar chain network, 46 coastal radar stations have been set up across the country's coastline. Under phase-II of the project, which is currently underway, 38 static radar stations and four mobile radar stations are being set up by the Coast Guard and are in advanced stage of completion. This will also enhance India's coastal security.

Chinese Trawlers on the Prowl in the Indian Ocean

The illegal, unregulated and unreported (IUU) fishing has been rated as the highest Maritime Security threat, more serious than piracy and Narcotic Smuggling, according to research undertaken by 'Caught Red Handed Project.' (IUU) fishing is one of the greatest non-traditional global Maritime Security threats facing nations due to the alarming depletion of fish in the sea. This concern has been flagged worldwide. However, it is blatantly disregarded by China, which is a member of the UNSC and a signatory to the UN Convention on the law of Sea. China, ranked as the worst offender in IUU fishing in 2019, has committed to the Sustainable Development Goals (SDG) of the Paris Conference 2015, as revealed by Indian Navy veteran Commodore Anil Singh to the Financial Express online.

As reported by the Financial Express online, India has observed an increase in the number of Chinese Vessels operating in the Indian Ocean, which, according to sources, is a matter of Maritime Security concerns for the countries of the Indian Ocean Region. These Vessels are likely to monitoring and surveying the seawater to improve their submarine capabilities and possibly engage in deep-sea mining. The area where the number of Chinese Research Vessels has increased is in the "Ninety Degree East Ridge and South-West Indian Ridge." Additionally, the number of Chinese fishing vessels has increased in the high seas of the Indian Ocean Region, particularly in the Central Arabian Sea and South West Indian Ocean.

Gaps in the fisheries regulation in high seas of the Indian Ocean, as per a report released by Trigg Matt Tracking (TMT), indicate that in just five years, squid fishing in one unregulated area grew by 830 percent. According to the findings of the report, on earth, the Indian Ocean has become home to some of the most important fisheries, accounting for over 14 percent of global wild-caught fish. However, 30 percent of assessed stocks in the region are already overfished, and unregulated fishing, which is not factored into the 30 percent calculation, is increasing in intensity, putting essential sources of revenue for millions of people and the wider ecosystem health at risk.

One out of five fish sold in the market is caught illegally. This results in a loss to the global economy estimated to be around $ 23 billion, according to an analysis undertaken by Global Fishing Watch.

Significance of Small Islands in the Indian Ocean Region

The Mission SAGAR is inspired by the Prime Minister Modi's vision of Security and Growth for All in the Region. Mission SAGAR -III is a part of India' HADR (Humanitarian Assistance and Disaster Relief) assistance to friendly foreign countries during the on-going pandemic. This mission is undertaken in accordance with PM Modi's vision of SAGAR and reiterates India's position as a dependable partner, and the Indian Navy as the preferred Security Partner and first responder. It also highlights the importance accorded to ASEAN countries and further strengthens the existence bonds.

India has sent INS Kesari to Maldives, Mauritius, Seychelles, Madagascar, and Comoros carrying Covid-19 related medicines, medical assistance teams and food items. Small Islands have historically played a very significant geo-strategic role in the Indian Ocean Region. From the ancient Persians' and Arabs' links with Pemba and Zanzibar on the Eastern African coasts to the more recent American military presence on the Diego Garcia, several small islands have been viewed with interests and used by regional and foreign powers for military purposes. Their location at sea and isolation from the continental land masses can provide very advantageous positions to armed forces for a wide range of activities, such as defence, surveillance, support and power projection from sea to land.

The military forces' interest in these islands has been greatly renewed since the beginning of the 21st century, as the Indian Ocean Region's growing importance in global geopolitics and the world economy. This is evident in the case of the United States with Diego Garcia in the Chagos Archipelago (BIOT), as well as for India with its island territories, Andaman & Nicobar, Lakshadweep and for France with its Indian Ocean Islands, Reunion and Mayotte. Many other small islands are already in use for ongoing military operations and are now integrated into strategic planning, such as the Seychelles, Mauritius, the Maldives, Oman's Masirah Islands, Yemen's Socotra island, Australia's Cocos (keeling) Islands and Burma's Coco Islands.

Therefore, Prime Minister of India Narendra Modi initiated a strategic approach towards small islands nations as part of his (India's) vision, using small islands for military forward presence in the Indian Ocean Region to face future challenges posed jointly by China and Pakistan.

Map 2.3: Western Indian Ocean Region

Source: www.googlemaps.com

Military forward presence has been defined as a country's military deployment and operations taking place outside its national territory, its extra- territorial maritime zones (EEZ & continental shelf), as well as its nearby aerial and maritime approaches in international areas. Therefore, the military forward presence consists of military deployment and operations taking place far from the national mainland, and consequently includes permanent and temporary military installations in other countries' islands or overseas territories.

Military bases or facilities operated by non-Indian Ocean countries in an Indian Ocean country include the bases of the USA at Djibouti, Oman,

Bahrain, France at Djibouti, UAE, Japan again at Djibouti and the United Kingdom at Bahrain. A military base operated by a non-Indian Ocean country in an Indian Ocean overseas territory is the US Navy support facility at Diego Garcia, located in British Indian Ocean Territory (BIOT). Overall, the military forward presence is quite impressive in the Indian Ocean and has been on the rise in recent years, especially in the wake of the radical Islamism terrorist outbreak in the early 2000s and the Somalia maritime piracy crisis at the end of the 2000s.

In accordance with the Indian Maritime Doctrine 2004, 2007 and 2015, India's Maritime Military Strategy calls for 'reach' multiplied by sustainability. Presence is used to express a resolve to deploy forces into or close to areas of interest or concern. In the Indian Naval context, forward presence is intended to (i) demonstrate India's commitment to regional stability, (ii) gain familiarity with overseas operational environments, (iii) keep areas of interest under surveillance and (iv) promote interoperability among the forces of friendly nations. This doctrine leads to the strengthening of India's infrastructure presence, the growth of its naval capabilities and increased deployments of these naval assets around the Indian Ocean.

On the whole, the Andaman & Nicobar installations are of much greater geostrategic significance as they have the potential to allow India to project large naval and aerial power through Southeast Asia and control the Andaman Sea, the Six Degree Channel and the Northern entrance of the Malacca Strait. Therefore, the Andaman and Nicobar Islands are instrumental in pursuing the security dimension of the Look East Policy initiated in 1991 by the Government of India. The Lakshadweep installations, however, are, much more modest and their role is limited to a first line of defence for the homeland and maritime security in its surrounding waters. This area is also of vital importance for maritime transportation as it is crossed by the Nine Degree Channel and projects India's maritime domain westward into the Southern Arabian Sea. Hence, India needs a strategy beyond the Andaman, Nicobar and Lakshadweep Islands in regard to small island nations in the Indo-Pacific region in order to project itself as a net security provider and challenger to face China's growing influence.

Mission SAGAR: Key to the Indian Ocean Region

INS Kesari returned to India on 28th June 2020, after travelling 7500 nautical miles over 55 days for Mission Sagar (Security and Growth for All in the Region) as the project was launched on 10th May 2020 to provide Covid-19 related assistance to the island nations of Maldives, Mauritius, Madagascar,

Comoros and Seychelles. While on the mission INS Kesari delivered essential food items, medicines and also deployed a Medical Assistance Team (MAT) to Mauritius and Comoros.

Due to the Covid-19 pandemic, the Indian Ocean Island nations were adversely affected due to their main source of economy was tourism, falling flat. Two of the Indian Ocean nations, Maldives and Seychelles are within the top five countries whose GDP is dependent on tourism and travel, being 32.5 per cent and 26.4 per cent respectively and the rest of the nations are in double digits. These islands are already facing the brunt of climate change—rising sea levels, had to face this new unprecedent reality.

During such a tumultuous and unexpected crisis, Mission Sagar is much needed. Helping the Indian Ocean Island Nations and to develop positive relations with them is strategically significant for India. As China woos the world with Covid-19 related assistance, India was also taking steps to spread its Medical Diplomacy net far and wide. While many countries like the US have purchased the anti-malarial drug—Hydroxychloroquine (HCQ) from India. The government of India has so far also provided it as grant assistance to 24 countries. In view of this prominence of the Indian Ocean sea Lanes of Communication have also been recognised by other powers like China, giving higher importance to India's maritime security China has been increasing its hegemony in the Indian Ocean Region by increasing Belt and Road Initiative and to increase presence of the People's Liberation Army Navy (PLAN) in the Indian Ocean. Although, historic reference to silk routes has been given, no Chinese ships controlled the Indian Ocean routes since, the Chinese explorer Zheng He sailed in the 15th Century, embarking on seven Voyages.

Looking at such an economic and strategic importance of Indian Ocean. Island is also recognised by other nations, SAGAR (Security and Growth for All in the Region) was launched by India in 2015. The main purpose for SAGAR was of tackling regional issues like providing humanitarian help to maritime neighbours and to counter non-state actors like pirates in the Indian Ocean. 2004 tsunami, repeated earthquakes, threat of rising sea level, water crisis in the Maldives and help that followed show the importance of this initiative. The overall objective of India is to gain legitimacy as the sole regional power in the Indian Ocean with the capability of providing humanitarian relief and security to the entire region. The SAGAR initiative, launched in 2015, works in tandem with Act East Policy, Sagaramala Project and Project Mausam. Keeping in line with the overall initiative of 2015, India extended help to the Indian Ocean littoral states, starting from the evacuation from Wuhan, China due to Coronavirus. Those evacuated, including Compassionate cases from Bangladesh, Myanmar, Maldives, South

Africa and Madagascar. Then the compassionate cases were also put into quarantine in India, before sending them back to their respective countries, due to which India got credibility as a responsible power. In Mission SAGAR, India became the first responder to Mauritius and Seychelles by sending a consignment of life-saving drugs including Hydroxychloroquine. PM Modi also gave full assistance to these countries. Such help on the top of 2018 agreement, a naval base on Assumption Island must have created a new bond between the two countries.

Covid-19 has given an important opportunity to India to extend its relationship with the Indian Ocean Island Nations and through Mission SAGAR, as the concept of SAGAR initiative was strengthened. With the amount of lives saved, capacity building and equipment supplied, Mission SAGAR became an important milestone in the relationship. The recent acceptance of India into the Indian Ocean Commission as an observer state in the presence of China shows that, India has gone a long way since the launch of Sagar initiative in 2015 under Modi government. Through the Indian Ocean Commission observer status, India can extend its influence to the Gulf countries and Indian Ocean stakeholder states to increase Indian legitimacy and build a positive image.

However, India should also be wary that it was the 5th member to be accepted as an Observer State, while China was already present. Also, India in order to protect its interests in the Indian Ocean Island Nations, needs to start building infrastructure, conduct military exercises and invest in the Stakeholder Countries to become a major player at the neck of Indian Ocean Sea Lanes of Communication—the Bab el-Mandeb and Eritrea, according to Nikunj Singh, Observer Research Foundation, New Delhi.

India's Vaccine Diplomacy

India's Vaccine diplomacy puts China on the back foot in the South Asia. India has gifted already the Covishield Vaccine manufactured locally by Serum Institute of India to all SAARC countries and other Asian countries. However, not surprisingly, Global Times has reacted with a propaganda against 'India's Maitri' initiative, raising India's capacity to manufacture vaccine, after the fire at the Serum Institute and also claiming that Indians in China were embracing Chinese Vaccine.

India told the UN Security Council recently, on 17th February 2021 that India had gifted 2 lakh Covid-19 shots to UN peacekeepers. Twenty-five countries have already received India made vaccines. India's External Affairs

Minister Mr. Jaishankar informed the UN Council that another 49 countries in Europe, Latin America, Southeast Asia and Pacific Islands will be supplied in the coming days. However, Chinese Foreign Minister Wang Yi told the UN Council that it had supplied vaccines to 22 countries.

In contrast to the Indian effort, China has had little to offer to countries in the region where it continues to otherwise rapidly expand its influence, both economically and politically. While Nepal's drug regulator is yet to approve the use of the Chinese vaccine, sources in the Maldives government said that delivery of Covid-19 vaccines by China so far, and even China's close ally Cambodia recently requested India for Vaccines despite having received a million doses of the Chinese vaccine. According to a Reuters report, China has been in vaccine deadlock with Bangladesh since the latter refused to contribute towards development cost of the vaccine.

India's Vaccines were being mainly supplying to South Asian countries as a form of aid. India, however, is also supplied vaccines on contractual or commercial basis to Saudi Arabia, South Africa, Brazil, Morocco, Bangladesh and Myanmar. By doing this India will gain good will from these countries.

India and Australia as Natural Maritime Partners in the Indian Ocean Region

Much of the initial focus of security cooperation between Australia and India in the coming years is likely to be on maritime security. These include issues such as piracy and maritime terrorism, illegal fishing, maritime environmental issues, people trafficking and Humanitarian and Disaster Relief (HADR). There are many opportunities for expanded cooperation in these areas on a bilateral or multilateral basis. Australia, India and the United States could sponsor for the establishment of disaster relief arrangements in the Indian Ocean Region, modeled on the successful FRANZ trilateral disaster relief arrangements conducted in the Pacific by France, Australia and New Zealand.[23] There are also opportunities for enhanced cooperation in anti-piracy efforts. Australia currently participates in the US-sponsored combined task forces 150 and 151 to combat piracy and terrorism in the Northeast Indian Ocean. Meanwhile, India conducts its own anti-piracy operations in the Gulf of Aden and doesn't formally participate in coalition counter - terrorism operations. The reason for this is political sensitivity in New Delhi over participation with a US-led military coalitions. There will be scope for Australia to explore creative ways to bridge this gap through promoting bilateral anti-piracy operations involving Australian and Indian Naval vessels.

India and Australia have shared interests beyond the Indian Ocean which extends into Asia-Pacific region and at a global level such as nuclear non-proliferation and disarmament and to control other weapons of mass destruction.[24] Both countries—Australia and India want to see the development of balanced multilateral institutions in the Asia-Pacific Region that are not dominated by any one country. India and Australia had also shared interests in ensuring safety and freedom of navigation in key Sea Lanes of Communication (SLOC) in the Asia-Pacific region such as Strait of Malacca and the South China Sea. Both countries have shared interests in promoting democracy, political stability and secularism in Southeast Asia, especially in Indonesia. This is an area where there can be considerable strategic collaboration between India and Australia in the future.

A major challenge that Australia will need to address in the Indian Ocean is how to navigate its important relationships with both China and India. China is Australia's leading economic partner and India is also rapidly becoming a key economic partner. India and China have a rapidly developing trade relationship, although they also have a number of bilateral issues that sometimes create significant threat, particularly on the Indian side. In engaging with India, Australia needs to be mindful of Indian concerns and differences in perceptions regarding China's security interests. Many Indian strategists are highly sensitive to any Chinese security presence in the Indian Ocean. Many view Chinese commercial interests in the region with suspicion and a sizeable number of Indian analysts believe that China has a long-term strategy of encircling or containing India.

Australia's strategy towards China in the Indian Ocean Region will also involve some difficult balancing of its interests in the Indian and Pacific Ocean. Australia, the US and others have concerns about China's increasing military power in the Pacific, particularly in the South China Sea. However, despite the growing interrelationship between Indian Ocean and Pacific Ocean security, it is not clear to what extent—or how these concerns in the Pacific should drive Australia's policy in the Indian Ocean. Some argue that Australia should work with the US and India to enhance their collective military capabilities in the Indian Ocean. Such an approach could sustain or even increase China's existing strategic vulnerabilities in the Indian Ocean Region. The consequences of this are not easy to predict. Others believe that Australia should work with the US, India and China in the Indian Ocean to find ways to accommodate the legitimate interests of all powers in the Indian Ocean Region. It may be in Australia's interests to facilitate the development of China's role as a legitimate and responsible stakeholder in Indian Ocean security.

Australia-China Relations hit a new low in the recent past. Cracks began to show in 2008, when Canberra blacklisted Huawei and ZTE for being involved in the rollout of its 5G networks. In that same year, Australia passed a new foreign interference law that was widely seen as aimed at increasingly widespread Chinese influence operations primarily targeting the Chinese-Australian community. The cracks widened into a gaping rift in 2020 when Australia in April 2020 called for an independent enquiry into the origin of the COVID-19 pandemic and criticized both China and World Health Organization (WHO) for the initial handling of the Coronavirus outbreak a move that enraged China and brought an increasingly troubled relationship into open discord. So, Australia in the coming years might need to choose whether it should work with its security partners to limit Chinese naval presence in the Indian Ocean. However, the viability of any long-term understanding with China in the Indian Ocean may depend on China's willingness to recognize India's legitimate security interests in the Indo-Pacific.

Fundamental shifts in the balance of power in the Indian and Pacific Oceans have highlighted the need for a closer security relationship between India and Australia. Australia's strategic posture can no longer rely on previous certainties and India faces strategic imperatives that are likely to position Australia an important security partner in the coming years. The primary focus of the future India-Australia security relationship is likely to be in the Indian Ocean Region, particularly on maritime security, where numerous opportunities for mutual benefit exist. A balanced security relationship will require cooperation with the United States in many areas, but should also move beyond the US in other areas. It will also require a balanced understanding of China's regional role. India and Australia need to pay significant attention to this aspect to shape their relationship for mutual benefit. This need is underscored by the deterioration of Australia-China relations in recent months,, following the outbreak of the Coronavirus in China and its subsequent global spread, particularly affecting Australia.

Importance of 'Oceania Region'

Oceania is a geographic region that includes Australia, Melanesia, Micronesia, and Polynesia, spanning the eastern and western hemispheres. It has a land area of 8,525,989 sq.km and a population of over 41 million. Compared to other continents, Oceania is the smallest in land area and the second smallest in population, after Antarctica. Oceania consists of thousands of islands throughout the Central and South Pacific Ocean, including, Australia, which is the smallest continent by total land area. The region includes 14 countries, 2 associated countries and 18 dependencies.

In Indian foreign policy and strategic discourse, island nations have gained special attention, particularly since 2014, when Prime Minister Narendra Modi recognised the significance of Small Island nations. This shift came in response to China's increasing presence in the Indian Ocean Region and the broader Oceania region. Oceana Region. The Modi government has acknowledged that regardless of their proximity to strategic sea lanes or the mainland, small island nations hold important strategic and commercial significance. This does not mean that other island nations were not important for India.

Map 2.4: Oceania Region

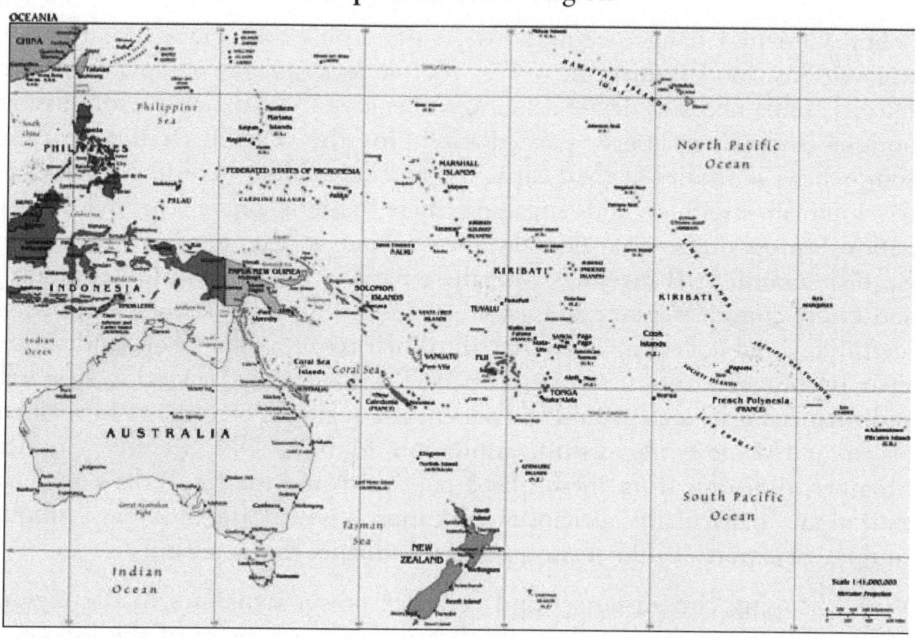

Source: www.googlemaps.com

Oceania is one of the regions where India's approach depends on information from larger neighbours, such as Australia and New Zealand. One of the severe limitations has been the lack of diplomatic missions and commercial liaison offices in many Oceania Countries, such as Fiji, Australia, New Zealand and Papua New Guinea (PNG). The Indian mindset needs to change, as any island nation can be a strategic asset, both in terms of monitoring and using that island nation as a refueling base or transit point. For example, the Cuban Missile Crisis is one instance in history when a small island nation became highly important for both the super powers i.e., the US and the former USSR.

The entry of China into this geostrategic theatre has forced countries, like Australia, the US and other major powers to recalibrate their strategies towards this region. Aid assistance, development, and infrastructure projects have become the new currency, utilised by these nations. Invariably, the superiority of the US and its allied partners in the region has been challenged. China's inroads into Timor-Leste and its constantly improving relationship with Fiji, PNG, and Vanuatu have created concerns in the minds of decision-makers in countries like Australia and New Zealandas well.

From the Indian point of view, there are several areas that need to be studied in the region to help shape India's policy towards small Island nations in the Oceania region. These areas include creating awareness about India's nuclear policy, Climate Change negotiations, its stand on world Trade Organisation negotiations, food security as well as its role as a globally acceptable player. Further, India needs to devise a strategy to engage these nations, with possible options including larger participation in the Pacific Island Forum, comprehensive studies of their capacities and capabilities, building sustainable development modules and engaging these nations under the developing nations' programme—Sagaramala programme is the need of the hour. Regular summit level meetings with these nations would build understanding and create complementary relationships. India should assist these nations in identifying and collecting data related to their resources, both on land and in their Exclusive Economic Zones (EEZ). The low cost of scientific Research and financial assistance would the benefit the region. For India to be a global player and achieve its intrinsic aspiration to be a UN Security Council Member, the votes from these island nations would matter. India's low cost education, particularly distance education, healthcare and agricultural equipment exports, could create a positive influence in the region.

With changing circumstances and complex power dynamics in the region, India will have to reach out to the Oceania region because of the following factors.

1. With the expansion of EAS and the inclusion of two Oceania nations, namely, Australia and New Zealand, it has become an imperative for India to reach out to these nations, under a comprehensive policy approach.
2. In order to diversify India's energy and mineral resource requirements, India will have to reach out to these nations including Timor Leste, PNG, and other nations in the region.
3. With the issue of the Climate Change gaining momentum, India being increasingly perceived as the recalcitrant nation, Pacific Islands might see it as counter to their development, existence, and sustenance needs.

4. India's diaspora in the region is increasingly identifying itself with India and needs a recalibrated policy approach.
5. India's aspiration for permanent membership in the UN Security Council would be fulfilled only if 2/3 of the members vote for its candidature in the General Assembly and this region has a large number of UN members.

Conclusion

India's ascendant stature as an Indian Ocean power is by no means a recent acknowledgment. India's geographical location, jutting out for a thousand miles into the Indian Ocean, and being walled off on three sides by land, has endowed it with a strategic security sphere over the entire Indian Ocean Region. This geo-strategic salience of India's situation acts as a security umbrella over the countries of Southeast Asia and the greater Asia-Pacific. The imperative of India safeguarding the Indian Ocean Region emerges from its extensive coastline of over 7516 km, an EEZ of 2.172 mn sq.km and a continental shelf of more than 1 million sq.km beyond the EEZ. In view of these considerations, the modern vision of the country's responsible power profile in the Indian Ocean has been emphasized by the Indian Naval Doctrine of 2004 and 2009.

The renewed emphasis of the Indian Navy in securing the Indian Ocean, while acknowledging the Navy's central role as a 'net security provider', can be viewed in the backdrop of Prime Minister Modi's visit to neighbouring countries in 2015, during which PM Modi demonstrated the region's priorities through New Delhi's Foreign Policy strategy. After becoming Prime Minister of India, Narendra Modi laid significant emphasis on small islands and island nations by visiting these nations, entering into bilateral agreements and providing assistance. Recently, PM Modi extended a $ 150 million line of credit to a group of Pacific Island nations for undertaking several projects based on their requirements. This move is in response to China's Aid Polices in the Indian Ocean and Pacific, aimed at growing its influence.

Prime Minister Modi's strategic approach is theoretically good, despite the scarcity of funds allocating to Defence and Navy Departments. But at least, an initiation has been undertaken and allocated good amount of funds to Andaman & Nicobar Islands to develop infrastructure in a integrated manner for army, defence and navy together under one Command keeping in view of the strategic Malacca Strait. As observed, the Indian Navy's allocation of funds is insufficient compared to China. To defend and to counter China in the Indian Ocean Region, India needs to enhance its budgetary allocation to defence sector and more so to Indian navy from existing 13.6% to 20%–25%. The assertive and aggressive China not only creating trouble to India at the borders but also in the Indian Ocean region on the guise of protecting its sea lanes of communication needs to re-look into the security aspects of the country. The Indian navy can shut down the Indian Ocean shipping lanes at the Six Degree Channel whenever necessary. Therefore, China should be mindful of its requirements when sending its nuclear submarines to the Indian Ocean. Narendra Modi's strategic approach requires a significant amount of funds to counter China, ensuring India's security and emerging as a net security provider in the Indian Ocean Region.

Notes and References

[1] Robert D., Kaplan, Monsoon: The Indian Ocean and the future of American Power, Random House, 2010.

[2] Panikar; K.M., India and The Indian Ocean: An essay on the Influence of Sea Power on Indian History (London: Allen and Unwin 1951); P.V. Rao (ed.) India and Indian Ocean (South Asian Publishers New Delhi 2003).

[3] The rate of increase of oil flow through Strait of Malacca is estimated to be above 3% per annum till 2025.

[4] Times of India (see clipping).

[5] Khalid, Nazery, Veni Vidi, V.L.C.C., "Some reflections on combating piracy in the Gulf Aden", December 8, 2008 at htpp://www.maritimeindia.org/modules.

[6] Sri Kanth Kondaplly, New Dynamics of the Indian Ocean Region and Indian Role, published in (ed.) book China in Indian Ocean Region.

[7] Ji, You and Kia, Lim Chee, "China's naval Development to Somalia and its implications" EA1 background Brief No. 454, May 29, 2009.

[8] See Krisha, Ananth, "China: Billion Dollar Fund of Maritime Silk Road" the Hindu May 20, 2014

[9] See, Ad Hoc Committee on Indian Ocean Adopts report to General Assembly, press release United Nations 25 July 2005.

[10] Ashley, Jackson, 'Britain in the Indian Ocean Region', Journal of the Indian Ocean Region, Vol. 7, No. 2, 2011 pp. 145–60.

[11] See, Ad Hoc Committee on Indian Ocean Adopts report to General Assembly, press release United Nations, 25 July 2005.

[12] Saibal, Dasgupta, 'China gets First ever chance to enter Indian Ocean for exploration, the Times of India 7/8/2011; China speeds up Indian Ocean exploration for minerals; The ET, 26/2/14.

[13] Robert D. Kaplan, Center stage for the 21st century; power plays in the Indian Ocean, Foreign Affairs, Vol. 88, No. 2, March/April 2009.

[14] For details visit official website of IORA at http://www.iora.net

[15] Mohammed Khalid, India in the Changing Geopolitics of the Indian Ocean; *Journal of Indian Ocean Studies*, Vol. 15, No. 1, April 2007, pp. 61–78.

[16] Rao, S.V. Seshagiri, "Indian Ocean neighbourhood—Narendra Modi's strategic Initiatives, 2nd November 2018, printed & published at Himalaya Graphics, Hyderabad.

[17] Seller, Hanns-Frank, The security Policy and Maritime Strategy of India in the 21st century, in Jurgen Schwarz, Wilfrroed A. Herrman, & Hanns-Frank Seller, (eds) maritime strategies in Asia, Bangkok: White Lotus Press., 2002.

[18] Rajeev, Savhney, "Redefining the Strait of Malacca" Maritime Studies, No. 148, May 0 June 2006.

[19] Qi, X.U., Maritime, "Geo-Strategy and the Development of the Chinese navy in the Early Twenty-First Century", Naval War College Review, Vol. 59, No. 4, Autumn 2006.

[20] Mokhzani Zubir, Mohd, Nizam Basiron, The Strait of Malacca: The rise of China, America's Intensions and Dilamma of the littoral States, Kuala Lumpur: Maritime institute of Malaysia, April 2005.

[21] Economic Times, dt. 5.9.2019.

[22] Mohammad Khalid, Somalia and its Lawless Coast: India's growing Security Responsibility in the Indian Ocean Region, *Journal of Indian Ocean Studies,* Vol. 18, no. !, April 2010, pp. 67–80.

[23] US Department of Defence (2010 b). Base structure report; Fiscal year 2010 baseline, office of the Deputy under-secretary of Defence, Washington DC.

[24] Banlaoi, R.C. (2005). Maritime Security outlook for South East Asia; in J. Ho and C. 2. Raymand, eds., The Best Times, The Worst Times: Maritime Security in the Asia Pacific, Singapore Institute of Defence and Strategic Studies, p. 59.

CHAPTER III

China's 21st Century Maritime Silk Road: Encirclement of India?

The geo-strategic and geo-political focus of global power has shifted from the West to East. India and the People's Republic of China (PRC) are two rising Asian powers that are constantly evolving their foreign policies to meet their burgeoning demands. China has shown remarkable growth since the end of the cold war and has an upper hand compare to other Asian and European powers. However, the PRC claims this development is peaceful, but its aggressive posture on neighbourhood issues has resulted in a hostile environment in the Region. Moreover, China's rise has altered the ecosystem in Asia and today Beijing has evolved as an opposing force to the dominance of the US in global affairs. Yet, at the same time it has provided opportunities for cooperation and collaboration through large-scale Chinese investments that have spread even to Africa, where China is involved in constructing roads, railways, and public utility buildings.

The 'Pivot to Asia' as part of the 'Grand Strategy' of the US to refine its strategic dynamics and engagement with Asia, along with the Trans-Pacific Partnership (TPP), has prompted China to revive of Silk Road diplomacy. China has sought to increase its sphere of influence and enhance cooperation with the Asia-Pacific, Central Asia and the Indian Ocean Region (IOR) through this initiative. The Maritime Silk Road initiative is part of its 'One Belt One Road' strategy aimed at fostering connectivity between China and countries in the region.

The Indian Ocean Region has witnessed a prominent rise of geo-political interest and commercial investments by states around the Indian Ocean, as well as from extra-regional powers. Today, the Indian Ocean Region today has become a centre stage in global politics. According to the Heidelberg Institute for International Conflict Research, more than 50 percent of the world conflicts occur in Indian Ocean. The significant increase in the importance of the Indian Ocean is due to its hosting of many of the world's important Sea Lines of Communication (SLOCs), major chokepoints, oil deposits like the Gulf and the capability of nearby states to influence petroleum exports among other factors. For quite a long time, the US largely dominated the Indian Ocean Region without any significant competitor. The rise of aggressive China in the region has challenged US power and brought the Indian Ocean back to the centre stage of geo-strategic and geo-political importance. China has been carefully crafting its military and maritime strategies for more than a decade. It has successfully expanded its wide-ranging influence in the Southeast Asia, South Asia and Africa through loans for national development, military exercises, political and technological assistance. China has also increased its submarine presence in the Indian Ocean Region.

China's Maritime Silk Road (MSR) appears to be part of its overall maritime strategy to consolidate its influence and at the same time, to neutralize the dominance of the US in the Indian Ocean Region. Even before the MSR initiative, the Chinese have addressed their energy interests through investments along the Indian Ocean littorals such as Pakistan, Myanmar, Sri Lanka, Bangladesh, Maldives etc. as part of their grand strategy and additionally under the MSR initiative. China has initiated several corridors to connect the Indian Ocean Region as an alternative routes for its energy supplies such as CPEC, CMEC, BCIM and OBOR, to bolster its influence in the region, secure its oil trade and expand its markets. The present chapter thoroughly discusses about the China's 21st Century Maritime Silk Road initiative and other corridors, how China's initiatives and corridors are attempting to challenge India's sovereignty and security in the Indian Ocean Region.

China's New Silk Road' concept is rooted in history as there existed an overland Silk Route and a MSR that connected China to countries across Asia, Africa and Europe. Drawing from past experiences and practices, China in recent years has built a network of highways and railroads from north to south and from east to less developed western and southwestern regions. With its achievements at the domestic level, China sees an opportunity to link the hinterland with South Asia, Europe, Africa and even the Americas.

The declaration of the MSR in 2013 by Xi Jinping opened up new vistas for expanding the footprint of China in the Indian Ocean and beyond to protect its sea-borne interests while simultaneously providing leverage to increase its influence in target countries in South, Southeast Asia and Africa. The developing cash starved countries in India's maritime neighbourhood would invite any investment on easy terms that would improve the livelihood and employment opportunities for its own citizens. From the Chinese point of view, it would have found new avenues in which to invest the surplus reserves expected to be in the region of three trillion by using AIIB and other banking sectors to facilitate the process. This will enable China to closely interact with the destination countries by employing its technology, manpower, etc.

The One Belt One Road (OBOR) initiative has caused ripples in economic, strategic, and political spheres not just in the neighboring countries but around the world. The ingredients such as surplus funds, utilization of surplus capacity and providing connectivity to find new markets are the success mantras of this century and beyond. Both the land and sea routes would provide China with opportunities to raise the bar in terms of becoming a superpower. The OBOR/BRI is a game changer in the region and India obviously has serious concerns about the possible impact of the OBOR in its neighbourhood. Except for some halfhearted efforts on projects such as Mausam[2], or the spice route, there is no concrete proposal to respond to the growing influence of China, which will alter the strategic balance in the region. This chapter seeks to examine the impact of China's MSR policy initiative implemented through the CPEC, BCIM and CMEC, which are the arteries that will carry goods through Central Asian Republic States and through Bangladesh, India and Myanmar, again opening up new vistas. While the China Pakistan Economic Corridor provides an exit to the Arabian Sea, the Bangladesh-China-India-Myanmar and China Myanmar Economic Corridors are providing an exit to the Bay of Bengal and will largely serve the markets of the world. The developments in Maldives have been worrisome for the Indian establishment, as the Chinese are now moving in a big way with investments and assistance that will create strong bonds that would be difficult to ignore from the security point of view.

MSR and Historical Perspective

The new grand initiative under the leadership of Xi Jinping to connect the entire world through both land and sea routes has received mixed reactions and responses from its Asian neighbor, India. The maritime initiative, called the 'Maritime Silk Road' (MSR)[3], was declared in 2013 in Indonesia. It aims to connect the continents by both land and sea routes. The Chinese government is committed to providing the necessary funds and assistance to build ports, harbours and related infrastructure projects in the destination countries in South East Asia, South Asia, Africa and beyond. Of course, this MSR initiative is undoubtedly a very ambitious plan on a gigantic scale that would provide the necessary impetus to the economic growth and integration of developing countries. The policy of the MSR, through various corridors, would immensely benefit both China and the recipient nations. Of course, it has been touted as the harbinger of prosperity and a key to joint development.[4]

Map 3.1: China's-One-Road-One-Belt-OBOR-Initiative

Source: www.googlemaps.com

The initiative reminds one of the long and arduous journeys undertaken by Admiral Zheng, He during the rule of the Ming dynasty, more than five centuries ago. The large fleet consisting of junks, auxiliaries, supporting vessels and merchant ships sailed the oceans from South China Sea to Indian Ocean and touched many parts in Asia and Africa, establishing maritime trade relations. The ancient maritime silk routes carried the special commodity called 'Silk' which was named for the exquisite quality of the cloth, which was manufactured under a special process known only to the Chinese at that time. The markets and empires around the world would go to any length to procure this exquisite material and it was used for battering with China and to increase the prospects for trade as other commodities from the west. Trade has a unique quality of bringing benefits to both trading countries.

By the 17th century, both China and India were rich nations, accounting for 40 percent of the global GDP. While China concentrated on silk, India used the 'spice' routes to transport the wonderful spices from the subcontinent to the rest of the world. This process also enabled the spread of the most vibrant Buddhist religious, particularly in East Asia. Trade enabled both China and India to reap rich dividends and achieve spectacular growth. It is the same trade routes that brought the East India Company to the shores of India purely for trade and commerce. As they say, it was only a matter of time before trade interests converted into the crown interests of Great Britain, as traders became masters and India was brought under colonial rule.

The Maritime Silk Route and Land Silk Route are sustained by China's phenomenal growth rates and its position as the manufacturing hub of the world. China has a long term strategy of protecting its overseas interests through OBOR and other corridors such as CPEC, BCIM and CMEC. China has the economic power and leadership that knows how to use the economy as leverage for promoting its interests in the Asian century. Today, China is a leading importer of energy goods from the Middle East and Africa. All this has to pass through the Indian Ocean and the Chokepoints in the Strait of Hormuz and the Strait of Malacca. The value of trade, including energy products, that pass through the South China Sea, is r more than three trillion USD. This amply shows the criticality of maintaining safe corridors that allow the passage of such large volumes without external threat.

China's Ancient Maritime Silk Road

The Silk Road is an ancient trade route that is well connected and organised network of roads. This network of roads was a route that connected East, West and South Asia. This route is called "the Silk Road" since ancient times. This route started from Far East, where China used to sell their silk. When it was found out by the western people that some people had been transferring culture, civilisation as well as the newest products through this route from the eastern countries to the western ones, they named it 'The Silk Road'. Currently, it has been discerned that the silk route is around 1700 years old.

The Silk Road is divided into two routes. One route is over land, and the other route is over the Sea. As per the below map 3.2, it is found that the "New Silk Road" based on land will start in the Xi'an, located in the Central China region. The route of this Silk Road runs southwest from Central Asia to northern Iran, through Syria and Turkey and eventually moves to North-Western Europe, where it meets the "Maritime Silk Road." The Maritime Silk Road will start in the Quanzhou in Fujian Province of China and will go through Guangzhou, Beihai and Haikou before going south to the Malacca Strait. Further, from Kuala Lumpur, the maritime Silk Road will reach Kolkata in India and will be crossing the rest of the Indian Ocean heading to Nairobi in Kenya and then to the Horn of Africa. After this, the MSR will move through the Red Sea into the Mediterranean and eventually join the land-based Silk Road.

As per the ancient maps, The Silk Road began from the city of Huang in China, moving up to Turkestan. After this, the route of the Silk Road passed through Central Asia, reaching Samarkand and Bukhara. After entering Iran, the route passed through the northern part of Iran, passing through Meru, Sarakhs, Nishapur, Gorgan, Saifabad, Ray, Qazvin, Zunjan and north of Hamadan. Then, the route ended at one of the harbours in Syria after passing through Yerevan.

Map 3.2: China's Ancient Maritime Silk Road

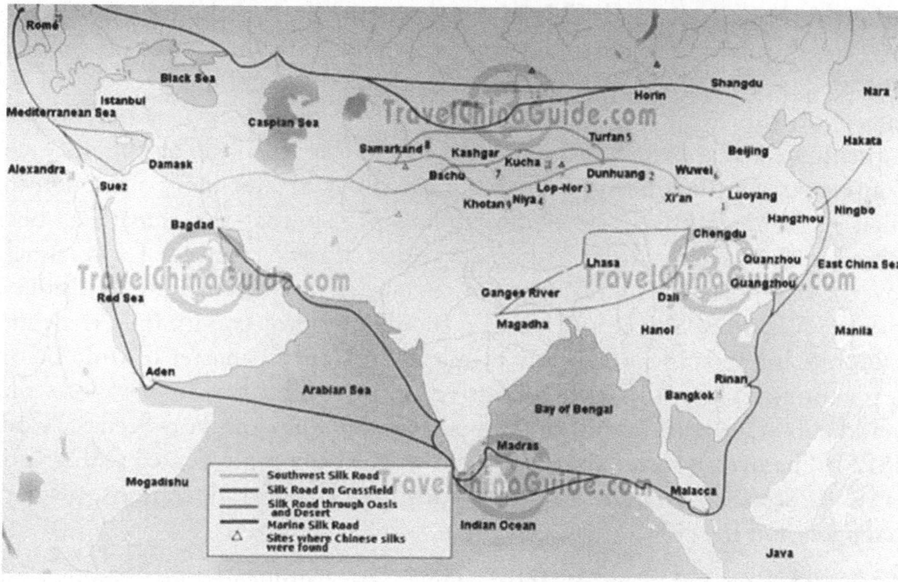

Source: www.googlemaps.com

Silk was the most traded product of this route, hence the name 'The Silk Road.' Many other products were also traded through this route and trading activities increased because of the ease of transportation. The Silk Road started flourishing during the Sasanian era. The empire earned its wealth by exchanging the products for silk along this route. Many traders were engaged in the export and import of various kinds of goods, such as a variety of carpets, precious stones, gems, fabrics, spices and as well as all types of high-consumption products through the ancient Silk Route. Even though the Silk Road declined in terms of trade for India, many countries considered it an interesting route for tourists and travellers. Hence, the Chinese people have been planning to develop tourism along this ancient route and China has decided to achieve economic progress through activities such as outsourcing of manufacturing to other Silk Road countries.

Challenges in the Maritime Domain in the Backdrop of MSR

While no nation wants to go to war today, all the maritime nations today are wary of non-state actors indulging pirates who have threatened safe passages and the lives of seafarers by including in unlawful acts. Piracy peaked between 2005 and 2009 in the waters of the African coasts[5]. At one time, there were more than a thousand hostages in the custody of the pirates raising concerns about the safety of merchant vessels and the seafarers. Since the beginning of the 2008, both India and China have maintained a continuous presence of their naval ships off Somalia. The threat of piracy on the waters off Somalia has receded until the recent past as a result of the combined actions of the navies of the world and also concerted efforts by the seafarers who implemented many onboard measures including carriage of the Privately Contracted Maritime Security Professionals (PCMSP) for transits through the High Risk Area (HRA). The unfortunate part is that the threat has been shifted to the Malacca Strait and South China Sea where more of such attacks have been reported. The relevance of the above to the MSR and to India is that the Maritime Silk Route is not a standalone project with only trade and economic interests in mind while primarily it is only a matter of time before more countries join the MSR initiative. This would provide new ports that would come under the ambit of the International Ship and Port Security Code (ISPS). The overall security environment would be complemented with greater levels of security awareness and training among port operations, owners, managers and the crew.

From the point of view of India which was subjugated to colonial rule through the trade initiatives of a British Company, it has bitter memories of trade being used by the British to serve the purpose of bringing India under its rule. India has a dominant position in the Indian Ocean thanks to geography. Also, since 1971 its navy has come of age and has become the most powerful regional navy[6] in the Indian Ocean, It has also engaged its maritime neighbours and contributing effectively to stabilizing the maritime environment. In its perception, the active engagement of China with the traditional allies of India has to pose a potential challenge.

India will continue to dither on whether to join in on the MSR initiative. There are serious concerns on how China will suffocate or encircle India with its huge economic investments in the ports related infrastructure, and hinterland connectivity in the destination countries through various corridors as mentioned in above Paras. This is the assessment of New Delhi that would gradually but steady increase China's capacity to wield influence in India's neighborhood. Consequently, India fears an erosion of its own power to wield influence in its traditional backyard in the Indian Ocean. However, India has maintained that it would support the 21st century Maritime Silk Road initiative subject to conditions of proposals and schemes, if that found suitability to India's interests. It is clear that India will constantly be suspicious of the long-term impact of China's presence in the Indian Ocean that India has conceded substantial strategic space to China is not in doubt anymore. Therefore, the actions of India are more akin to damage control.

India is not in a position to take a confrontational stand against the initiatives of China as they are economically oriented and supported by funding agencies through strong banking systems such as Asian Infrastructure Investment Bank (AIIB). The estimation of the requirement in the region is about 800–900 billion dollars annually in the region and the AIIB would meet a substantial portion of this development need.[7]

At this juncture India would not like to be seen as a silent spectator also that is only allowed to watch the proceedings in its backyard. Despite its reservations about the long-term impact of MSR on the strategic landscape, ultimately India showed its interest selectively to some of the projects in India like BCIM, initially. There are both supporters and detractors of MSR and the advantages have been shown to outweigh any disadvantages, particularly with a focus on developing the economy of the region. These views have been well orchestrated by R. Chowdary in the Economic Times on 9th April 2015.

China's vision in building a network under the sea-route strategy of MSR involves financing projects in Myanmar (Sittwe), Pakistan (Gwadar) and Sri Lanka (Hambantota). While the primary focus is to seek commercial benefits, China in is also concurrently building naval power in to safeguard its maritime trade routes. Most importantly, the sea route will serve China's core interests in the South China Sea, where it faces a severe threat—"as the Malacca Dilemma" at the Strait of Malacca—a strategic chokepoint affecting China's free flow of trade and energy supplies.

Beijing with its MSR is seeking to co-opt strategically located states in economic and security alliances led by it, is working specifically to acquire naval-access outposts through agreements for refueling replenishment, crew rest and maintenance. Its efforts involve gaining port projects along sea lines of communication, securing new supplies of natural resources and building energy and transportation corridors from China through Myanmar and Pakistan. The China Pakistan Economic Corridor (CPEC) and Bangladesh China India Myanmar Economic Corridor and China-Myanmar Economic Corridor and the proposed 'Kra' canal projects are closely related to the overall Belt and Road Initiative under 21st century Maritime Silk Road concept.[8]

Despite Beijing pledging US $ 40 billion in the Silk Road Fund to develop infrastructure along the route and backed by more than $ 100 billion fund drawn from AIIB, lack of specifics and clarity about the MSR not only makes it hard to decipher its real purpose, but it also gives credence to suspicions of China's geo-political game. Therefore, this chapter will thoroughly discuss the various corridors that China has planned under MSR/OBOR initiatives such as CPEC, BCIM, CMEC, Kra canal project, Digital Silk Road and Polar Silk Road etc. and their implications on India's security and sovereignty in detail below.

China-Pakistan Economic Corridor (CPEC)

The CPEC is claimed by China as a developmental mega project that aims to connect Gwadar port in Southeast Pakistan to China's northeast autonomous region of Xinjiang via a network of highways, railways and pipelines to transport oil and gas through Indian Territory called Pakistan occupied Kashmir (PoK). The economic corridor central to China-Pakistan relationship runs about 3000 km from Gwadar to Kashgar, is an extension of China's 21st Century 'New Silk Road' initiative. The CPEC also provides Pakistan with Tele communication and energy infrastructure.

Map 3.3: China Pakistan Economic Corridor

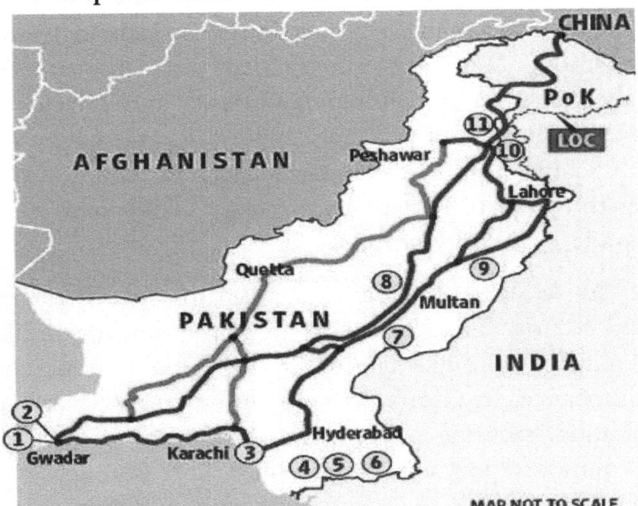

Source: www.googlemaps.com

The US Secretary of State for South Central Asia, Alice Wells, stated earlier that, Pakistan will face long-term economic damage with little return if China continues its giant infrastructure push under One Belt One Road (OBOR) initiative, as the Corridor (CPEC) comes potentially at an unsustainable cost to Pakistan.[9] The US Assistant secretary (Wells) informed that, Washington shared India's concerns over OBOR projects that do not have economic basis and leads to countries ceding sovereignty, highlighting Sri Lanka's case where the Seaport of Hambantota was handed over to China in 2017 on a 99year lease after it failed to meet debt obligations. Well's further informed that, it has crystal clear that, there are geo-political elements of the China's 21st century maritime projects.[10] India is the only major country in the world to have opposed the OBOR projects on the grounds of territorial sovereignty, particularly the CPEC passes through Pakistan- occupied Kashmir.

China Pakistan Economic Corridor is the collection of infrastructure projects that are currently under construction throughout Pakistan. Originally valued at $ 46 billion, the value of CPEC projects are enhanced to the worth of $ 62 billion as of 2017. The CPEC is intended to rapidly upgrade Pakistan's required infrastructure and strengthen its economy by the construction of modern transport networks, numerous energy projects, and special economic zones. In November 2016, CPEC became partly operational when Chinese cargo was transported overland to Gwadar port for onward maritime shipment to Africa and West Asia, while some major power projects were also commissioned by late 2017.

A vast network of highways and railways are to be built under the aegis of CPEC that will span the length and breadth of Pakistan. Inefficiencies stemming from Pakistan's mostly dilapidated transportation network have been estimated to cost the country's annual GDP. Modern transportation networks built under CPEC will link seaports at Gwadar and Karachi with northern Pakistan, as well as points further north in western China and central Asia. A 1100 kilometer-long motorway will be built between cities of Karachi and Lahore as part of CPEC, while the Karakoram highway from Hasan Abdal to the Chinese border will be completely reconstructed and overhauled. The Karachi-Peshawar main railway line will also be upgraded to allow for train travel up to 160 km per hour by December 2019. Pakistan's railway network will also be extended to eventually connect to China's Southern Xinjiang Railway in Kashgar. The estimated $ 1.1 billion required to modernize transport networks will be financed by subsidized concessionary loans.

Over $ 33 billion worth of energy infrastructure are to be constructed by private consortia to help alleviate Pakistan's chronic energy shortages under CPEC, which regularly amount to over 4500 MW, and have shed an estimated 2.25 percent of Pakistan's annual gross domestic product. Over 10,400 MW of energy generating capacity came online by the end of 2018, with majority developed as a part of CPEC fast-tracked "Early Harvest" projects. A network of pipelines to transport liquefied natural gas and oil will also be laid as a part of the project, including a $ 2.5 billion pipeline between

Gwadar and Nawabshah to eventually transport gas from Iran. Electricity from these projects will primarily be generated from fossil fuels.

CPEC potential impact on Pakistan has been compared to that of the Marshall Plan undertaken by the United States in post-war Europe. Pakistani officials predict that CPEC will result in the creation of upwards of 2.3 million jobs between 2015–2030 and add to 2 to 2.5 percentage points to the country's annual economic growth. Should the initial $ 46 billion worth of projects be implemented the value of those projects would be roughly equivalent to all foreign direct investment in Pakistan since 1970, and would be equal to 17 percent of Pakistan's 2015 gross domestic product. From the initial project, the scope has expanded from a net worth of $ 46 billion to $ 60 billion according to a report published in The Times of India on November 23rd 2019. The CPEC is seen as main plank of Chinese President Xi Jinping's Belt and Road initiative.

According to official statistics, 20 percent of CPEC is debt-based finance, while 80 percent of CPEC are investments in joint-venture (JV) enterprise between Pakistan and China, with the project contributing to 40,000 jobs for local Pakistanis and 80,000 jobs for Chinese. The total CPEC loan is 6 percent of Pakistan's GDP, however, the Indian government has labeled the project a debt-trap. Nevertheless, officials countered that 3.5 percent of Pakistani GDP per annum is lost due to poor transportation network, which the CPEC investment aims to remedy leading to added benefits for any lag in Pakistan's growth statistics.

Economic analysts have stated that tangible benefits of this initiative include an end to the major energy shortages in Pakistan which had previously crippled economic growth.

Plans for a corridor stretching from the Chinese border to Pakistan's deep water ports on the Arabian Sea date back to the 1950's,[11] and motivated the construction of the Karakoram Highway beginning in 1959. Chinese interest in Pakistan's deep-water harbour at Gwadar had been rekindled in 2002 and China began construction at Gwadar port which was completed in 2006. Expansion of Gwadar port then ceased thereafter owing to political stability in Pakistan following the fall of late General Pervez Musharraf and subsequent conflict between the Pakistan state and Taliban militants. In 2013, the then Pakistan President Asif Ali Zardari and Chinese Premier Li Keqiang decided to further enhance mutual connectivity. A memorandum of understanding on cooperation for long-term plan on China-Pakistan Economic Corridor between the two governments was inked by Xu Shao Shi and Shahid Amjad Chaudhry.

Gwadar forms the crux of the CPEC project, as it is envisaged to be the link between China's ambitious One Belt One Road (OBOR) project, and its 21st century maritime Silk Road project.

The Strait of Malacca provides China with its shortest maritime access to Europe, Africa and Middle East about 80% of its Middle East energy imports also pass through the Strait of Malacca. As the world's biggest oil importer, energy security is a key concern for China while current sea routes are frequently patrolled by the US navy.

In the event that China were to fare hostile actions from a state or non-state actor, energy imports through the Strait of Malacca could be halted, which in turn would paralyze the Chinese economy in a scenario that is frequently referred to as the Malacca Dilemma. In addition to vulnerabilities faced in the Strait of Malacca region, China is heavily dependent upon sea-routes that pass through the South China Sea (SCS), near the disputed Spratly Islands and Paracel Islands, which are currently a source of tension between China, Taiwan, Vietnam, The Philippines and the United States. The project CPEC will allow Chinese energy imports to circumvent these contentious areas and find a new artery in the west, and thereby decrease the possibility of confrontation to suggest that any pipeline from Gwadar to China would be very expensive and would encounter a number of logistical difficulties, including difficult terrain and terrorism, which would barely make any impact on China's overall energy security.

In addition to potential weakness with regard to the United States Navy, the Indian Navy has recently increased maritime surveillance of the Strait of Malacca region from its base on Great Nicobar Island. India has expressed fears of a Chinese 'string of pearls' encircling it. Were conflict to erupt, India could potentially impede Chinese imports through the Strait of Malacca. Indian maritime surveillance in the Andaman Sea could possibly enhance Chinese interest in Pakistan's Gwadar port—the Kyaukpyu port, which is currently in Myanmar and operated by the Chinese government as another alternative route around the Strait of Malacca, will likely be vulnerable to similar advances by the Indian Navy. The proposed Bangladesh-China-India-Myanmar (BCIM) corridor would also be vulnerable to Indian advances against China in the event of conflict, thereby potentially limiting the BCIM corridor usefulness to China's energy security and thereby increasing Chinese interest in CPEC.

Even the CPEC faces potential conflict with India as the corridor passes through Indian territory of Pakistan occupied Kashmir (PoK), that is why Indian government objected to the CPEC project as it impinges on India's security and sovereignty,[12] if in near future, the Modi government were to take over the PoK, as announced in the Indian parliament by Amit Shah, Home Minister of India, the entire project may have 'implications of detrainment'. The India and Pakistan guards have occasionally exchange fire across the 'Line of Control', is known fact.

The government of India, which shares tense relations with Pakistan, objects to the CPEC project as upgrade works to the Karakoram highway are taking place in the Gilgit Baltistan territory that it claims as its own. During the visit of Indian Prime Minister Modi to China in 2015, reportedly told Chinese Premier Xi Jinping that projects passing through Gilgit-Baltistan are 'unacceptable'. Former Indian Ambassador, Phunchok Stobdan, alleged that, China and Pakistan intend to develop the CPEC corridor not just for its economic benefits, but also ard motivated by the strategic intent of besieging India.

The Karakoram Highway known by its initials KKH, also known as N-35 or China-Pakistan Friendship Highway, is a 1300 km (810 miles) national highway which extends from Hasan Abdal in the Punjab province of Pakistan to the Khunjerab pass in Gilgit-Baltistan, where it crosses into China and becomes China's National Highway 314. This highway connects the Pakistani province of Punjab and Khyber Pakhtunkhwa plus Gilgit-Baltistan with China's Xinjiang Uyghur Autonomous Region, and was built by the government of Pakistan and China. It was started in 1959 and was completed and opened to the public in 1979. The highway, connecting the Gilgit-Baltistan region to the ancient Silk Road, runs about 1300 km from Kashgar, a city in the Xinjiang region of China to Abbottabad of Pakistan. As part of the $46 bn China Pakistan Economic Corridor, reconstruction and upgrade works on the Pakistan portion of the Karakoram Highway are underway. The KKH spans the 806 km long distance between the China Pakistan border and the town of Hasan Abdal.

India has slammed China and Pakistan for reference to J&K in a joint statement released by them and said that it expects other countries not to comment on is internal matters and should respect its sovereignty. The Kashmir issue has been figured in the talks between Chinese President Xi Jinping and his counterpart Arif Alvi in Beijing on Tuesday, March 17, 2020. Both sides exchanged views on the situation in J&K. The Pakistan side briefed the Chinese side on the latest development, including its concerns, position, and current urgent issues.

In response to this development, India's external Affairs spokesperson Raveesh Kumar asserted that the UT of J&K is an integral part of India and issues related to it are the country's internal matter. India would like to strongly object to and reiterate its concerns to both China and Pakistan on the projects in the so-called illegal CPEC, which passes through the territory of India that has been illegally occupied by Pakistan since 1947.[13] India is resolutely opposed to any action by other countries to change the status quo in Pakistan occupied J&K. We call on parties concerned to cease such actions. Such illegal activities will never be accepted by India.

BCIM—Economic Corridor

BCIM Economic Corridor is an initiative connecting India and China through Myanmar and Bangladesh as a corridor. In 2015, China proposed including the corridor as part of its vision for the Belt and Road Initiative (BRI), China's signature global connectivity initiative.[14] The BRI was boycotted by India from the beginning. In May 2019, the BCIM was not mentioned in the list of 35 corridors and projects in a joint communiqué issued by the state leaders attending the 2nd Belt and Road Initiative Forum, indicating the BCIM has been dropped from the BRI. In the same year, India sought to keep the BCIM intact by sending a delegation to the 13th BCIM Forum in Yuxi.

The proposed corridor will cover 1.65 million square kilometers, encompassing an estimated 440 million people in China's Yunnan province. Bangladesh, Myanmar, and West Bengal in Eastern India via the combination of road, rail, water and air linkages in the region. The BCIM envisages greater market access to goods, services and energy, elimination of non-tariff barriers, better trade facilitation, investments in infrastructure development and a joint exploitation and development of minerals, waters and other natural resources.

The BCIM came to the fulfillment during the meeting between Chinese Premier Li Keqiang and Indian Prime Minister Manmohan Singh in 2013. Li's visit marked the first-time high-ranking officials discussing the high-level corridor. Earlier in the year, the first-ever BCIM car rally was held between Kolkata and Kunming via Dhaka to highlight road connectivity in the four countries. In December 2013, the four nations drew up a long- discussed plan, emphasizing the need to quickly improve physical connectivity in the region, over two days of talks in the south western Chinese city Kunming the provincial capital of Yunnan, which borders Myanmar.

The economic advantages of the BCIM trade corridors are considerable, most notably, access to numerous markets in Southeast Asia, the improvement of transportation, and infrastructure creation of industrial zones. The BCIM

Forum for Regional Cooperation is a sub-regional organization of ASEAN nations aimed at greater integration of trade and investment between four countries and the economic corridor has been coined out of it. Through linking the ASEAN Free Trade Area, ASEAN-China Free Trade Area and the ASEAN-India Free Trade Area, the corridor would constitute one of the largest free trade areas. Bangladesh-China-India and Myanmar expected to create a corridor that would effectively combine road, rail, water and air linkages in the region. This will also improve foreign trade of the BCIM countries and empower bilateral trading.

Map 3.4: BCIM—Economic Corridor

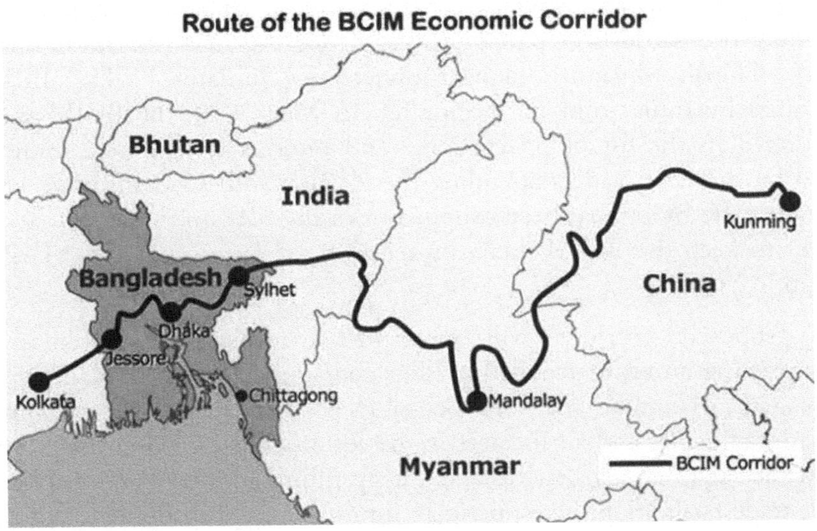

Source: www.googlemaps.com

Though the BCIM came into being more than a decade ago, only now it is coming to the centre stage as member countries realize that it can play a unique role in creating economic cooperation among themselves with the rest of the region. A successful BCIM Economic Cooperation Venture would enable India to be a significant part of East Asian economic architecture. An added advantage is that—China's ambitious Belt and Road initiative, which would entail huge investments in connecting vast regions across continents, will help create appropriate infrastructure. There is an urgent need to recast India-China relations discourse with a greater focus on economic engagement, for it will be the principal determinant of the Indo-Pacific's new order.

The issue is why the BCIM matters to India now than ever before, probably one of the backward and least integrated with the rest of India is the North-

have motivated China to push forward the BRI and improve ties with the Myanmar government.

Map 3.5: China-Myanmar—Economic Corridor

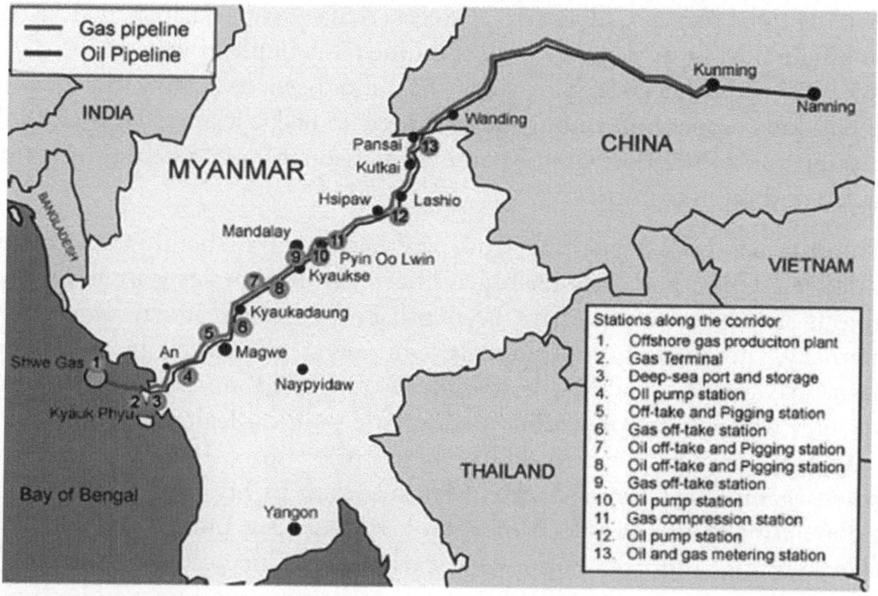

Source: www.googlemaps.com

Subsequently, relations improved when Aung San Suu Kyi's party (NLD) came to power in 2016. This coincided with increasing international condemnation of Myanmar for its handling of the Rohingya crises, particularly after August, 2017. China aligned itself with the Myanmar government's interests on the Rohingya crisis and the ethnic peace process. This allowed Beijing to minimize the role of other external players while obtaining strategic projects in Myanmar.

China and Myanmar signed an MoU on cooperation with 'The Framework of the Silk Road Economic Belt' and the Myanmar counselor attended the 1st Chinese BRF. After five months, the CMEC was proposed and an official agreement on the 'Y'-shaped corridor was signed in September 2018 to connect China's Kunming to Mandalay and then extended east and west respectively to Yangon and Kyaukpyu. In August 2018, Myanmar renegotiated the Kyaukpyu deep-water seaport. The 7.3 billion USD project was agreed in 2015 between the two governments of that time. However, the Myanmar government decided to scale down the project to 1.3 billion USD, with just two jetties, which can be expanded later if so required.

The Myanmar government is moving beyond the question of whether or not to be part of BRI, as the Myanmar government appears to be pursuing a diplomatic balancing act of securing China's support to take forward the ethnic peace process and protect it in international fora. In return, Myanmar is willing to be part of Chinese BRI projects that seem mutually beneficial, but not binding. Most of the deals reached in the past couple of years have no legal force. Towards the end, Naypyidaw has also been leveraging the growing geopolitical competition among major powers to hedge against the BRI. In the renegotiation of the port deal, Myanmar had sought and received help from the US and other countries.

Myanmar has been benefiting from alternative infrastructure development initiatives. Tokyo and New Delhi have been involved in key port and railway projects in Myanmar and have been collaborating in regional connectivity. Internally, the growing opposition to Chinese mega-projects in the country means Myanmar's political leadership would need to deal with China's pressures without compromising its domestic political legitimacy. Just before Aung San Suu Kyi's visit to China in the recent past, there was a massive protest against the Chinese backed Myitsone dam in Myanmar. The growing unpopularity of the Myitsone dam project may have pushed the Myanmar leadership to abandon the project, in exchange for guarantees to the CMEC projects. Strategically, the CMEC is far more critical to China and both sides may consider such possibilities as a way out. Aung San Suu Kyi indicated at the BRF a desire on the part of the Myanmar leadership to reflect the concerns of the country's people. The BRI projects should not only be economically feasible but also socially and environmentally responsible, and most importantly, the projects must have the confidence and support of local people.

Very recently, China and Myanmar inked 33 BRI deals in January 2020[16] to speed up infrastructure projects in the Southeast Asian nation as Beijing seeks to cement its hold over a neighbor increasingly isolated by the West. But no major new projects were accepted during the two-day visit by President XI Jinping, the first of any Chinese leader in last 19 years. Myanmar was very cautious of investments by Beijing and was also careful ahead of the elections at the end of the year 2020. But, still Xi and San Suu Kyi signed 33 agreements, shoring up key projects that were part of the flagship Belt and Road Initiative, China's vision of new trade routes described as a 21st century Silk Road. The most significant part that appeared to be a concession and shareholder's agreement for the Kyaukphyu Special Economic Zone in the Bay of Bengal with a deep-water port, is the terminus of the 1700-kilometer-long

China Myanmar Economic corridor—a major link in the Belt and Road Initiative whose other end is in China's Yunnan province.

The Kyaukphyu project concerns India as the Myanmar Corridor provides China with shortcut route to the Indian Ocean, on the Bay of Bengal, a major goal of Chinese strategic planners. An outlet to the Indian Ocean allows China's sizable oil and gas imports from the Persian Gulf to bypass the Strait of Malacca, and could conceivably serve a future military purpose. China has also acquired Pakistan's Gwadar port and Sri Lanka's Hambantota port, raising concerns over the theory of 'String of Pearls' to encircle India by Beijing.

During the meeting between Xi and Myanmar state counselor, they did not address the controversial $3.6 billion Beijing backed mega dam, where work has been stalled since 2011, reflecting the cautiousness of Chinese investment in Myanmar, which is uncomfortable with the way Beijing has over its smaller neighbor. A creeping fear is that Beijing is creating debt traps across the developing world and monopolizing profits has compelled Myanmar officials to suspend or renegotiate hydropower and port deals done earlier. Despite 33 agreements signed, there are no Big Bang projects felt by Richard Horsey, a Yangon-based analyst with the international crisis group. By this time, Myanmar is being very cautious about Chinese investment.[17]

The Myanmar State Counselor, Suu Kyi specifically emphasized and urged that all economic projects must avoid environmental degradation and be beneficial to local people.[18] Ahead of the state visit, Xi Jinping wrote an article in Myanmar newspapers expressing his ideas about the proposed projects in the economic corridor, which will be part of China's Belt and Road Initiative. Xi further stated that both sides—China and Myanmar—need to deepen result oriented Belt and Road cooperation and move from a conceptual stage to concrete planning and implementation in building the CMEC. Xi further elaborated in the newspapers that, China provides finance, materials and construction capability in Belt and Road projects and doesn't seek any contribution from its partners like Pakistan. The relationship between the two countries, China and Myanmar has warmed since 2017 when China refused to join the international outcry against the military campaign to force the Rohingyas to flee across the border to Bangladesh.

Despite cautious measures taken by Myanmar's State Counselor on signing agreements with Chinese President Xi Jinping. Many in Myanmar view China warily. Infrastructure projects have been deeply unpopular, uprooting thousands of villages and wreaking environmental damage. People have protested outside Chinese embassy in Yangon to oppose the exploitation of natural resources in Myanmar, including the $ 3.6 billion Myitsone hydro power dam project, which was suspended in 2011, but expected to restart after Xi Jinping's state visit.

Thai Canal Project/Kra Canal

India is spooked by China's push to expedite work on the Thai (Kra) Canal across the Isthmus, the narrowest part of the Malay Peninsula in Southern Thailand, to counter the increasing Chinese presence in the Indian Ocean, India is working on the military up-gradation in its Island territories. The Thai Canal, also known as Kra Canal, refers to a proposal for a canal that would connect the Gulf of Thailand with the Andaman Sea across the Isthmus in southern Thailand. It is believed that such a canal would improve transportation in the region, similar to the Panama Canal and Suez Canal. The 120 km long canal is an integral part of China's Maritime Silk Road initiative, which in itself is a key constituent of the ambitious One Belt One Road project.[19] The Kra Canal is China's attempt at solving the Malacca problem.

The canal would provide an alternative to transit through the Strait of Malacca and shorten shipments of oil to China and Japan by 1200 km. China refers to it as part of its 21st Century Maritime Silk Proposal (MSR). The proposal for canal construction was made in 2015, with measurements of 120 km in length, 400 meters in width and 25 meters in depth. Plans for the canal have been discussed and explored at varies times, but have not been implemented so far. To counter China's strategic move, India plans to upgrade its Island territories. Accordingly, the airstrip at INS Kohassa Shibpur in north Andaman and the Campbell Strip at Nicobar will be transformed into full-fledged fighter bases. Similarly, the airstrip at Agatti in the Lakshadweep Islands will also undergo upgrades for military operations, securing both the Bay of Bengal up to the Malacca Strait and the Arabian Sea up to the Gulf of Aden.

The two Island territories will serve as new aircraft carriers for India, significantly extending the Navy's operational reach in the region, far from the mainland. Both the islands sit on the busiest sea lanes of the world with more than half of the world trade going through this route.

According to Lt. Gen. Prakash Katoch (Retd.), he expressed his views on Kra Canal on 3rd September,20. Many feasibility studies for the project have been undertaken in the past. In Feb2018, Thai Premier Prayut Chan-O-Cha declared the canal was not a government priority. However, in January 2020, the Thai House of Representatives agreed to set up a committee to study the canal project, possibly due to behind the scene Chinese efforts. But to China's Chagrin, Thailand has finally dumped the canal project at this movement and instead plans to build two-deep-water seaports on either side of the country's southern coasts, linking them with a 100 km rail-road land bridge.

Map 3.6: Thai Canal Project (Kra)

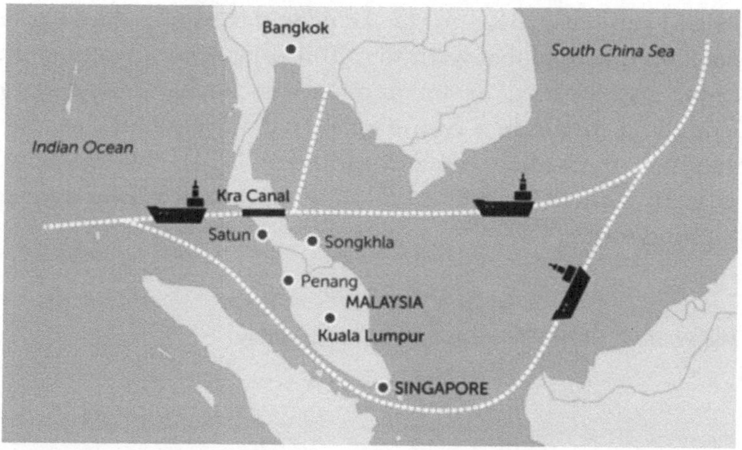

Source: www.googlemaps.com

Amid the border stand-off between India and China, the latter has suffered a severe blow from Thailand. Thailand declared that it will scrap the Thai Canal project, which Beijing desires to shorten its access to the Indian Ocean and avoid the Strait of Malacca. Moreover, the Thai government has also given in to the public pressure and delayed the purchase of two Chinese Submarines worth $724 million. However, according to a recent report by TFIPOST, China still holds hopes for the Kra project, aligning with Beijing's long-term ambitions to bypass the Strait of Malacca.

Had the Thai Canal come up, China would have taken control of it in probability like the Hambantota port in Sri Lanka giving it a tremendous strategic advantage. Beijing will still try to invest in the land bridge and the two sea-ports planned by Thailand. In that case, also, the Chinese oil tankers and warships can't avoid the Strait of Malacca, a strategic waterway between Indonesia and Malaysia through which the majority of Chinese imports pass.

Cancellation of the Kra Canal will increase the significance of the China Myanmar Economic Corridor (CMEC) of which Kyaukphyu could be the future naval base of China. Chinese President had termed the CMEC "Priority of Priorities", during his visit to Myanmar in 2020 (January). China is putting its weight behind Aung San Sau Kyi and her National League for

Democracy (NLD) to win in the upcoming November 2020 elections, according to Lt. General Prakash Katoch (Retd.), 30th September 2020.

After OBOR, China pushes Polar Silk Road

China has outlined its ambitions to extend President Xi Jinping's signature Belt and Road Initiative (BRI) to the Arctic by leveraging shipping lanes that have opened up due to global warming. In its first official Arctic policy white paper, China has declared its intention, to encourage enterprises to build infrastructure and to conduct commercial trial Voyages, paying the way for Arctic Shipping routes that would constitute a "Polar Silk Road." China is willing to work with all parties to build a Polar Silk Road by developing the Arctic Shipping routes.[20]

Map 3.7: Polar Silk Road

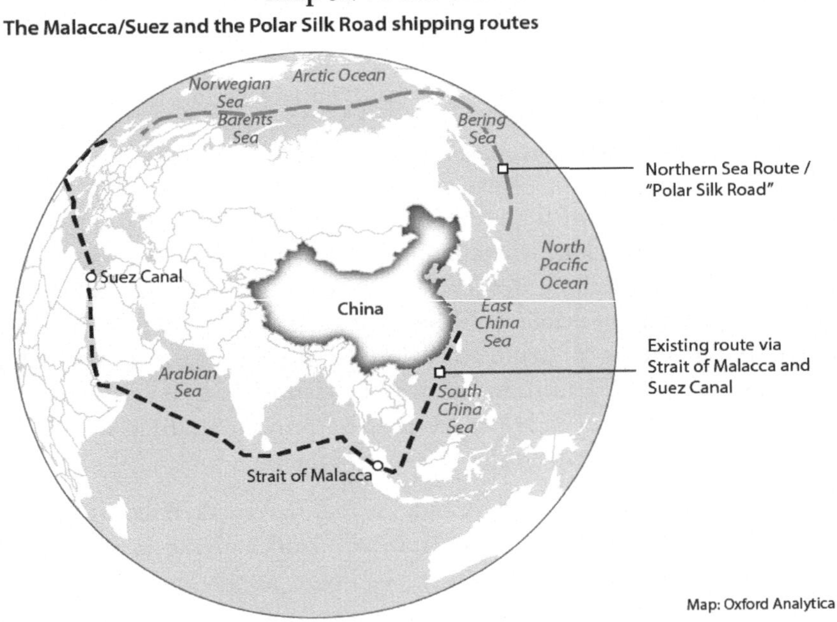

Source: www.googlemaps.com

China despite being a non-Arctic state is increasingly active in the Polar region and became an observer member of the Arctic Council in 2013. Among its increasing interests in the region is its major stake in Russia's Yamal liquefied natural gas project which is expected to supply China with 4 million tonnes of LNG a year. China's increasing prominence in the region has prompted concerns from Arctic States over its long-term strategic objectives, including possible military deployments. This clearly indicates that China is not leaving any piece of land or region for its expansionist purpose and to lure available resources from that region. The Polar Silk Road (PSR) essentially refers to the shipping routes comprising the Northwest Passage, Northeast Passage and Central Passage that cross the Arctic Circle and connect the Economic centers of North America, East Asia, and Western Europe, as shown in the above map.

The Arctic policy of China outlines its approach to foreign relations with Arctic countries and its plans to develop infrastructure, enhance military capabilities, conduct research, and exploit resources within the Arctic Circle. A major component of this plan is to the construction of a Polar Silk Road, a network of trade routes through the Arctic aimed at expediting global shipping delivery. China has released its official Arctic policy document, which draws a picture of how China views the economic possibilities the region offers. With this, China has vowed to actively participate in Arctic affairs as a "New Arctic State" and a major stakeholder in the Arctic. China has also focused on developing military projection capabilities that would extend into the Arctic Region. China has anticipated that with global warming and melting of Polar ice caps, more resources will be available for exploration and exploitation, leading to increased interest and investment in the region.

Interest in the Arctic region is not limited to littoral states, as many non-Arctic countries have been admitted in the Arctic Council. China has been steadily asserting its presence in the region, despite describing itself as a non-Arctic country. The only unanimity among public voices appears to be that the Arctic belongs to humankind and not to any single country or group of countries.

India's Arctic Policy

India's Arctic Policy must address the double standards of rich countries. The Arctic is crucial for stabilizing the earth's climate, arguably, even more so than the Antarctic. Its sea ice plays a critical role in moderating the global climate. In turn, it is also sensitive to changes in climate. Consequently, the Arctic is warming more rapidly than global average, and its ice has decreased dramatically since the late 1970s. The warming of the Arctic is also speeding the melting of the Greenland ice sheets. Recent studies indicate that Greenland ice is melting on average seven times faster today than in the 1990s.Consequently, these changes in the Arctic have significant implications for sea level rise, aquatic ecosystems, and weather patterns worldwide, including the monsoon.

But the melting sea ice has also opened up the fabled Northwest Passage, significantly shortening the route between the Arctic and Pacific oceans. Additionally, Arctic sea bed is now accessible for oil, gas extraction and deep sea mining. An estimated 40 per cent of the current global oil gas reserves are in this region, leading to a scramble over shipping lanes and resources, particularly among Arctic states, such as the US, Russia, Canada, Norway and Denmark. However, other countries, notably China, are also staking claims over the region's resources.

India is an observer at the Arctic Council and has recently released a draft Arctic policy. Regrettably, the draft policy lacks objectivity. It is an all-of-the above policy with contradictory goals. On the one hand, India's Arctic policy envisions India's role in exploring and exploiting hydrocarbon and encourages investments by Indian companies. It also expresses deep concerns regarding the impacts on the country due to the changes in the Arctic including the monsoon. The draft terms the Arctic as the common heritage of humankind and calls for sustainable responsible and transparent human activity. The irony is that, the world's wealthiest people living in the already wealthy Arctic states will gain the most by exploiting the resources. However, the costs will be borne by the world's poorest, living in the coastal areas of the global south. China's major stake in Russia's Yamal liquefied natural gas project which is expected to supply China with 4 million tonnes of LNG a year.

If India wants to be a serious player in the Arctic, then its policy must address the irony and double standards of Arctic states. The bottom line is that India will not gain economically but is likely to incur massive losses due to coastal flooding, monsoon disruptions and changes in the ocean systems. Therefore, India's Arctic policy should push for international legal mechanisms, similar to the Antarctic treaty, to save the Arctic's pristine ecosystem and earth's climate.

Digital Silk Road Project of China

The 2nd summit of the Belt and Road Initiative concluded in the 1st week of May 2019 amid great fanfare in Beijing. Headlines in the Newspapers proclaimed BRI's inexorable expansion to new countries and China's growing footprint in the Digital Silk Road project, which could prove to be a game changer in the world.

Ever since the Silk Road was launched in 2017, China has been building up an 'information expressway' of fibre optic links to Myanmar, Nepal, and Kyrgyzstan. It plans to connect Africa to China by laying cables across the ocean from Pakistan, which is being linked to China through its China

Pakistan Economic Corridor. China has offered help to countries as far away as Cuba, Egypt, Saudi Arabia and Turkey to advance cloud computing, big data, The Internet of Things, and artificial intelligence (AI). China's advance as a digital connector and leading provider of 5G technology, which would form the backbone of autonomous vehicles, facial recognition technology and AI to an ever-growing number of developing countries, raises the possibility that Chinese-style surveillance states will proliferate.

Though China loftily describes its Digital Silk Road as a community of common destiny in Cyberspace, its growing control over the cyberspace—its own and that of its partners—would in fact allow Beijing to bend that common destiny towards the interests of its one-party line. However, the US keeps issuing warnings about the espionage risks of using Chinese 5G network equipment, yet infrastructure projects keep growing. Despite lamentations of a Cassandra like Washington, Huawei and ZTE are acquiring access to larger markets, making an end run around their Western rivals. Less visible than ports and railways of BRI, China's expanding control over the world's digital communications networks would give Beijing unparalleled influence. Its growing clout in surveillance tech, combined with its lead in developing superfast 5G, promises to make China a global tech challenger to the US. This significant development comes despite repeated American warnings that it might reconsider sharing sensitive intelligence with allies as a member of the 'Five Eyes' intelligence-sharing group that includes the US, UK, Canada, Australia and New Zealand. Even the UK, which as a member of the 'Five Eyes' intelligence sharing group once supported a tough stand against Huawei, has now decided to allow the firm to build parts of its 5G network. Major BRI partners don't even have an option; they are supposed to use only Chinese 5G suppliers, which hold 36 per cent of all 5G patents worldwide, potentially leading to security issues in their countries.

Cyber Threats to Indian Infrastructure have Escalated

Since the Galwan tussle, cyber threats to Indian infrastructure have escalated. Chinese hostilities along the border are not the only incursions India needs to be alert to. A study by the American company, 'Recorded Future' underlines systematic cyber incursions by Chinese State-Sponsored groups attempting to gain a foot-hold in "critical nodes across the Indian power generation and transmission infrastructure." The October 12 blackout in India's financial Capital (Mumbai), is being linked to this cause, with Maharashtra energy Minister affirming the possibility of sabotage, though the link remains unsubstantiated. It bears reminding that Mumbai's grid failure brought its trains and financial markets to a screeching halt, leaving hospitals scrambling for generators in the high moon of the pandemic, making it plain in just a couple of hours how extensive economic damage caused by digitally crippling the power structure can be. Another recent report points out that the Chinese groups are targeting Serum Institute and Bharat Biotech. According to insiders in the government, additional safeguards have been deployed after October 12, 2020, to protect the national power grid, with CERT (Indian Computers Emergency Response Team) helping to deflect various malware (software that is especially designed to disturb, damage or gain unauthorized access to a computer system).

So, cyber security needs broader strengthening because the Pandemic has pushed many sectors through an unprecedented digital transformation. For this, international collaboration is necessary and urgent. Towards this, India must work closely with like-minded countries to share intelligence and neutralize cyber-attacks, while protecting the privacy of citizens. The Chinese armed forces are as prepared in cyber warfare as they are fighting pitched battles on the ground. This is a reality that the Indian government is grappling with after the Galwan Valley clash. According to reports, Chinese hackers attacked India's power grid immediately after the clash, indicating how the nature of war is changing.

The Indian government has since decided to beef up its digital attack and defence capabilities by introducing Artificial Intelligence (AI) in everything, from Missiles to Surveillance to ship building, with the help of academic institutions, such as the International Institute of Information Technology at Hyderabad (IIIT-H), and defence institutions, such as, Secunderabad based Military College of Electrical and Mechanical Engineering (MCE-ME). India has received a lot of Artificial Intelligence related requests following the Chinese incursion last October 2020.

Recently, Telangana and some other states were alerted by the Central agency on a day the Central Minister denied reports of Chinese cyber-attacks causing a major power outage in Mumbai last year. Telangana's top electricity authorities said that they had received alerts about Chinese malware entering 40 Substations from the Central Electricity Authority. In the first week of March 2021, the Indian Computer Response Team (CERT) reported from a trusted source that a China based threat actor group's command and control servers were trying to communicate with systems belonging to the Telangana State Load Dispatch Centre (SLDC) and instructed the Telangana power utilities to take all protection and safety measures. The SLDC monitors the power supply situation in the State and the malware had entered 40-sub-

Stations, but the efforts by the hackers were successfully thwarted by state government agencies. After the Telangana State government got alerts from the central authorities, it removed all malware in 40 sub-stations in SLDC and strengthened the firewall, according to Telangana Transco & Genco Chairman and Managing Director, Prabhakar Rao.

In view of the above, the Government of India has changed rules to firewall telecom infrastructure from the China threat. In a move that will restrict the business of top Chinese vendors such as Huawei and ZTE in India's 4G telecom expansion and upcoming 5G, the government has taken decisive steps towards securing the mobile ecosystem by making amendments to the license rules. The amendments mandate that post June 15, equipment can be procured only from 'trusted' sources that have been approved by a Designated Authority. This move comes amidst growing concerns in the government over meddling by Chinese elements in India's critical infrastructure. The current amendments have been necessitated by the need to secure the vital and burgeoning Indian Telecom space from untrusted Vendors.

So, India warded off cyber-attacks from foreign countries, especially, China and Pakistan, during the coronavirus induced l lockdown by implementing measures to ensure safe work from home practices. In the present situation, robust cyber security mechanisms are imperative for the effective implementation of the Digital India program.

China's growing 5G clout could soon enable it to play a big brother role to the world, as ZTE sells its products and services in more than 160 countries worldwide. Despite the US issuing warnings about the espionage risks of using Chinese 5G network equipment, infrastructure projects continue to grow. Despite the lamentations of a Cassandra—like Washington, Huawei and ZTE are gaining access to larger markets and circumventing their Western rivals. Less visible than the ports and railways of the BRI, China's expanding control over the world's digital communications networks would give Beijing unparalleled influence. Its growing clout in surveillance tech, combined with its lead in developing superfast 5G, promises to make China a global tech challenger to the US in the near future.

ZTE Corporation on NBR Radar

ZTE is a Chinese Corporation technology company that specializes in Telecommunications. Founded in 1985, ZTE is a global leader in Telecommunications and Information Technology. Zhongxing Telecommunications Equipment has been committed to providing integrated end-to end services. ZTE is listed on both Hong Kong and Shenzhen Stock Exchanges.

The Chinese company has had business transactions worth $ 500 million with different entities in the country over the last few years. The National Board of Revenue (NBR) has launched an investigation into ZTE Bangladesh, a subsidiary of the Chinese ZTE Corporation, which has many business operations in different sectors of the country, to see if the company is involved in tax evasion, according to The Business Standard on December 20th, 2020.

As a part of the investigation, the revenue board has already sent separate letters to different entities with whom it has its business deals. With aim of protecting the property safety of Bangladesh and upholding local laws and regulations, the revenue authority has launched the probe as the company's operations are deemed to have an intention of tax evasion. The ZTE Corporation, listed on the stock exchanges of Hong-Kong and Shenzhen, sells its products and services in more than 160 countries. According to the Shenzhen Stock Exchange, the total revenue of the ZTE Corporation in 2019 was 9073 crores Chinese Yuan. Meanwhile, the US lawmakers passed a law to create US $ 1.9 billion fund to replace telecom equipment from China's Huawei and ZTE. The US lawmakers passed the bill late on Monday, the 20th December 2020, endorsing $ 1.9 billion to fund a programme to remove telecom network equipment that the US government says poses to its national security risks, as a part of a year-end spending bill and Covid-19 bill, according to a report published in The Economic Times on December 20, 2020. The Federal Communications Commission informed in June 2020 that it had formally designated China's Huawei Technologies Co and ZTE Corporation as threats to the US.

History of Chinese Economy and its Rise in the Indian Ocean Region

Since the introduction of economic reforms in 1978, China has experienced a high growth rate over the last few decades, becoming the world's second largest economy, pushing Japan into the 3rd position. It ranked 9th in the national gross domestic product with USD of 214 bn and after 37 years today, it jumped to second place with 9.2 trillion USD. The country, aiming to overcome backwardness, decided to shift from a hard core capitalist economy to a communist socialist society with a high growth rate of 10.6 percent in 2010. Until Mao Zedong's death in 1976, China was more backward than India. Only after Den Xiaoping, the 2nd generation of Chinese leadership, pushed reforms that reshaped the country's economy with the introduction of a market driven mechanism and reduced government control over economy. When Xi Jinping became president to lead the fifth generation of Chinese leadership, he unveiled an ambitious reform agenda from a capitalist economy to market economy with the highest growth rate in the world. However, the Chinese economy has been struggling with high debts, languishing exports and a continued slowdown in its economic growth rate since 2011, from a double digit growth rate of 10.6 in 2010 to 6.9% in 2015 and in 2018, the growth rate recorded 6.5%, the slowest growth rate in the last 30 years.[21]

The People's Republic of China (PRC), under the reforms and policies initiated by Deng Xiaoping in 1978, has surpassed the US in several economic performance metrics, achieving exponential growth. China has net assets of $ 2.3 trillion compared to the US's of 2.5 USD trillions. The value of Chinese exports surpassed that of the USA in 2007 and Chinese fixed capital investment overtook US investment in 2009. Similarly, manufacturing output and energy consumption exceeded US levels in 2010. Chinese defence expenditure will surpass the US in absolute terms by 2025. Above all, China became world's second largest economy in 2010 overtaking Japan and is estimated to surpass the US by 2027. China's military expenditure four times more than India at present, the second largest spender after the US with $ 250 bn.[22]

In the ancient period China's Maritime forces has mainly centered on the pacific, but with the changing international status quo supremacy over Asia's Maritime sphere, especially over the waters between the Indian Ocean Region and the South China Sea, has become a Beijing's one of the primary strategic goals. Due to this, China's national security is heavily dependent on the safety and security of the sea routes to sustain its rapid economic development and increasing power projection. The quest for security can be understood in the context that more than 70 percent of China's energy imports are transported through shipping lanes in the Indian Ocean Region (IOR), with major strategic chockpoints at Malacca Strait.[23]

Hence, to secure its strategic goals, China is expanding its military posture and naval modernization in the Indian Ocean. Srikanth Kondapally notes that with this "China could be testing the waters in the Eastern Indian Ocean, including its ability to its bases in the region. The strategic interest of China in the Indian Ocean is driven by its deep-seated security dilemma which drives its ambition to build an ocean capacity to become an active player in the region, to project power in the Indian Ocean Region in rivalry, not only with India but primarily with the US. This is primarily driven by the need to secure freedom of navigation in the Indian Ocean, whereby China faces a Malacca

Dilemma, as 80 percent of its petroleum imports, pass through the Indian Ocean from 'the Strait of Malacca' China may face obstacles from US and India.

China's security dilemma vis-a-vis the US is posed by the US Navy's dominance of high seas stretching from the Persian Gulf to the Indian Ocean to the South China Sea. China's strategic thinking in the Indian Ocean is guided by a fear of US containment of PRC—by roping, in Indian Ocean littorals within the Indo-Pacific framework and America's prowess in holding China's sea-dependent economy hostages in times of crisis, mainly the Malacca Straits which is a maritime portal for virtually China's Persian Gulf Oil.[24]

It is not an exaggeration to say that whoever controls 'The Strait of Malacca' will also have a strong hold on the energy route. Excessive reliance on this strait has brought an important potential threat to China's energy security. Apart from the US security threat, China's interest in the Indian Ocean is also guided by the dominant presence of India in the region. India, by its geographic location and given its potential to be a great power together with its aspirations runs antagonise to a rising China's quest to gain strategic and hegemonic spare as an off-shore region.

Furthermore, China recognizes India's requirement for energy security, which it anticipates as another challenge to its own energy procurement. This external influence on China's Indian Ocean seems apparent in the official statements and observations of authoritative scholars confirming that, China's dominant thinking on the Indian Ocean is primarily driven by the presence of two dominant powers, the US and India. Hence, China's strategic interest in the Indian Ocean Region is to safeguard its expanding national interests—trade and energy.

China's responses to its energy vulnerabilities and quest for great power in the Indian Ocean vis-a-vis India and the US are seen as a soft power policy with a long term aim to secure a strong maritime position. But China's Indian Ocean strategy in terms of its military presence in the Indian Ocean Region has raised concerns among the regional players particularly for India. China's strategies in the Indian Ocean Region encompass its naval activities, String of Pearls strategy and Maritime Silk Road strategy.

The People's Liberation Army Navy (PLAN) has been expanding and reconfiguring its role in view of changing circumstances and the growing importance of the Indian Ocean. The PLAN's increasing operations in the Indian Ocean reflect China's desire to improve its ability to combat perceived threats to sea routes vital to its economic development. PLAN strategists and academics argue that the USA uses the 'First Island' chain to "encircle" or contain China and to prevent the PLAN navy from operating freely beyond China's immediate periphery. A Chinese nuclear submarine "Changzheng-2" along with the support ship "Changxing Dao" docked from 7–14 September 2014 in the Colombo International Container terminals, in which China has invested $ 500 million. This clearly signals the possibility of using commercial infrastructure and built by them for military purpose. The PLA navy has been progressively increasing its Maritime influence by transforming itself from coastal defence navy to a force capable of sustained open-ocean operations, which is reasonably commensurate with China's super power status.

Apart from this, China has deployed submarines in the Indian Ocean which has raised concerns for the Indian navy. In the past China deployed its Jin-class submarines in 2008 at the submarine base near Sanya in the Southern tip of Hainan, raising alarm in India as the base is merely 1200 nautical miles from Malacca strait and is its closet access point to the Indian Ocean. It is also reported that the Chinese navy appears to be building "Expeditionary Maritime Capabilities"[25] and could also use nuclear-powered submarines such as the DE-21D, anti-ship ballistic missiles to threaten India within the region frequently. China's nuclear submarines are also docking in the Indian Ocean littoral countries ports, such as Gwadar port in Pakistan, Hambantota port in Sri Lanka, Djibouti port in Africa on the pretext of protecting its sea lanes of communication. For this purpose, China has developed a strategy to establish ports for both naval and military purposes, called the 'String of Pearls' plan of action. China is building railways, ports, power plants, roads, bridges and to other infrastructure facilities aimed at improving connectivity both on land and at sea, known as the Chinese BRI Strategy.

Therefore, China's Indian Ocean Strategy which aimed to protect and enhance its interests in the region—is in turn generating apprehensions in Indian strategic circles, thereby endangering a classic security dilemma between two Asian giants. Naturally, India has its fear and apprehension about the perception of China's growing naval prowess in the Indian Ocean that is driving Indian naval posture through its pearls strategy.

China's 'String of Pearls' Strategy

The Indian Ocean is no longer just the Ocean of Indians; armed conflicts in this area are also taken into account. It is often argued that the 21st century will be the century of Asian countries. From the Industrial Revolution to the end of World War II, it was a European century. Asia is witnessing the emergence of three major powers—China, India and Japan. Among them, China and India are seen as 'Rising Powers'.

China's 'String of Pearls' Strategy describes its rising geopolitical influence through efforts to increase access to ports and airfields in Indian Ocean littoral countries, from the middle east to southern China. These 'Pearls' take the form of naval bases or electronic eavesdropping ports built by China in Myanmar, Bangladesh. Pakistan, Sri Lanka, Djibouti in Africa and with a focus on Maldives to protect its oil shipments. India sees this as China's 'Encirclement Policy'.[26] This strategy as argued, is seen as an attempt of Beijing to establish a serious of naval airports in the Indian Ocean, with a presumed aim of keeping the Indian Navy from consolidating its influence over its own strategies backyard. The 'pearls' include Gwadar in Pakistan, the Hambantota Port in Sri Lanka, Chittagong in Bangladesh, Sittwe and Coco Island in Myanmar, Djibouti in Africa and in the Maldives.

Map 3.8: China's 'String of Pearls'

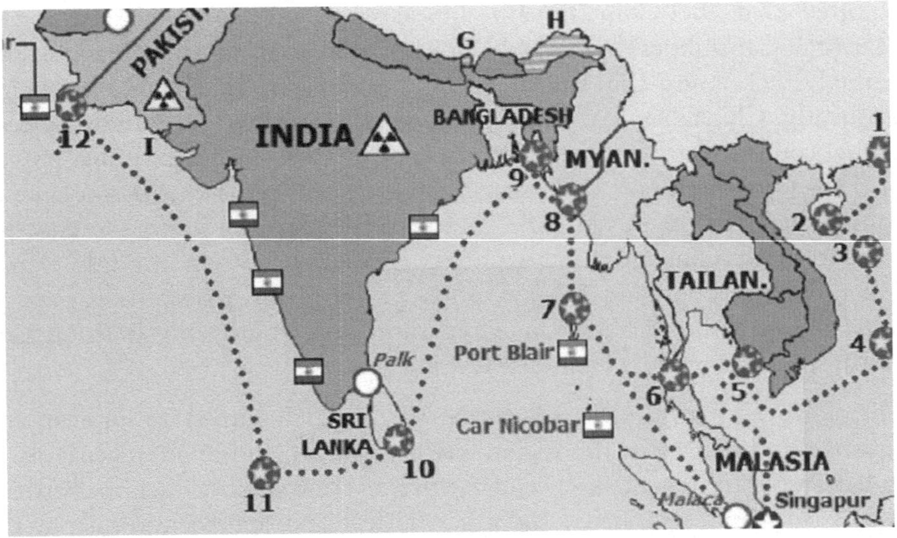

Source: www.googlemaps.com

As per Indian claims, the 'String of Pearls' strategy, apart from the strategic ports, also includes electronic intelligence gathering facilities on Islands in the Bay of Bengal, funding for the construction of a canal across the Kra Isthmus in Thailand, a military agreement with Cambodia and building up of forces in the South China Sea. These 'Pearls' help in building strategic ties with several countries along the sea shores from the Middle East to the SCS (South China Sea).

Concentrating with the littoral states in the Indian Ocean Region the China-Pakistan Economic Corridor (CPEC), and Bangladesh, China, Indian Myanmar (BCIM) Economic Corridor and China-Myanmar Economic Corridor, which are launched the projects will unleash a massive inflow of Chinese funds to Myanmar which can further weaken Indian influence over its eastern neighbor. This corridor though aimed to building basic infrastructure, enhancing telecommunication facilities and improving transport and agriculture in Myanmar. The corridor would connect the Chinese Province of Yunnan and three important economic centre's in Myanmar. Several challenges can create problems, based on ethnic conflicts in different parts of Myanmar and anti-Chinese sentiment among a section of people. There is also fear of a debt-trap in Myanmar, which has earlier cancelled the construction of a Chinese financed dam project.[27]

With these mega projects and heavy investment, China intends to mitigate the security concerns in the MSR, ranging from territorial disputes in the South China Sea to transnational threats such as piracy, armed robbery and terrorism. These initiatives, which intends to deeper Chinese economic and maritime links with both South-East Asia and Indian Ocean Region countries, are perceived as an attempt to reframe the regional ambition about China's growing military and naval presence amid many disputes both at land and sea called as a response to the 'String of Pearls' Strategy.

After the establishment of its first overseas naval base at Djibouti in the Horn of Africa in 2017, China now wants to host marine infantry combat vehicles and helicopters in Pakistan, Cambodia, Vanuatu and other countries for additional military bases to enhance its strategic footprint and emerge as power in the crucial Indo-Pacific region.[28] The Djibouti base, where China is now constructing a 450-meter pier capable of berthing four warships by the end of 2019 and probably follows naval bases at other locations, signaling a turning point in the expansion by PLA in the IOR and beyond.[29]

Belt and Road Initiative

China appears to be rebranding its multi-billion dollar Belt & Road Initiative (BRI), bracing for competition with the US President Joe Biden's Build Back Better World (B3W) Initiative which emphasizes transparency and democratic values.

After Xi Jinping was successfully endorsed by the Chinese Plenum meeting as President of China for the third term, China enunciation on BRI's strategy under which BRI adopts new circumstances and new vitality by laying great emphasis on green Belt and Road development giving importance to green infrastructure, green energy and green finance. The Chinese President Xi declared in his UN address that China will not build coal-fired power projects abroad in response to climate change. China further assured that greater emphasis will also lay on the inclusive development of BRI cooperation.

The Build Better Back World (B3W) Initiative was unveiled by the US President Biden during the G-7 summit in June 2021 with an aim of creating a 'values driven high standard transparent infrastructure partnership' to help finance projects in developing countries. China, however, played down the initiative B3W as any competition to its BRI project which Xi launched in 2013 to fund infrastructure projects across the world. China felt that at present there is a huge gap in infrastructure investment in the world, especially in developing countries. The trade volume between China and BRI partners has exceeded $ 9.2 trillion in 2020, while direct investment by Chinese companies has nearly touched $ 14 billion. However, analysts have cautioned Beijing about the US plan saying that the B3W initiatives stated goals are targeting China.

AUKUS

'AUKUS' is a security alliance between Australia, the UK and the US aimed ostensibly at countering China's growing influence in the Indo-Pacific region. This is a military alliance involving the transfer of top-tier military technology. The Quad is also aimed at countering of China has largely economic orientation.

On the Indo-Pacific, there are some apprehensions that AUKUS could dilute the strategic cooperation envisaged under the Quad, relegating the Quad grouping to just issues like Climate change, Covid Vaccines and similar topics. In this regard, the US assured India that the new trilateral AUKUS military pact is aimed at discussing challenges posed by the China in the Indo-Pacific, stressing it will not detract from either bilateral cooperation with New Delhi or multilateral ones like the Quad.

Under the AUKUS, Australia will get the wherewithal to build at least eight nucleated-powered attack submarines to counter China's expanding naval footprints in the Indo-Pacific. It is to be noted here that, the US has over the years refused to discuss nuclear reactor propulsion technology for submarines or aircraft carriers with India.

Quad countries share the vision of a free open, transparent and inclusive Indo-Pacific region. Quad has adopted a wide array of initiatives global on issues like the Pandemic, new and emerging technologies and climate change. But,

AUKUS is a purely security alliance involving three countries. According to the US, the AUKUS is neither relevant to Quad nor will it have any impact on Quad's functions.

China's Belt and Road Drive reaches Latin America

China's expansion programme reaches Latin America under the OBOR initiative, to build ports and other trade-related facilities is creating ripples in Washington over Beijing's ambition in the region, as the American leaders since the 19th century have seen it as off-limits to other powers. China is hardly a newcomer to the region but now it focuses on countries in Central America such as Panama. Though, it is very small country, possessing just 4 million people, but its canal linking the Atlantic and Pacific Oceans makes it one of the world's busiest trade arteries strategically important both to Washington and Beijing. American authorities expanded Alrum at Beijing's ambition in the US-dominated region. Italy becomes the 1st G-7 nation to join China's OBOR initiative in spite of opposition from its own government,[30] inking an agreement worth 2.5 billion contracts to lift the economy out of third recession in a decade. Few EU leaders also cautioned Italy for quickly aligning itself with China. However, the US, Japan, Russia, India and other governments felt that Beijing gaining economic and strategic influence at their expense. India termed in the past while lashing out at the initiative, branding it a colonial enterprise that China adopted new imperialism in the developing and less-developed countries.

India Opposed to China's OBOR Initiative

Since the announcement of the OBOR initiative in 2013 by Chinese President Xi Jinping in Central Asian countries, India cautiously observed China's purpose and motive behind the initiative, which involves 10 billion Yuan ($1.66 n) funds to build ports and other infrastructure to boost maritime connectivity with Southeast Asian and Indian Ocean littoral countries.

India turned down an official invitation from China to attend even the 2nd Belt and Road Forum (BRF) meeting held in month of April 2019. India also boycotted the first meeting held in Beijing in 2017, which attracted 19 head of government, including Russia's President Putin and Turkey's Recep Tayyip Erdogan. The US sent only a Joint Secretary official to the summit, while the government of India maintained its stance that China's BRI undermines India sovereignty, particularly through the China Pakistan Economic corridor passing through Pakistan Occupied Kashmir (POK). Despite countries like Japan, Britain, Germany and France participating, India stood firm in its opposing BRI, underscoring its strong reservations about the Chinese initiative. This marked the first setback to China's attempts to establish itself as a global leader through the BRI. Since then, several other setbacks have compounded China's challenge.

India has opposed China's BRI on the grounds of not only sovereignty issue, there are other equally significant concerns, it has highlighted such as China's constant attempts to block India's bid at the UN to declare Jaish-e-Mohammed Chief Masood Azhar as a global terrorist for a long period (it has resolved now), inclusivity issues, financial and environmental sustainability and the unilateral nature of BRI.[31] Bhutan, India's immediate neighbor boycotted the meet in 2017 too, aligning itself with India's sovereignty concerns.

A number of countries that had joined the BRI bandwagon initially are now having second thoughts, and are echoing Indian views. Southeast Asian nations like Malaysia & Myanmar have recently expressed concerns about China's "debt trap diplomacy" emanating out of BRI. From the Maldives and Sri Lanka to Malaysia, Pakistan and Thailand, doubts are being raised about the future viability of many of the Chinese projects.

Newly elected Malaysian President Mahathir Mohamad shocked China when he slaved the project, soon after he came to power. It is the opinion of the President, that the project contracted by the previous government was unfair and imposed a major financial burden on the country, as the condition, laid on the project and the rate of interest on the investment is unviable and Malaysia wants to cut the project.

In response to the Malaysian decision, China had agreed to hugely lowered price for China's rail line under OBOR slashing 30% from the original cost to the 648 km rail link. Only after the announcement by China, Malaysia reopened a closed Chinese rail construction project after slashing 30% from original agreement. It became desperate for China to present a strong global infrastructure programme under OBOR initiative while land grabbing in the island nation like Maldives.[32]

The decision to slash the price might result in a chain effort with countries implementing BRI, like Pakistan also demanded price cut for its China-Pakistan Economic Corridor (CPEC) project. India, one of the countries skipping the BRI meetings, was among first to highlight the negative aspects of the programme, including financing systems that could trap poor countries in debt.

China was subjected to continue allegations for its expansionist plan with neighboring countries both on the borders (land) and in the water of Oceans its shares borders and some of the countries are openly alleging that China's land grabbing in poor countries. For example, Maldives leader of opposition and former foreign minister, openly accused China's land land-grabbing activities in the Island nation, with the potential of developing them into a military outpost.[33] China has also undertaken similar activities across the region from Djibouti to Hambantota port in Sri Lanka and now potentially the Maldives giving cause for concerns in the region, hence, the Pentagon has warned China about its land-grabbing activities in Maldives and in other poor and small nations.

China's Trillion-dollar OBOR Initiative Runs into Debt Jam

China's massive and expanding Belt and Road trade infrastructure project is running into speed bumps as some countries have begun to grumble about being buried under Chinese debt. Malaysia, Pakistan, the Maldives, Sri Lanka, and many more are falling into the debt trap, with some questioning whether the cost outweigh benefits. First announced by Chinese President Xi Jinping in 2013, the initiative, also known as the "New Silk Road" project, envisions the construction of railways, roads and ports across the globe, with Beijing providing billions of dollars in loans to many countries.

After seven years on, President Xi Jinping finds himself defending his cherished idea amid growing concerns that China is setting up debt-traps in countries that lack the means to repay the Asian giant. Xi has described in his address a year ago marking the initiative that the Chinese trade with Belt & Road countries has exceeded $ 5 trillion, with outward direct investment surpassing $ 60 billion. However, some are beginning to question whether the benefits justify the costs.

During visit to Beijing, Malaysian Prime Minister Mahathir Mohamad expressed concern that his country would 'shelve' three Chinese backed projects, including $ 20 billion railway. The Pakistan's Prime Minister Imran Khan after he became PM, vowed more transparency amid fears about the country's ability to repay Chinese loans related to the multi-billion dollar China-Pakistan Economic Corridor. Meanwhile, the exiled leader of the opposition in the Maldives said that Chinese actions in the Indian Ocean archipelago amounted to a "land grab" and "colonialism", with 80 per cent of its debts held by Beijing. In Maldives, China has acquired several islets in that heavily indebted Indian Ocean archipelago. While the terms of the lease agreements have not been disclosed, the acquisitions have come on cheap. For instance, China paid just $ 4 million for Feydhoo Finolhu, an island that previously served as a police training Centre.

Sri Lanka has already paid a heavy price for being highly indebted to China. The Island nation had to grant a 99-year lease on a strategic port to Beijing due to its inability to repay loans for the $ 1.4 billion project. The Sri Lankans experience has been a wake-up call for other countries with outsize debt to China. A number of Belt and Road Initiative partner states have begun trying to renegotiate their deals with Beijing. Some have decided to cancel or scale back projects. Malaysian PM Mahathir Mohamad declared during his visit to Beijing the cancellation of Chinese projects worth about $ 23 billion. Additionally, close ally to China, Pakistan has downsized its main BRI rail road projects by $ 2 billion.

In Djibouti, the IMF has warned that the Horn of African countries faced a "high risk of debt distress" as its public debt jumped from 50 per cent GDP in 2014 to 85 per cent in 2016, within 2 years only. Africa has long embraced Chinese investment, helping make Beijing the continent's largest trading partner for the last decade. Beijing has leveraged big credits to gain even military presence, as its first overseas naval base at Djibouti illustrates the case. Trapped in a debt crisis after borrowing billions of dollars, Djibouti was left with no option, but to lease land for the base to China for $ 20 billion an annual rent.

Sierra Leone has become the latest country to scrap an OBOR project cancelling a $ 318 billion airport deal with China. After smooth sailing, BRI now encountering strong headwinds, as partner nations wary about sovereignty eroding debt traps. In multiple countries, OBOR projects are being scraped or scaled back.

China is similarly seeking to employ its leverage over cash-strapped Pakistan to build a naval base next to Gwadar port. Pakistan in recent periods retained in regard to its earlier decision on China Pakistan Economic Corridor deal over unfair benefits to Chinese firms. Prime Minister Imran Khan's government discussed thoroughly renegotiating the agreements reached under China's ambitious BRI, as it is unfairly benefiting Chinese companies. The projects concerned one part of the multi-billion CPEC plan—the most ambitious part of OBOR, which seeks to connect Asia and Europe along the ancient Silk Road. The CPEC was launched in 2015, in a planned network of roads, railways, and energy projects linking China's resource-rich Xinjiang region with Pakistan's strategic Gwadar port on the Arabian Sea.

The huge endeavour brings much-needed infrastructure improvements to developing countries while giving China a destination to stock up on its raw materials. But a study by the Centre for Global Development—a US think-tank found" serious concern" about the sustainability of the sovereign debt in eight countries receiving Silk Road funds. Those were Pakistan, Djibouti,

Maldives, Mongolia, Laos, Montenegro, Tajikistan and Kyrgyzstan. The cost of the Laos railway project $ 6.7 billion represents almost half of the Southeast Asia countries' GDP. Stevenson Yong expressed that, China's loans are quoted in dollar terms, but in reality, they are lending in terms of Tractors, Shipments of Coal, engineering services and thing like that and ask for repayments in hard currency.

Against the background of China's actions, India's brave, principled stand against BRI initiative by Prime Minister Modi, stands fully vindicated. India can prove itself as the intellectual leader that helped shine a spotlight on BRI financial and security risks and thereby moulded the international debate. The larger international pushback against China's predatory practices is likely to intensify in the coming years, putting greater pressure on the Chinese BRI initiative.

The Chinese navy has grown the fastest in the world over the last 200 years, according to Admiral Sunil Lamba, the Chinese navy was present in the Indian Ocean in 2008, having added a phenomenal 80 ships to its navy in the past five years. He further said that at any given time there are six to eight Chinese navy ships in the northern part of the Indian Ocean in the form of anti-piracy operations. China has also deployed submarines for this purpose.[34] But the Indo-Pacific panel of the navy chief of India, Australia, Japan, France and the Indo-Pacific command Chiefs of the USA, thorough discussion and expressed apprehensions about the presence of Chinese military and its security implications for the Indian Ocean littoral countries.

Keeping in view of these, in the mind India under leadership PM Modi, has virtually allocated an exclusive fund Rs. 5650 crores for the military infrastructure development plan spread over 10 years for the strategically located Andaman & Nicobar archipelago, which will allow the stationing of additional warships, aircraft, drones, missile batteries and infantry soldiers, against the backdrop of China's rapidly footprint in the Indian Ocean Region. The 10-year infrastructure development plan for the Andaman & Nicobar Command (ANC), which is the country's only Theatre Command with assets and manpower of the army, navy, Air force and coast guard under one operational agencies under agency of defence planning committee. The initial plan was pegged at around Rs. 10,000 crores for the purchase of land that was already under acquisition by the ANC.

Strategically located, the572 Islands of the Andaman and Nicobar archipelago straddle major global trade routes. About 70,000 ships sail through the Strait of Malacca annually. This strategic location will act as a pivot to counter China's strategic moves in the Indian Ocean Region and ensures the security of sea lanes of converging towards the Malacca Strait. It also secures India's 5.95 lakh sq km of Exclusive Economic Zone, a 30% of total in the region. The government of India, parallelly, has a comprehensive plan for force accretions of the armed forces in a phased manner at the Andaman and Nicobar Command (ANC) by 2027. Under this plan, the proposal for an increase in Army manpower and assets is pegged at about Rs. 5970 crores.

India and Indonesia joined hands to counter expansionist China recently.[35] The two countries agreed to develop a naval port in 'Sabang', a strategic location on the tip of Sumatra Island and at the entrance of vital Malacca Straits. The move, which comes at the time, when China is expanding its maritime footprint in the region, was the most significant decision by the two countries. The two countries have also agreed to step up defence and maritime front, largely due to fears of China's expansionism. The two countries have agreed to negotiate the issues of the maritime boundaries, based on the principles of International law including that of 1982 UNCLAS. China has encroached on Indonesian's exclusive economic zone with its nine-dash-line to the extent that Indonesia has now renamed its sea as the 'Natuna Sea'.[36]

India may not be the economic powerhouse of that level, but plans are underway to counter China's expanding strategic footprint in the Indian Ocean Region (IOR) with Chinese warships and submarines making regular forays into the region. The government of India has given approvals for the contribution of 56 new warships and six submarines for the Indian Navy. The Indian navy currently has 140 warships and 220 aircraft, already 32 warships are under construction in domestic shipyards at a total cost of Rs. 1.26 lakh crores to replace its aging fleet and plug operational lapses.[37]

Since the annual defence budget in India has not registered any tangible hike for the last five years, to ensure the navy comes anyway close to its original target of 212 warships and 458 aircraft force by 2027. But the admiral Sunil Lamba expressed confidence ahead of Navy Day recently that India is good enough to tackle an aggressive and expansionist China in India's strategic backyard. The navy chief further added that the entire world's attention is focused on IOR where our navy is increasingly seen as a net security provider. Our maritime environment is free from all forms of threats (Traditional & non-traditional)

The former US President Trump acknowledged the threat from China's OBOR project, which over five years, has bankrolled mega projects across Asia, Africa and Europe to expand its sphere of influence through various corridors, under OBOR/BRI. The US president wants to counter China's growing geo-political influence and perceived threat, hence he signed a bill that created a new foreign aid agency, called the US International Development Finance Corporation, and gave it authority to provide $ 60 billion in loans, loan guarantees and insurance to companies willing to do business in developing nations. The move by US President was a significant reversal from his earlier decisions, desire to block Beijing's plan for economic technological and political dominance.

China's trillion-dollar OBOR initiative runs into debt jam—Malaysia, Pakistan, Maldives, Sri Lanka and Djibouti are worried about Chinese investment/loans under OBOR in the form of dollar terms, but in reality Chinese are lending in terms of tractor, shipments of coal, engineering services and thing like that and they ask for repayment through hard currency with heavy rate of interests.[38] Therefore, the IMF chief has raised concerns about debt problems for these countries as these countries' lack of means to pay back to the Asian giant.

Keeping in view of the situation, Chinese President Xi Jinping has announced at the end of the three-day BRF in China in April 2019 that Beijing is modifying the structure of the infrastructure re-building programme under OBOR. Xi further declared that BRI would adopt market-driven practices, as China has been criticized for allowing companies to take away 90% of the business and dictating its financing terms to borrowers.

Blocks to OBOR Initiative

India's stand was vindicated as China's grandiose OBOR plans run into resistance from the member countries after experience and falling into a debt trap, which affected sovereignty and integrity of nations. Apart from others, Sierra Leone has become the latest country to scrap a Belt and Road project, cancelling a $ 318 million airport deal with China.

India was the first country to come out against the popular BRI initiative. India boycotted Xi's much-hyped BRI summit, held to garner global support for his initiative, held in 2017 and also in the 2nd BRI summit held in 2019 India has boycotted and publicly termed BRI as a non-transparent, neocolonial enterprise aimed to ensnare smaller/poor cash strapped states into debt trap to advanced China's geopolitical agenda by using geo-economic tools. The European Union openly echoed India's concerns by agreeing that, BRI did not include commitments to transparency and social and environmental substantiality. The USA also a long back cautioned the BRI initiative of Xi Jinping as the dawn of a new colonial era and further called the initiative a' new—imperialist power, whose practices are reminiscent of European colonialism.

The International Monetary Fund has also warmed that Chinese loans are subjected to lead into unsustainable debt burdens, which can erode respective countries' sovereignty, self-respect and integrity. The handover of Hambantota port on a 99-year lease to China was seen in Sri Lanka, as the head of a heavily indebted farmer giving away his daughter to the cruel money lender.

India's constant silence about the MSR has mainly been due to uncertainty about how the MSR and other corridors and projects will be implemented, along with concerns and doubts as to whether it will have a geo-economic rationale or a security perspective the MSR appears to be a hindrance to India's interests and security. Already when China is posing a strategic challenge to India and its influence in the region, apart from distrustful of each other's intention including in maritime maneuver and enduring India-China border problem, it is difficult for India to think of joining or cooperating with the MSR. The history of Chinese projects/corridors in the neighbourhood where Beijing brings in its men, material and equipment not to speak of funds providing access to the MSR initiative looks to be perilous.

China has proved it has become a danger to humanity in the light of the Covid-19 virus, killing millions of Tibetans, incarcerating thousands of Uyghurs in Aushwitz-like concentration camps in Xinjiang and promoting terrorism in neighbouring countries like India and Myanmar. It would be natural for the world to exploit China's vulnerabilities at sea and target its strategic arteries like CPEC and CMEC as well as overseas bases if China initiates continuous conflicts with neighbouring countries without any reason.

Conclusion

India is planning its strategy under Prime Minister Modi on how to contain China's expansionist inroads in the Indian Ocean Region and through the OBOR initiative, with a massive investment funding of one trillion dollars in more than 100 countries of Asia, Africa, Europe and Middle East countries. The government of India has initially allocated 10,000 crores for the defence department and 5,000 cfor an integrated military infrastructure development plan for the strategically located Andaman and Nicobar archipelago near the Malacca Strait. Additionally, the government of India floated the Indian Development Assistance Scheme (IDEAS) to counter China's OBOR initiative. As declared in the Indian parliament recently, as the world's six largest economy, the government plans to provide more funds for the scheme, enabling India to provide concessional financing for development projects in the neighbourhood countries. Given India's position in the world, the size of its economy and its status, alternative development models including private sector equity, multilateral financing, contributions from corporate, non-residents, etc. are being considered for the scheme's success.

Project Mausam, considered by the Modi government, as the most significant foreign policy initiative designed to counter China's MSR. India is using its history, culture and geography as a multidisciplinary, transnational project to compete and answer China's OBOR.

As an expansionist, economically and militarily strong China looms large over India's north-eastern border and in the Indian Ocean neighborhood. To overcome this, India needs good governance and economic development are essential for India to make the economic progress that will empower it to face the enduring challenge from China. So, India must rise to the occasion to deal with China, which requires politically guided doctrine and comprehensive military capabilities needed to counter and face the collusion threat from China-Pakistan.

Besides, India and Indonesia have agreed to develop a naval port at 'Sabang' site, a strategically located tip of Sumatra Island and at the entrance of the vital Malacca Strait, which may also be useful for counter China, as the move comes at a time when China is expanding its maritime footprints in the region. It is to be remember that, China's huge oil imports from gulf countries and its excess capacity exporting to African, West Asian and European countries use the vital Malacca Strait. Further, to contain China's expansion and assertiveness India along with the US, Japan and Australia are consistently voicing together against China in the Indian Ocean under 'Quad' and conducting 'Malabar' naval exercises in the Indo-Pacific Oceans to show naval power.

It is now the Indian armed forces will need to respond to China's rapidly expanding military might, especially its growing naval footprint in the IOR, within their budget limitations and other constraints, as per the opinion of Admiral Singh, India has to watch carefully after looking Beijing released its white paper recently, through China was striving to promote security, stability along the India-China border. To face or overcome the threat from China, India requires long-term fiscal support to build a naval base and navy, that is only the way out left for us to counter the Chinese encirclement policy of India.

Notes and References

[1] Deepak, B.R., "One Belt One Road", China at the centre of the global Geopolitics and Geo-economics", South Asia Analysis, paper. No. 5838, December 4, 2014.

[2] Project-Mausam-India-answer-to-China's-maritime-silk-road/report on deployment accessed on 03-12-2015.

[3] Maritime Silk Road issues highlighted during the speech of the Chinese premier XI Jinping on 2nd October 2013, available http://www.asean-china-centre.org/english/2013-10/03/c1330-6267-5.htm accessed on 07-01-2016.

[4] Global Times had organized a forum in October 2014 and the views of different speakers reinforced the view that, MSR is for joint development of ASEAN and provide connectivity of the three continents, http://www.globaltimes.com/content/889599.html accessed on 05-Jan. 2016.

[5] Boom, Krishna E. and Lovelace, Douglas C. (Jr.), Piracy and International Maritime Security: Developments through 2011, Vol. 125, Oxford Press 2012, pp. 194–197.

[6] Muhammad, Anwar, Friends Near Home: Pakistan's Strategic Security Options, Author House Bloomington, 2006, p. 45.

[7] Cho, Lee-Jay and Lee, Chang Jae, Financing Economic Integrations and Functional Cooperation for Northeast Asia, North East Economic Forum Publication 2014, p. 38.

[8] OP. Cit. Vision and Actions, March 28, 2015.

[9] 'US warns Pakistan against China's infra push' Times of India, dt 23rd November 2019.

[10] China prez promises Myanmar a similar BRI deal as Pakistan's, Times of India, dt 18th January 2020.

[11] Sidda, Goud R., 'China Pakistan Economic Corridor Game-Changer in Indian Ocean Region', published in Indian Ocean Digest, Vol. 35, No. 1, issue 55, January–June 2015, ISSN: 0925-8240.

[12] Ibid (pl. write).

[13] New Delhi Slams Beijing refer to CPEC illegal occupied Indian Territory, dt 17-3-2020 routed through net.

[14] 12th BCIM Forum Regional cooperation was held in February 2015 in Yangon but unfortunately hardly any details on outcome are available.

[15] Naidu, G.V.C., BCIM Economic Corridor and prospects for India-China Cooperation, published in edited book Sino-Indian Relations, by Allied publishers, New Delhi, 2016. ISBN 978-85926-22-8, editors, Sidda Goud R, & Manish Mookherjee.

[16] China Prez Promises Myanmar a similar deal as Pakistan, Times of India, dt January 18th 2020.

[17] 'China, Myanmar ink 33 BRI deals', Times of India, dt January 19th 2020.

[18] 'Xi courts an isolated Myanmar in first state to visit of the year', Times of India, dt 17th January 2020.

[19] "Time to revisit Canal project" (opinion). Bangkok Post, 20th January 2020. Retrieved 20th January 2020, & Proposed Kra Canal not priority project for Thai Govt.", The Straits Times, 13th February 2018. Retrieved 13th February 2018.

[20] Trump Aleksander Eiterjord, "The growing institutionalization of China's Polar Silk Road", The Diplomat, 7th October, 2018.

[21] China's trillion-dollar OBOR project runs into debt jam, published in Times of India 03/09/2018.

[22] Wolf Jr, Charles, Wang Xiao, Warner, Erict, 'China's Foreign Aid' and 'Government Sponsored Investment Activities', www.lowyuistitute.org/issues/china-pacific

[23] Eye on China, government finalises 5 k Cr def plan for Andamans; Times of India dt. 27/01/2019.

[24] Yamaguchi, Hiroichi, East Asian Scenario: A Japanese Perspective, published in Indian Ocean Survey—A journal of Indian Ocean Research Group, Volume 4, No. 142; January –December 2008.

[25] "The geo-Political Interests and Strategies: Chinese Strategy of String of Pearls" conference paper presented by J.A.D. Nisunsalu Kalpani Jayakodi, 13th–14th November 2014, at International Conference, on China in Indian ocean Region, Osmania University, Hyderabad.

[26] Khalid, Mohamad, China in Indian Ocean, 'From sink shios to effective naval presence, published in edited book, china in Indian Ocean Region, R. Sidda Goud and Maneesh Mukherji.

[27] Mokhduni Zubir, Mohd, Nizam Basiron, The Strait of Malacca: The Rise of China's American's Intensions and the Dilemma of the Littoral States, Kuala Lumpur, Maritime Institute of Malaysia, April 2005.

[28] Italy becomes lot G-7 nation to join China's OBOR plan, Times of India.

[29] Xi allays BRI projects debt fears at meet, published in Times of India, dt. April 27th 2019.

[30] China's trillion-dollar OBOR project runs in to debt jam, Times of India, dt. 03/09/2018.

[31] Chinese land grab in Maldives is a cause of concerns, says US, Times of India in a column "Our neighbours New, Worrisome friends.

[32] China seeking to expand military rule, warns US, Times of India, dt. 04/05/2019.

[33] Eye on China, government finalizes Rs. 5K crores def plan for Andaman's, Times of India, dt. 27/01/2019.

[34] India, Indonesia joins hands to counter exparnist China, Times of India, dt. 31/05/2019.

[35] Trump green-lights $ 60 bn answer to China's OBOR, Times of India, dt. 16/10/2018.

[36] China—warry govt. clears plan for 56 ships, 6 subs, Times of India, dt 4/12/2018.

[37] Rao, S.V. Seshagiri, India's Ocean neighbourhood, Narendra Modi Strategy Initiatives, 2nd November 2018, printed at Himalaya Graphics, Bhagyanagar complex, RTC X roads, Hyderabad, India.

CHAPTER IV

China in the Indian Ocean Region: Impinge on India's Security and Sovereignty

China is growing its influence in the Indian Ocean Region day-by-day by adopting several initiatives causing concern to India both in the waters and at the borders. Chinese String of Pearls strategy, BRI, CPEC, CMEC and BCIM-Economic Corridors are aimed at encircling India and positioning China to emerge as a superpower controlling the entire Indian Ocean Region. With its strong military, economic and defence power, China is sending nuclear powered submarines to the Indian Ocean under the guise of securing its Sea Lines of Communications (SLOCs). At any given time, China deploys 6–7 warships in the Indian Ocean Region, which is a cause of concern for New Delhi. China recently reorganized its 2.3 million PLA into Five Theatre Commands, with the Western Theatre command meant to look after the entire Line of Actual Control of the 4057 km border with India. China spends four times more than India on defence to boost its offensive capabilities and establish a better command and control structure. In 2020, the navies of China and Pakistan conducted nine-day exercises in the Arabian Sea to enhance their all-weather strategic partnership. For the first time, submarines were deployed, providing significant exposure to the Chinese navy in the region, which is a serious matter of concern for New Delhi.

The Arabian Sea region is strategically important for India as its major ports including Kandala, Okha, Mumbai, Navi Mumbai, Mormugao, New Mangalore and Kochi are located. To limit and to control China's influence in the Indian Ocean Region, India needs re-look its security landscape, by allocating more funds to the Indian Navy to project power & guard strategic interests from Persian Gulf to Malacca Strait and to deter Pakistan. India needs to build a powerful blue-water navy to protect the daily transit of sea trade worth $ 2 billion and offshore assets and should further strengthen the Andaman & Nicobar Islands Command, its only theater Command, along with the Lakshadweep Archipelago. India should focus on creating a Command specially to control any threat from China at the India-China borders from Eastern Ladakh to Arunachal Pradesh, especially to guard the strategically located Siliguri 'Chicken-Neck' corridor, which is strategically very important. However, India can give a fitting reply to China in the event at the Strait of Malacca as the Andaman & Nicobar Islands are being strengthened by PM Modi in all respects recently.

China's interest in the Indian Ocean Region (IOR) can be traced back to the early 1960s when it began expressing solidarity with some of the beleaguered Afro-Asian states through economic and military aid. Ever since, Beijing has been increasingly deepening its presence in the IOR for a variety of reasons: oil, trade, security, etc. Over thirty per cent of China's seaborne trade worth above US $ 300 billion presently transits across the IOR. Sharing a quarter of the world's population, China faces ever increasing demand for energy. According to a recent OPEC report, while it consumed more than 10.1 million barrels of oil a day—one-ninth of the world's total but the country produced only 4.2 million barrels a day. China used only half as much energy as the United States in 2000. Nine years later, it surpassed the United States as the No. 1 oil importer. China has little choice but to look beyond its borders for its energy needs. About 77 per cent of its oil imports are sourced from West Asia and Africa and these are transported through the Indian Ocean. Thus, China's dependence on the Indian Ocean continues to grow for energy imports from the Gulf, to import resources from Africa and trade with Europe. China has been employing several soft power strategies, and in extreme cases, even force to satisfy its growing hunger for energy to fuel its economic growth.

Sea Lanes of Communications (SLOCs) in the IOR are not only vital for the world's economy, but also for India too. According to K.M. Panikkar "while only to other countries the Indian Ocean is one of the important oceanic areas, to India as it is a vital sea. Her lifelines are concentrated in that area, her freedom is dependent on the freedom of that water surface." India imports about 70 per cent of its oil through the Indian Ocean Region to its various ports. Consequently, it has been enhancing its strategic influence through soft power by becoming a major foreign investor in regional mining, oil, gas, and infrastructure projects. As the ability of China's navy to project power in the Indian Ocean Region grows, India is likely to feel even more vulnerable despite enjoying distinct geographical advantages in the region. China's growing naval presence around the Indian Ocean Region restricts India's freedom to maneuver. Of particular note is what has been termed China's 'string of pearls' strategy, which has significantly expanded China's strategic depth in India's backyard. China to protect its strategic sea lane has a 'string of pearls' strategy of bases and diplomatic ties that include the Gwadar port in Pakistan, naval and electronic intelligence—gathering facilities on the Burmese islands in the Bay of Bengal, port access and modernization of Chittagong in Bangladesh, construction of Sri Lanka's harbor like Hambantota and serious plans for a canal across the Kra Isthmus in Thailand.

With China's maritime presence in the Indian Ocean set to expand along with its economic interests, the question for India is how to cope with this new geo-political reality. India is deeply apprehensive about the Chinese assertive or even aggressive attitude towards its neighbours and India. China has territorial disputes with all nations it shares borders with and eight other nations (Afghanistan, India, Malaysia, Mongolia, Nepal, Philippines, North Korea, Russia, Singapore, South Korea, Japan and Vietnam). Some of these countries however do not belong to the IOR. India being a strong advocate of 'freedom of navigation in the sea' has made known its 'concerns' over China's aggressive postures in the South China Sea.

Given such Chinese assertive policies, India is compelled to carefully devise its strategic responses. In the existing situation, one can't build a cordon against China's maritime presence nor does its growing influence in the Indian Ocean for free navigational rights to ensure energy security. However, many Indian strategists view that the Indian Ocean is India's 'rightful domain' and India has to play a mammoth role in ensuring prospects for peace and cooperation in the IOR. Thus, maritime friction is likely to grow as the Indian Navy tries to expand its footprint in the South China Sea and the Western Pacific even as the Chinese Navy increases its presence in the Indian Ocean.

China recently announced 10 billion Yuan ($ 1.6 bn) fund to take forward its ambitious "Maritime Silk Road Plan" to build and boost maritime connectivity with Southeast Asian and Indian Ocean littoral countries, in support of infrastructure projects under the umbrella of the Silk Road plan. The Maritime Silk Road plan has become a key initiative of Chinese president after a high-profile trip to Southeast Asia in October 2013. Hence, China is keen to set-up free-trade zones to link its coastal areas with countries in Southeast Asia and in the Indian Ocean, attempting to revive the ancient maritime 'Silk Road' that connected China with the region. India, Sri Lanka, Malaysia, Singapore and Gulf countries have been sounded out about the initiative. The new Chinese plan focuses on 'infrastructure constructions' in Pakistan, Sri Lanka, and Bangladesh, where China has already involved in the port projects. This clearly indicates Chinese intent to establish its footprints in the Indian Ocean Region.

While China and India are potential competitors for power and influence in IOR, they also share common interests in maintaining regional stability by combating the growing Islamic fundamentalist menace, exploiting economic opportunities, maintaining access to energy sources and markets and enhancing regional cooperation. Bilateral cooperation on the above challenges can enable the two Asian powers to balance US influence and increase their negotiating positions with the sole superpower. On economic, environmental and cultural issues, they may have far more reasons to build synergies. Improvement in China-India relationship will also depend upon Beijing's assessment of India's evolving political cohesion, economic growth and military potential. China doesn't see India as a serious nuclear threat, but resulting change in the India's stature as a rising power and its improved ties with USA, is a new variable in China's geo-political calculations. 'Freedom of Navigation' is vital for China's and India's economic development as they both depend on the sea for trade and transportation. Thus, China and India's Indian Ocean strategies can mutually promote shared objectives, underpinning the greater cooperation, rather than competition in the IOR.

Chinese Voyages in the Indian Ocean

History reveals that, Chinese envoys sailed into the Indian Ocean from the late 2nd Century BC, reaching Kanchipuram (Tamil Nadu), even up to Ethiopia. During late 4th and early 5th centuries, Chinese pilgrims and monks travelled by sea to India. In 674, the private Chinese explorer Daxi Hong tong was among the first to end his journey at the southern tip of the Arabian Peninsula, after traveling through 36 countries west of the South China Sea. China had never been a maritime power but to consolidate the tributary system, it extended its maritime thrust towards Southeast Asia and the Indian Ocean. Chinese Junk Ships were even described by the Moroccan geographer Al-Idrisi in his geography of 1154, along with the usual goods they traded and carried aboard their vessels.[1] As China became internally weak, it had to suffer many internal wars and it gradually became overly dominated by the outside powers. It did not think of having presence in the Indian Ocean for a long time.

To explore new territories and expand commercial and diplomatic relations with the states of South and Southeast Asia and demonstrate the power of the Ming Empire, China sent its fleets consisting of trading ships, warships and support vessels in 1403 onwards. During the 1414-15 period, a Chinese fleet called at the ports of Champu (now port of Vietnam) Java and Sumatra (Indonesia) reached the Strait of Hormuz and entered the Persian Gulf. Chinese voyage went to Bengal, Coast of Malay, Sri Lanka and the Maldives. This voyage marked the height of Chinese sent another massive voyage which sailed to Indian Ocean and called at the ports of Indonesia, India, Malacca Straits, Sri Lanka and Maldives. Ships from this fleet explored further to the Arabian Coast from Strait of Hormuz to Aden and the East Coast of Africa.

A similar voyage was sent in 1421–22 to explore more of the coast of Africa. In 1424 Emperor Zhu died and was succeeded by Zhu Zhanji, who continued the tradition and sent voyages—the 7th voyages in 1413 which remain in sea for two years when admiral Zheng, the main architect of these voyages, died in 1433. After his death China lost track of the waters of the Indian Ocean. By the time Vasco Da Gama arrived at Calicut on May 20, 1498 is the most important turning points in the history of the Indian Ocean Region. The Chinese had already retreated from the Indian Ocean.

The Indian Ocean had been a centre of vibrant trade and commerce from the time immemorial. It has seen nurturing of great civilizations in the past. China, though touching shores of North Pacific Ocean, has been deeply interested in the Indian Ocean. It has shown its presence in the Indian Ocean in myriad ways for a couple of centuries. During this time, Chinese fleets visited all major ports of India, the African continent, Persian Gulf and the Red Sea. After the death of Emperor Zhu in 1424 and admiral Zheng in 1431, Chinese forays in the Indian Ocean receded and China lost track of the waters of the Indian Ocean. During the colonial period, the Chinese rulers surrendered their powers and responsibilities to the colonial masters. After Second World War, as the cold war set in, China remained busy and confined to itself and its immediate vicinity and hence could not show any kind of effective presence in or around the Indian Ocean littorals.

Economic reforms were introduced in China in December 1978 by Deng Xiaoping. Its thrust in the beginning was decollectivisation of agriculture and the opening of the economy to foreign investment and permission for entrepreneurs to start-up businesses. In the late 1980s and early 1990s, China privatized and contracted out the state-owned industry, lifted price controls, protectionist policies and regulations which led to the remarkable growth of the private sector. China's economy became the largest economy, after the United States and is projected to become the world's largest economy by 2025.

The rapid industrialization has forced China to ensure uninterrupted supplies of raw materials, especially oil which comes from the littoral of the Indian Ocean Region. Twenty-eight littoral states and Six Island Republics of the Indian Ocean Region offer converted markets for Chinese products. In order to protect its interests, China is steadily spreading its presence in the Indian Ocean Region on two fronts—economic and strategic. It has sought and successfully established economic-diplomatic relationship with the countries of the Indian Ocean Region, especially from Africa. China has set up its network of military and commercial facilities and relationships called as String of Pearls along its sea lanes of communications extending from the Chinese mainland to Port Sudan. The sea lines run through several major maritime choke—points in the Indian Ocean Region such as Babal-Mandep, the Strait of Malacca, the Strait of Hormuz and the Lombak Strait. This move is indicative of China's growing geopolitical influence: increasing access to ports and airfields, expanding and modernizing military forces and fostering stronger diplomatic relationships with the littorals of Indian Ocean. India has reasons to worry and has to counterpose as the presence of China is detrimental to its economic and strategic interests. This chapter is an attempt to elaborate on the issue of increasing Chinese presence in the Indian Ocean Region and the Indian response.

With the booming economy, China is emerging as the key player in the Indian Ocean Region and possibly as a dominant superpower in the Asia-Pacific. The rise of strong, aggressive, assertive China has changed the geopolitics in the region as well as in the international order. Today, China has become the most important economic partner with Asian countries and their footprints are growing by leaps and bounds, dramatically transforming international relations. Indian Ocean or to say Indo-Pacific has become the centrefield for power play or power balance between rising powers and the US. In turn, the evolving geopolitics of the Indian Ocean Region with Chinese power projection has posed major challenges to the statusquo in the region with consequences for its neighbours and other powers, such as the United States of America. This heightens endeavors of both regional and external powers like the US, Japan and India to reposition themselves to protect their national interests are linked with the sea lanes of communication of this region. Significantly, the rise of China has led India with its own capabilities and power projection to meet the challenges in the strategic area.

In the light of the above facts, this chapter seeks to assess how the rise of China has impacted the geopolitics of the Indian Ocean Region and the challenges posed to India's security. In this chapter, an attempt has been made firstly to outline the significance of the maritime domain which represents a confluence of interests ranging from economic to strategic, followed by the historic relevance of the Indian Ocean. In this context, an attempt is made to analyze the present strategic setting of the Indian Ocean and the challenges posed by China's rise in the region. Vis-a-vis PM Modi's initiatives to counter China in the Indian Ocean Region.

China is geopolitically so located that on the east of it is the vast Pacific Ocean. Historically, its lands on the Pacific littoral were barren, sparsely populated, and without any commercial activity. China considered the South China Sea and countries of Southeast Asia as its natural sphere of influence and the area was devoid of any noticeable trade and commerce. On the other hand, the Indian Ocean had been a centre of vibrant trade and commerce from time immemorial. Some of the world's great civilizations—The Babylonia, The Egyptian and the Indus have developed on its coasts. Apart from the commercial activity, the migrations of the people generating a cultural amalgam have been a significant trait of the lands and peoples of the Indian Ocean Region.

Maritime Domain: Confluence of Interests

In the recent years, the maritime domain has grown in its relevance as a field of study within international relations and in the political economy. Several factors have contributed towards the increasing relevance of the study of the maritime sphere and have its impacts on the power of nations, such as: (i) the oceans have been used for centuries as carries of trade and enabled economic engagement between regions (ii) cultural exchanges occurred simultaneously (iii) the oceans formed the roadways for expedition and later paved way for the colonial powers to establish and consolidate their supremacy. Apart from these aspects, the Oceans also became the key pathways for energy transportation. Therefore, the maritime domain, when considered in its entirety, depicts a confluence of interests, wherein economic interests are intermingled with security concerns, ranging from naval interests to energy security.

The multiple roles played by the maritime sphere are abundant from the theoretical standpoint, the significance of the waterways was communicated in the work of Alfred Thayer Mahan's—the influence of sea power upon History. The conceptualization of the opportunities of the maritime domain from the prison of power Mahan formed a turning point in how nations perceived the oceans. Mahan provided a framework for nations to not only comprehend the power of the sea's but to use this potential for outward expansion.

The supremacy of naval power in safeguarding economic and strategic interests of nations was also articulated before Mahan as well. The US Secretary of State William Seward understood the power held by the maritime sphere. He sought to expand the US interests by purchasing Islands and to form bases. In this regard, Seward tried to impose the US commercial interests in Asia by purchasing Alaska in 1867. In a similar way, Seward attempted to purchase Islands in the Caribbean wherein naval bases were to be built.[2] Therefore Seward tried to use the potential of the maritime domain in expanding the US influence. When the two cases of Mahan and Seward are considered, it becomes apparent how the utility of sea for commercial purposes was deemed as significant. Moreover, both scholars stressed on exploiting commercial interests and expanding that into strategic interests through sea power.

It must be noted that Mahan's work has been interpreted mostly in context to naval strategies and propagating the need for stronger naval forces to protect maritime interests. However, for a large part, he presents the need for a strong navy by first conceiving the sea as a highway or a wide-common. He then builds the case for the expansion of naval capabilities by calling for far-sightedness as it is essential for military preparedness.[3] Therefore, the significance of protecting interests at sea is enumerated through various elements of sea power by first indicating the diversity of interests that the maritime domain inherently possesses. Though, the concept of sea power has been interpreted narrowly with specific attention to the navy and its building or capabilities the maritime domain connotes wider access to the sea and its resources for economic and strategic interests.[4] Despite the growth in the ambit the maritime power of relevance of Mahan's work, even today stems from the attention he paid to the significance of sea power during peace time. This aspect of Mahan's work aptly depicts the diverse role the navy plays and the myriad of interests a nation can seek to obtain from the maritime domain has therefore, made it significant even in the contemporary situation wherein nations are devoting attention to protecting economic and strategic interests by actively using the potential of the oceans.

Maritime Power in Indian Ocean Region: Historical Perspective

As outlined, the maritime landscape encompasses trade, commerce, energy and security, while nations develop naval capabilities to meet economic and strategic interests. It provides useful platform for diplomatic signaling and offers a gamut of opportunities for nations to integrate military and non-military interests. Therefore, the maritime landscape which represents a plethora of interests becomes crucial in the present scenario wherein nation-states rely on the maritime sphere to expand their influence and grow.

Reflections of history consistently showcase the significance of maritime trade routes and the overreaching strategic interests they serve. The success of the colonial powers such as British, Dutch and Portuguese were credited to the investments these powers made to consolidate their maritime power.

Tracing back to Minoans, Phoenicians, Greeks and Romans exhibited a strong proclivity for maritime power which later provided a precursor to the European maritime trade patterns.[5] In the context of the growth of the powers of the colonial nations the maritime routes through the Indian Ocean become crucial.

The Indian Ocean is the third largest water body in the world. The Indian Ocean Region forms one of the most important sea lanes for trade and commerce. Geographically, to the west of the Indian Ocean lies Africa, stretching to the Cape of Agulhas. To the north, the Indian Ocean is bordered by the Indian Subcontinent and Iran. Here, it stretches from the Suez Canal to the Malay Peninsula and Singapore Straits going up to Australia, encapsulating the most significant sea lanes of communications in the world, while Tasmania lies to the east of the Indian Ocean and it stretches to the latitude 60 degree south as per the Antarctic Treaty of 1959.[6] Thus, the Indian Ocean covers crucial continents and hence becomes a significant trade route.

Many have argued that a historical analysis of the trading patterns of the Indian Ocean Region indicates that over a period of time, the Indian Ocean became integrally tied to the Mediterranean region. This historic linkage between the two water bodies provided an insight into the presence of the colonial powers and their eventual domination of Asian region. The Indian Ocean hence became a link in connecting the West to the East. Significantly, it has been noted that the Portuguese established a stronghold in the trade route through the Indian Ocean that in turn led to monopoly. However, there was constant conflict between the Portuguese and the Dutch, French and British. Interestingly, the withdrawal of the Portuguese from the Indian Ocean not only led extra-regional colonial powers to try and dominate the strategic ocean, but revived the maritime interests of the indigenous littoral states within the Indian Ocean Region. This was seen in how Oman emerged as a regional naval power and boasted of deep-sea penetration capability.[7] Also, the Mughals emerged as a dominant force in the Bay of Bengal and also developed a naval base at Jangir and Cambay.[8] Further, the Marathas have also been credited with maintaining strong naval forces. However, these were limited to littoral waters lacking capability to enter the deep sea.[9]

The littoral states of the Indian Ocean Region were reinvigorating their maritime capabilities. They would remain outflanked by the maritime powers of the colonial powers especially, the British who attended maritime pre-eminence after defeating the Spanish Armada in 1588.[10] This pre-eminence, to a large extent, has been attributed to the control the British

Royal Navy exerted on the Indian Ocean. The strategic significance of the Indian Ocean which connects the west to the east, led to European rivalry to claim control of these waters. Therefore, with the growth of the British Empire the Indian Ocean was described as a 'British Lake' with Britain being called the 'Colossus' of the world.[11] However, with growing unrest as colonies the maritime supremacy that the British had created that had lasted for a century began to wane.

The Indian Ocean has been a significant theatre for extra-regional powers, particularly, with the waning influence of the British following the world Wars saw rising competition between the US and the Soviet Union. These developments at the international level were witnessed in the Indian Ocean. For instance, the purchase of Diego Garcia by the USA from the British was seen as a significant move by the US to establish a naval base in the center of the strategic Indian Ocean. Moreover, the presence of the extra-regional powers in the Indian Ocean was opposed by the littorals given the colonial history and the past supremacy of the British in these waters. Through the course of the negotiations for installing a naval base in Diego Garcia, Indian Government opposed the idea on the grounds that it produced big-power competition in the Indian Ocean area.[12]

In a conversation between Indian External Affairs Minister (Dinesh Singh) and British Foreign Secretary Stewart, stated that, the Indian Government was very unhappy with the increasing presence of the extra-regional powers in the Indian Ocean Region and outlined how the Chinese showed interest in the Indian Ocean, while the Russians were seeking refueling facilities and the Americans seeking to establish a naval base in Diego Gracia made the Indian Ocean Region central to unwanted rivalries of the big powers. The Soviet Union in light of the cold war politics also, began to view the Indian Ocean Region as an important theatre to increase their presence. The naval presence of the Soviets can be traced to 1968 with a goodwill visit by four ships from Vladivostok to Kenya, India, Sri Lanka, Somalia, Pakistan and South Yemen.[13] In this connection, Afro-Asian nations of the Indian Ocean Region led by India began their tryst with destiny opposing the growing presence of big-power rivalries in the Indian Ocean.[14]

India and Pakistan war of 1971 became a significant instance of the direct involvement of the big powers—the US and the Soviet Union in the Indian Ocean. The entry of 'S' of the US aircraft carrier enterprises into the Indian Ocean coupled with the presence of the big powers in the strategic waters. However, after the disintegration of the Soviet Union, the US emerged as a dominant power in the Indian Ocean. It has a considerable presence in the

Western region of the Indian Ocean, specifically in the Persian Gulf and Arabian Sea which is directly linked to the dependence of oil and gas coming from the regions. While the naval base in Diego Gracia depicts its presence in the central Indian Ocean Region, the US continues to maintain its presence in the Eastern Indian Ocean through its allies, such as Singapore and Australia.[15] Therefore, through these countries, the Indian Ocean has become a central trading route, significant to energy politics and its strategic location made it a playfield for extra-regional powers.

Indian Ocean Strategic Approach

In the contemporary context, the Indian Ocean has become highly significant with the rise of Asia. The industrialization of Asia is traced to the 1920s with the growth of the Japanese economy followed by the growing economies of South Korea and Taiwan.[16] However, the present setting, the growth of China and the rising economy of India have captured the attention of the international community. The growth of these Asian nations has been attributed to multiple factors such as ship building, high-level service sector, manufacturing of high-density microelectronics, etc.

Nations with growing economies are voracious consumers of energy and raw materials. The first wave of industrialization in Europe led to competition among the colonial powers to get raw materials and energy. Currently, the burgeoning economies of Asia have led to similar patterns with China and India's increasing appetite for energy and materials. As outlined earlier, the use of sea-ways to meet the demand of a growing economy becomes inevitable. The confluence of interests in terms of the economic benefits, trade routes and strategic advantage possessed by the maritime domain become intrinsically used by growing economics. Contextualizing this aspect to the Asian landscape, the significance of the Indian Ocean becomes manifold.

The Indian Ocean has been described as more than a geographic feature stating that, it is an idea that combines its vast geographic extent with the growing energy politics of rising powers in the Asian region to depict a multilayered, multipolar world.[17] The strategic setting of the Indian Ocean in the current context can be understood by first assessing the use of ocean waters for trade and transport, the energy politics played out and how these factors are intrinsically linked to the rise of China and India. Also to be noted is how the economic growth of the Asian nations has intensified the military modernization drives specifically in the context of the maritime domain. These factors, in turn, have made the Indian Ocean central to the power politics unfolding in the 21st century as emphasized by Kaplan.

In a global context, the maritime traffic has risen by 300 percent since 1992 showcasing the growing dependence of nation-states on the maritime domain. In such a scenario, the rise of Asian nations has catapulted the Indian Ocean Region as an important conduit of trade, commerce and also a platform to project power. The Indian Ocean is said to carry 50 percent of the world's container traffic while the ports of the Indian Ocean Region handle about 35 percent of global trade. Further, about 66 percent of the world oil seaborne trade traversed to have 55 percent of known oil reserves and 40 percent gas reserves.[18] The strategic significance of the Indian Ocean can be further assessed by considering the seven choke-points, such as the Mozambique Channel, The Babel Mandeb, The Suez Canal, The Strait of Malacca, The Strait of Hormuz, the Strait of Sunda and The Strait of Lombok. Significantly, the Strait of Hormuz and the Strait of Malacca have been described as the world's most important strategic choke points based on the volume of oil transit.[19]

The strategic significance of the Indian Ocean in terms of the energy sea routes became a tangible reality with the oil crisis of the 1970s. With the Organization of Petroleum Exporting Countries (OPEC) decision to increase the price of oil deeply impacted the West and the US which depended on the hydrocarbons of the Persian Gulf. Significantly, in the current situation, the passage of energy trade through the Strait of Hormuz and Strait of Malacca are dubbed as 'dilemma' for China and India. The dilemma was outlined by former Chinese President Hu Jintao in 2003 stressing on the need to find an alternative to overcome China's dependence on the Strait of Malacca wherein nearly 80 percent of oil of its imports through these straits.[20]

Similarly, India is also presented with the 'Hormuz Dilemma' wherein a large number of crucial imports of India pass through the Hormuz Strait which is located close to Pakistan's Makran Coast.[21] Therefore, the growing economies of Asia depend significantly on the trade routes of the Indian Ocean which in turn has made the significant choke-points into strategic vulnerabilities. Apart from the strategic significance of the energy routes and high-level marine traffic trading through the Indian Ocean. The presence of extra-regional powers especially, the US lends another dimension to the strategic setting. A case in point of this complex interaction of strategic interests of China, the US and India was recently when Iran threatened to block the Strait of Hormuz. With the increasing US pressure on Iran to shut down the latter's nuclear programme, Iran threatened to block the Strategic choke-point of Hormuz. The dependence of China and India who depends on the Straits for their economic and energy imports Iran's threat could prove fatal. Although China was friendly towards Iran in the light of the sanctions imposed by the US and the West, the threat of such a blockade could result in China isolating Iran further. India needed careful diplomatic treading in the light of the threat of the blockade. Therefore, these incidents depict how the delicate the confluence of interests in the Indian Ocean is and the presence of extra-regional powers coupled with the growing powers of the Asian nation states, the strategic approach of the Indian Ocean is bond to become more complex.

Chinese Expansion in the Indian Ocean after the end of the Cold War

China's expansion towards the Indian Ocean had two aspects—economic and military. In recent years China has steadily spread its wings in the Indian Ocean Region with its rapidly growing well well-equipped navy with all logistic support. China has established several access points through a series of arrangements for refueling, replacement, crew rest and low-level maintenance facilities. By doing so, China is mainly trying to ensure the protection of its sea lanes for critical energy needs. To assume a role beyond its natural geographic and historical maritime boundaries—China began to set up a series of bases to project its power. Its secured land borders helped to build a strong navy and increasingly concentrate on the South China Sea and as well as the Indian Ocean where supplies of oil, natural gas, and other commodities were critical to China's economic growth. China has developed naval and ports in Bangladesh, Maldives, Pakistan, Sri Lanka, Myanmar and in other countries of the Indian Ocean littorals.[22]

China has made series of attempts to wean Bangladesh and has supplied it with arms and other defence equipments. Bangladesh Armed Forces today are pre-dominantly equipped with Chinese military hardware. China signed Defence Cooperation Agreement with Bangladesh in December 2002—the first of such agreement ever signed by Bangladesh in its history. China sold missile-guided frigates in 1988 and later torpedo boats to enhance the striking capabilities of Bangladesh Navy. China built a port in Chittagong by funding the transportation of its coastline at an estimated cost of $8.7 billion.

China is the most important supplier of military aid and maintains extensive strategic and military cooperation with Myanmar. Since 1989 China has supplied Myanmar with jet fighters, armored vehicles and naval vessels and has trained its army, air force, and naval personnel. China has access to Burma's ports and naval installation providing it with strategic influence in the Bay of Bengal. China has developed a deep-water port of Kyankpyu (Western Myanmar) in the Bay of Bengal. It has also built an 85-meter jetty, naval facilities and major reconnaissance and electrical intelligence systems on the great Coco Island, located 40 km off the northern tip of the Andaman Islands, giving China capabilities to monitor India's military activities, including missile tests at Wheeler Island of the Odisha coast on the Bay of Bengal.[23] China has assisted in the construction of a naval base in Sittwe (Akyab), a strategically important seaport of Myanmar just 542 km flight distance away from the port of Kolkata. China has funded the construction of the China-Burma road to the ports of Yangon and Sittwe, providing the shortest route to the Indian Ocean from Southern China.[24]

Sri Lanka's geographical location in the Indian Ocean has promoted China to develop a strategic relationship with Colombo. China intends to use the partnership with Sri Lanka to enhance its influence over strategic sea lanes from Europe to East Asia and oil tanker routes from the Middle East to the Malacca Straits. China has entered into oil exploration business in Sri Lanka and has built bunker facilities creating an oil tank farm at Hambantota, Chinese insist is a purely commercial move.[25] China's help is likely to boost Sri Lanka's annual cargo to about 23 million from just 6 million. Hambantota also had developed factories producing cement and fertilizers for exporting. This makes Sri Lanka welcome Chinese investments. This promoted Sri Lanka to allocate a block in the Mannar Basin to China for petroleum exploration. This provides presence to China just a few kilometers from India's Southern tip. These militaries are aimed to augment its power projection in the Indian Ocean.

In Pakistan's western province of Balochistan, Gwadar is located about 533 km from Karachi and 120 km from the Iranian border and 380km from northeast of the nearest point on Oman across the Arabian Sea. Gwadar port is located at the mouth of the Persian Gulf, about 600 km outside the Strait of Hormuz, near the key shipping routes in and out of the Persian Gulf. China is developing the port as its military-commercial base.[26] The Gwadar port offers several key benefits for both China and Pakistan. The Gwadar port is seen as having the potential of edging against a possible Indian blockage of the port of Karachi, which currently handles about 90 percent of Pakistan's sea-borne trade. For the Chinese, who have funded much of the $1.2 billion construction, the Gwadar port represents an important strategic foothold. China has set up electronic eavesdropping posts at Gwadar to monitor ship traffic through the Strait of Hormuz.

Chinese companies have also constructed a railway link between Khartoum, the capital of Sudan and port Sudan-country's major port on the Red Sea. It has invested over $10billion in infrastructure projects in the country to take

advantage of its substantial oil reserves. China has also financed to building a US $10 billion port in Bagamoyo, Tanzania which is expected to handle about
20 million shipping containers annually.[27]

Marao is one of the largest of the 1192 coral islands grouped into atolls that comprise Maldives and lies 40 km south of Male, the capital. In May 2011, Wu Bangguo, Chairman of the standing committee of the National People's Congress visited Maldives and he underscored the increasing importance of the Maldives to China's regional strategic calculations. Though no evidence suggests a Chinese military presence of any kind in Marao but the Atoll is regarded as a potential Chinese military base of operation.[28] Maldivian government had cancelled a $ 511 million contract to expand Male airport which signed with India's GMR infrastructure. This contract has now been again given to a Chinese firm and the agreement was signed on September 15, 2014, as the Chinese President Xi Jinping toured Maldives. It should be a great concern for India.

Chinese Naval Outreach in Indian Ocean

Chinese naval presence though not substantial, threatening has increased into the Indian Ocean Region in recent times. It is understood that China aims at building a strong navy which is able to project power across the greater Indo-Pacific. China is heavily focusing on its navy and building an increasingly sophisticated fleet. With its 26 shipyards, it has emerged as the world's fourth largest shipbuilder and its naval expansion is aimed at assured access and control over its adjacent ocean's, especially the Indian Ocean. This has given roots to China's naval diplomacy from the Suez down the east coast of Africa. China's naval build-up is not only because of its phenomenal economic growth and military power, but also because of its ambition and determinate drive towards achieving global power status.[29] The Chinese, however, always argue that, their initiatives towards the Indian Ocean are guided by both strategic and economic compulsions and capabilities, as about 85 percent of its sea borne trade passes through the Indian Ocean.

Rise of China as a sea power is one of the biggest developments after the end of cold war. Dominance in South China Sea and the East Sea makes China a great regional power, but its presence in the Indian Ocean makes it a great naval power. Being a state from outside the region, it is difficult for China to deploy its naval forces permanently in the Indian Ocean. To meet this difficulty, it has made Pakistan, Myanmar, Sri Lanka, the Maldives and other littoral countries of Indian Ocean Region and islands in the region as its allies. By increasing its presence in the Indian Ocean, China can also control its supplies and threaten to disrupt supplies; it needs to be, to its economic rivals such as India, Japan, South Korea and Taiwan, etc. To expand its footprints in the region through naval presence, China has pumped massive economic aid and assistance to many littoral states and small island nations of the Indian Ocean.

Time and again, Chinese nuclear submarines have made frequent forays into the Indian Ocean. By doing so, Chinese submarines are probably trying to determine the Indian navy's ability to detect under sea objects. United States Naval Institute has warned that these operations are going to pose sub-surface (undersea) challenges to India in future. These submarines are believed to be the South Sea Fleet based at Sanya on Hainan Island, off China's Southern Coast. These forays can be seen in the connection of the proposal made by President Xi Jinping during his visit to Southeast Asia in 2013, so as to create a Maritime Silk Route (MSR) to foster cooperation and goodwill between China and the ASEAN countries.[30] It was further extended to the entire Indo-Pacific region as China's outreach subsequently expanded to Sri Lanka, India and even to Africa. It was known to all, that the MSR is aimed to involve the construction of ports, logistical stations, to create infrastructural and storage facilities and free-trade zones. The rationale behind it is the leveraging of Chinese soft power and its legitimate interests in the Indian Ocean Region.

An important aspect of the growing Chinese presence in the Indian Ocean stems from the anti-piracy exercises that the PLAN has been involved in, especially in the Gulf of Aden. This has been interpreted as a possible precursor to future PLAN presence in the Indian Ocean Region. The notion behind such an analysis stems from the strategic stakes that China has in the Indian Ocean coupled with the need for power projection by a rising power. In this context, the naval drill conducted by PLAN in the Strait of Lombok in 2014, near Indonesia indicates that China is paying close attention and seeking to expand operations in the East Indian Ocean also.[31] The drill was seen as significant because of the use of the largest amphibious landing ship, the Changbaishan accompanied by two destroyers.[32] The use of such a squadron and the location of the exercise depicted the increasing priority the Chinese were giving to the Indian Ocean. Recently Chinese seven warships deployed in the Indian Ocean in the waters of Sri Lanka along with an amphibious ship without any requirements is a great concern to India. More so, China has deployed sophisticated and new weapons during its current military exercise in the Tibetan region, recently bordering India to send out signals to other countries including India (7/1/2020, Times of India report).

China spends Four Times more than India on Defence

Chinese military expenditure is almost four times that of India. The US of course, is the world's largest spender on defence with a military expenditure almost equal to the next eight countries combined. The latest data released by global think-tank Stockholm International Peace Research Institute (SIPRI) shows that the total world military expenditure will rise by 2.6 percent to $ 2.1 trillion in 2021. The biggest five spenders in the world were the USA 801 billion USD, China 293 billion USD, Saudi Arabia 55 billion USD, India 76.6 billion USD and France 56.6 billion USD, which together accounted for about 60 percent of the global military spending.

China continues to rapidly modernize its war-fighting from nuclear-capable missiles and submarines to cyber warfare and ante-satellite weapons, even as it looks to set up military bases around the world to project hard power as well as to guard its multi-billion-dollar One Belt One Road (OBOR) infrastructure projects. After setting up its first overseas military base at Djibouti on the Horn of Africa in 2017, apart from its submarines regularly using Karachi. China's target locations for military basing could include West Asia, South East Asia, and the Western Pacific region. China's expanding military capabilities are as of now, mainly geared towards preventing any US military intervention in the Taiwan Strait, South and East China Seas as well as protecting its energy supply routes in the Indian Ocean Region. India, however, has no option but to keep a close watch on China's strategic moves in the Indian Ocean Region and along the 4057 km long line of 'actual control', stretching from Eastern Ladakh to Arunachal Pradesh.

China in early 2016 set up '5' theatre commands to boost offensive capabilities and to establish better command control structures. The Western Theatre Command (WTC) is responsible for conflict with India and managing terrorism in Western China. The WTC handles the entire 4,057 km line of Actual control, from Eastern Ladakh to Arunachal Pradesh. The Western Theatre Command includes '2' "group armies" (each with 6 combined-arms brigades & 6 combat support brigades), 3 air force bases, 1 rocket force base & a whole host of other forces. China has also built 14 airbases, an extensive rail, network & over 58,000 km of roads in Tibet. So the People's Liberation Army (PLA) can swiftly induct & sustain 30-32 divisions (each with over 12,000 troops) along the Line of Actual Control. Whereas India with no theatre command has '4' Army & 3 IAF commands for northern borders with China.

Taking note of the 73-day troop face-off between India and China at Doklam in 2017, Chinese leaders are adroit at employing tactics short of armed conflicts to pursue China's country strategic objectives in dominating the Indo-Pacific region. These tactics are particularly evident in China's pursuit of its territorial and Maritime claims in the South China Sea and East China Sea as well as along its borders with India and Bhutan. (Times of India report dt. 4-5-2019 and 30-4-2019).

Implications and Challenges to India

The real questions in the world today is that the changing geopolitics and rise of China mean security problems for the region and in particular for India's security given the Chinese "String of Pearls Strategy" and Chinese Belt and Road Initiative (BRI), apart from other corridors. The rise of China impacts the region directly and also shapes the geopolitics of global. The rapid growth of Beijing has played a very important part in reshuffling the relationship between the regional powers and major actors, noticeably, some of the countries have shown an inclination to accommodate China by recognizing its significance, its economic power, its military strength, while others like India have enhanced multilateral partnership with other powers like Japan and Australia in the Indian Ocean Region to protect its interests. The US dominant power has rebalanced its strategy to the Indo-Pacific from its current focus on the Middle East. In fact, the China's inexorable rise has forced countries such as Vietnam, Japan and Australia too to look beyond their traditional partner like the US. Indian strategic partnership with Vietnam, Japan and Australia emphasized the potential of greater cooperation in the Indian Ocean Region that can mutually advance shared objectives and interests.

As Indian strategic and security interests go behind the Malacca Strait with New Delhi's dependent on access to vital offshore natural resources and economic prospects in Indo-Pacific markets, it becomes inevitable for India to adapt to the changing geo-political. Today India's economic and political interests are more widely dispersed beyond its perimeter. India is focusing on strengthening its ties with Japan and Australia, which are considered as natural and indispensable partners in the Indo-Pacific. Through, these partnerships New Delhi wants to show that it has legitimate interests and strategic presence beyond the South China Sea.

Rising maritime interests for which building substantive naval capabilities has created new challenges for India which have traditionally followed a principle of 'non-alignment' and 'strategic autonomy' in its international relations. India like other powers in the region was compelled to act tactically to cope with the Chinese ability to project power in the Indian Ocean

Region. Indian policymakers began to formulate a new maritime strategy which was aimed to secure its interest in the South China Sea and ASEAN where it becomes essential for India to protect freedom of navigation in high seas and sea lanes of communication. As the economic growth and prosperity of India are tied to the resources and market outside its territorial waters it becomes essential for India to act swiftly at the same time tactically to counter any threat that emerges from the assertive and aggressive Beijing in the seas. The Chinese expanding territorial claims and development of anti-access and anti-denial strategies are cases in point.

However, the major challenges that India faces in the maritime domain in the Indian Ocean are to maintain its strategic autonomy and at the same time please the expectations of the other littoral who see India as a net security provider in the region. Even though India assists littorals like Vietnam in building their capacities, it doesn't really want to take a clear stand on many of the issues in the Indian Ocean Region in relation to China. For example, though it is concerned at the developments in South China Sea it doesn't consider it as its own turf. This predicament in fact shown in the habitation of India in taking responsibility and being a proactive player in the region. As a desiring global power, India needs to allow more courage and take responsibility in standing by the smaller littorals that are inclined to India.

Another major challenge that India and other powers like Japan and Australia face is their commitment to stand by each other during the time of crisis in the future. While they have worked out a bilateral partnership aimed at protecting their mutual maritime interest in the Indian Ocean Region, but the question is whether they can work to form a great power concert, since there is a perception that the USA can't be expected and trusted in standing by their side in any eventuality against China the above concern remains significant.

Thus, government of India should deepen its engagements—defence and economic with the littorals in Indo-Pacific and small islands of the Indian Ocean and utilize its advantage as here lies India's strategic and security interests and the only way to deal with the emerging geopolitical implications.

China's Trade and Commerce with Indian Ocean Region

Apart from naval presence, China has substantially expanded its trade with the countries of the Indian Ocean Region. It is estimated that trade between China and African countries reached US $ 166.3 billion in 2011, an increase of 31 percent compared to 2010. China's top African trading partners in 2021 are, South Africa, Nigeria, Angola, Egypt and the Democratic Republic of Congo (a central African country) countries trade values of exports and Imports are, $ 54 bn, $ 26 billion, $ 23 billion, $ 19 billion and $ 14 billion respectively. Nigeria, South Africa, Egypt, Ghana, Kenya were the African countries that are imported the most goods from China in 2021. Combined their imports made up and half of all imports of Chinese goods to Africa in 2021. Exports from China to Africa were US $ 73.1 billion and imports from Africa were 93.2 billion. Similarly, China invested in 2021 more than US $ 50 billion in Africa, by which more than 2000 companies are operating and providing huge job opportunities to the local people.

Africa and China relations began centuries ago and continue in the present day. Several bilateral trade agreements have been signed between China and 40 countries on the continent. Nowadays China seeks resources for its growing consumption and African countries seek funds to develop their infrastructure. Large-scale structural projects often accompanied by soft loans are proposed to African countries, which are rich in natural resources. China commonly funds the construction of infrastructure such as roads, railroads, dams, ports, airports. While the relations are conducted through diplomacy and trade, military support via provision of arms and other equipment. In 2018 China export to Africa to the extent of US $ 104.91 billion, an up of 10.8 percent and China's import from Africa were US $ 99.28 billion an up of 30.8 percent. The growth rate of China's trade with Africa was highest in the world by 15 percent points. In 2019 up to October total export and import value with Africa was $ 101.86 billion USD, an up of 2.9 percent year-on-year basis. Trade between China and African countries is growing as per the General Administration Customs of China recently noted that, bilateral trade between two amounted to $ 254.3 billion in 2021.

China's trade with Mozambique was almost a billion dollars in 2011, which was a 37 percent increase on 2010. Mozambique was China's 23rd most important trading partner. In 2018 the trade value between China and Mozambique has increased to 2.515 US billion dollars, an increase of over 35 percent on 2017. This makes Mozambique to emerge into fourth largest trading partner. As per the Chinese customer services exports from Mozambique to China grow by 23 percent to 651 million US dollar, while imports increased to 40 percent to 1.866 billion USD. In September 2022, China exported $ 339 million and imported $ 130 million from Mozambique, resulting a positive trade balance of $ 209 million.

Trade between China and Tanzania reached over US $ 205 billion at the end of 2012, making China as Tanzania's single biggest trading partner, accounting for 15 percent of its trade. The bilateral trade between China and

Tanzania has increased to 3.88 billion USD in 2016. China is also Tanzania's 2nd largest source for Foreign Direct Investment Centre, while more and more Tanzanian's are entering into partnerships with Chinese companies. In September 2022, China exported $ 727 million and imported 107 million from Tanzania, resulting in a positive trade balance of 619 million between 2021–22. The export of China has increased by 77 million which imports $ 10.2 million. China has invested 3.976 billion US dollar in Tanzania. The total investment in Tanzania has exceeded $ 7 billion USD, which makes the Asian giant, the largest foreign investor in the country.

China is the second largest trade partner of Kenya with bilateral trade amounting to 2.8 billion USD in 2013, an up from 186.37 million in 2002. China's imports from Kenya mainly black tea, coffee and leather. China was Kenya's largest trading partner in 2017. In September 2022, China exported $ 786 million and imported $ 15.6 million from Kenya, resulting a positive trade balance of $770 million.

China had good trading relations with Somalia but have suffered due to continuous violence in that country. The total trade value in 2002 was 3039 million USD. Somalia exported 1.56 million USD of goods to China and imported 1.83 million USD. Seven Chinese development projects were launched in Somalia, these initiatives include 1.6 million USD worth of Economic assistance. In 2022, China exported $ 102 million and imported $ 660 K from Somalia, resulting in a positive trade balance of $ 101 million.

The trade volume between China and Djibouti reached 197 million USD in 2009, an increase of 55 percent over the same period of 2008. China exported $ 294 million and imported $ 14.6 million from Djibouti, resulting in a positive balance of $ 280 million. Beijing has funded to Djibouti for various projects such as development finance to Djibouti to the amount of 16.6 million USD, 8.2 million USD funded to construction of hospital in Asta, 2.4 million USD granted for construction of New Head Quarter for Djibouti Foreign Minister, 1.75 million USD grant given to food aid during a drought in Djibouti in 2005. In 2016 construction began on a Chinese naval outpost on Djibouti with an estimated cost of 600 million USD. The 90-acre plot would likely house only 300 Chinese troops and would require the Chinese government to pay the Djiboutian government 20 million USD per annum for ten years with an option for an additional period of ten years.

The trade value between China and Eritrea came to 6.029 million USD in 2002, of which the export from China was 6.025 million USD. Eritrea has borrowed from China 3 million USD in 1994 to buy Chinese agriculture machinery. In 2002 China constructed a 200-bed hospital in Eritrea capital city of Asmara. The IMF and world economic outlook forecasted total debt of Eritrea to China 52.518 ERN billion in December 2019. Apart from this, China cancelled Eritrea's debt by granting Eritrea a grant for the same amount of 3 million USD. In 2006, China granted Eritrea a loan of 23 million USD to improve communication infrastructure. China-Eritrea relationship was much beyond the trade and investment. China supported the Eritrea independent movement through the Eritrean Liberation Front beginning in 1967. Today Eritrean President Isaias Afwerki received military training in China. In 2022, China exported $ 8.33 million and imported $ 68.6 million from Eritrea, resulting in a negative balance of $ 60.2 million

China is Sudan's largest trading partner mainly due to its oil imports. The relation between two countries refer to the bilateral between PRC and Sudan, as biggest trade partner importing oil from Sudan, while China exporting low-cost items as well as armaments to Sudan. In September 2022, Chinese exports value $ 198 million to Sudan and imparted $ 61.6 million, resulting in a positive trade balance of $ 136 million.

China bilateral trade with Egypt reached from 4 billion in USD in 2007 to 7 billion USD in 2011. Egypt was the fifth largest trading partner of China in Africa. The trade volume between two countries reached to 13.8 billion USD in 2018. Trade exchange between Egypt and China increased by 27.8 percent during 2018, recording 13.8 billion USD, according to economic report of Egyptian-Chinese trade economic relations. Egyptian exports exceeded 1.8 billion USD with an increase of 37.8 percent on year-on-year basis. More than 7 billion USD investment worth 134 companies of Chinese are operating in Egypt in various fields and industrial sector. Finally, China-Egypt bilateral trade volume recorded 5.43 billion USD during January–May 2019, an increase of 5.2 percent on year-on-year basis. China's exports to Egypt hit 4.87 billion of 2019 in the same period, while Chinese imports from Egypt reached 0.56 billion during the 2019. China has exported $ 1.28 Billion in 2022 to Egypt and imported $ 45.1 million, resulting in a positive balance of trade an amount of $ 1.23 Billion.

China is aware that its future depends on the capacity of the Gulf Co-operation Council (GCC) countries to provide a steady flow of oil for the coming decades. Among the countries of Arabian Peninsula, China considers Jordan as its gateway to Middle East and in 2013 organized its 10th annual China Fair the "Largest China Fair" in the Near East. The exhibition featured over a thousand Chinese suppliers displaying 12,000 made-in-China products for customers from across the Middle East. In June 2014, China organized, China-Arab States Corporation Forum in Beijing and called upon its Arab counterparts to upgrade their strategic relationships by deepening bilateral cooperation in areas ranging from finance and energy to space technology. China's trade volume with Arab countries has been growing stronger for more than a decade. Trade has increased from 25.5 billion USD in 2004 to 238.9 billion USD in 2013 and further increased to 30,000 million USD in 2016. China is Arab countries' main bilateral trade partner with figures amounting to $ 330 billion in 2021. According to Ministry of Commerce of PRC in 2017, the Direct Chinese investment in the Arab states reached to 630 million USD, an increase by 25.6 percent year-on-year basis. China was the 2nd largest trading partner of Arab states had fall down to seventh largest trade partner as per the Ministry of External Affairs of the People's Republic of China in 2016, in spite of that China's 'March West' into Arab world is a bold effort to translate its economic might into enduring regional, and ultimately, global influence. Beijing has exporter $ 10.5 billion in 2021 in BRI and energy related projects in Iran, the third largest supplier of oil to China after Saudi Arabia and Russia.

Among the countries of Southeast Asia an Indian Ocean littoral, China-trade with Pakistan has reached about 13 billion USD in 2018 as on 5th November. In 2017–18 China-Pakistan trade volume totaled 13.2 billion USD, accounting a 16.4 percent of Pakistan total trade volume. China exported to Pakistan in 2021 to the extent of $ 24.24 billion, according to United Nations COMTRADE data base on international trade. So, Pakistan has a trade deficit in the balance of Payments. Pakistan exports to China include cotton products, grains, minerals, sands and calx, garments and optical. The trade between China and Sri Lanka reached 3.6 billion USD in 2013, increased from 1.1 billion USD in 2006. There was a significant rise in Chinese imports after 2010 from 2011 to 2018 Chinese imports increased by almost four times. By 2017, the imports to GDP ratio had dropped down to 23.8 percent, while the Chinese imports to GDP ratio had increased to 4.8 percent. This significant increase in Chinese imports came even without China having a Free Trade Agreement (FTA) with Sri Lanka. Finally, in 2020, China exported $ 4.01 billion to Sri Lanka and in the same year Sri Lanka exported $ 266 million worth of goods to China.

China-Bangladesh trade was 6.778 billion USD in 2012–13. Bangladesh is the third largest trade partner of China in South Asia. But bilateral trade between these countries highly tilled towards Beijing. China's exports to Bangladesh increased to 1489149 USD THO from 1332025 USD THO in August 2019. As per World Bank report Bangladesh export volume to China amounted to 723 million USD in 2015, which was only 3 percent of the country's total exports. Bangladesh exports to China also fall down largely in the 2017–18 worth of 694 million USD. When it comes to 2021, Bangladesh total exports to China reached to $ 38.95 million as per CEIC data and China's exports to Bangladesh was $ 24.09 billion during 2021 according to UN COMTRADE data base.

In South Asia, China had 4.46 billion USD trade volume with Myanmar in 2013–14. Myanmar-China bilateral trade hit by 6.3 billion USD. The volume of bilateral trade with China was 10.8 billion USD in 2016–17. The volume of Myanmar trade with China as on October of this year 2019 reached to 6.3 billion USD—consisting of 2.83 billion USD in exports and 3.5 billion USD in imports, according to commerce ministry. Myanmar exported $ 5.378 Billion to China and China's trade volume to be exported to Myanmar during 2021 was $10.53 billion USD, according to UN COMTRADE data base. China was also the largest trading partner of Singapore and Malaysia in 2021 with bilateral trade of Singapore dollars 122.30 billion USD and 176.8 USD respectively. Malaysia has been China's top trading partner within the ASEAN. In 2014, China and Malaysia pledged to increase trade volume to 160 billion USD in 2017. The bilateral trade developed rapidly in recent years between China and Singapore and maintained first position among ASEAN in their trade with China.

It is the second largest trading partner of Indonesia in 2021. The bilateral trade between Indonesia and China grown by 58.6 percent from previous year to $ 124.4 billion USD. China trade with Australia reached AUD $ 150.9 billion in 2013. Australia is the Chinese' six largest trading partner. China has exported $ 8 billion and imported $ 11.7 billion from Australia, resulting in a negative trade balance of $ 3.668 billion during 2021. The bilateral trade in 2017–18 reached to 194.6 billion USD. China has free trade agreements with Pakistan, Thailand and Singapore and its companies have heavily invested in almost all the countries of the Indian Ocean Region. To develop close relationship with these countries, China has funded many welfare projects, including building parliament houses, super markets, school buildings, hospitals, stadiums, railway lines and other infrastructural projects in these countries.

India's Trade with China is on Rise

Amid China's upping the ante in the border areas the bilateral trade between India-China zooms to around $ 100 billion in 2021, according to Times of India report dated 1st January, 2022 despite the Chinese aggression and the military standoff along the borders continuously since mid-May 2020. Further, Chinese decision to renaming 15 places inside Arunachal Pradesh to be used in the China map, shows its rough behavior and its mindset of encroachment of neighborhoods.

In spite of India's actions in 2020 banning Chinese mobile apps to restricting Chinese companies' access to Indian government contracts many had helped assuage public anger at home over the aggression, but did little to influence China's behavior. China's exports to India are booming amid its aggression, allowing it to have its cake and eat it too. India's trade deficit with China dips to $ 44 billion in 2020–21 from $ 53.57 billion in 2018–19, according to Ministry of Commerce and Industry. Imports from China marginally reduced from $ 70.32 billion in 2018–19 to 65.21 billion in 2020–21. So, measures initiated by the government of India showed little impact because India is continuously depending upon China's products amid its aggression along the border.

The rapid expansion of India-China bilateral trade since the beginning of this century propelled China to emerge as our largest goods trading partner by 2008, a position which China continues to hold today. Since beginning of the current decade, bilateral trade between the two countries recorded exponential growth. In 2017 and 2018, the bilateral trade has registered robust two-digit growth. In the year 2019, India was the 12th largest trade partner of China. The bilateral trade in the first 11 months of 2020 touched $ 78 billion, amidst border tensions between the two countries in Eastern Ladakh. The two countries traded about $ 96.68 billion worth of goods in 2019.

Since May 2020, Indian and Chinese military has been engaged in a standoff at multiple friction points in Eastern Ladakh. Following the death of 20 Indian soldiers at a violent face-off, India took several economic measures against China including ban on Chinese IT firms, mobile applications, restrictions on Chinese FDI and cutting Chinese firms out of 5G trials. It is to mention here that market access to Chinese market for Indian products had always been problematic for Indian exporters, even after signing several trade agreements in various bilateral negotiations between India and China.

China has been working for quite long to ensure that it is not left out of any regional equations in the Indian Ocean Region. It intends to be a major player in the Indian Ocean, alongside the US and India. There are deep worries in India over increasing Chinese presence in the Indian Ocean, where India's geographical edge is being chipped away by billions of dollars in aid from China and big Chinese construction projects and investments.

In view of the facts mentioned above, India needs to focus more on the littoral countries of the Indian Ocean Region including small islands by way of promoting trade and commerce with these countries. Therefore, India should place more focus on the Small Island nations, as they played a very significant geo-strategic role in the Indian Ocean since ancient times. Merely focusing on the Indian Ocean Region as a unit to provide security to India and the region is a difficult task. Therefore, India should reach to each of the countries and islands independently with bilateral and multilateral treaties, and agreements separately and with other groups, such as ASEAN, SAARC, Southeast Asia, etc.

India's interest in multi-lateralism dates back to the pre-colonial period, when an Indian delegation participated in the 'Bretton Woods' conference in 1944. India un-willing to compromise its cherished policy of non-alignment, India showed little interest in the multilateral engagements during the Cold War period. However, in the post-Cold War period, India began to evince interest in multilateral organizations meant for global peace and prosperity, while addressing domestic issues of immediate and greater importance such as security, economic development and infrastructure development at a later stage. One of the fascinating developments of the post-world-war period has been the growing recognition of the significance of multilateralism, though India has followed bilateralism continuously to survive and remains a channel for achieving national goals. Therefore, PM Modi has adopted bilateral mechanism with small countries and islands in the Indian Ocean neighbourhood, with particular emphasis showing towards the Maldives, Sri Lanka, Seychelles, Mauritius, Madagascar and Comoros etc. are strategically important, those that falls under the Western Indian Ocean Region.

To consolidate India's presence in the Indian Ocean Region, the Western Indian Ocean, is a region where China is continuously and rapidly expanding its presence both economically and militarily. The Ministry of External Affairs, the government of India recently decided to bring these countries in this region under one umbrella, namely, the Indian Ocean Region Division which handles Sri Lanka, Maldives, Mauritius and Seychelles. This division will also now deal with Madagascar, Comoros and the French re-union in the Western Indian Ocean.

The government of India, under Prime Minister Modi, hoping this move will help it make strategic inroads into the Western Indian Ocean, a region China sees as its gateway to Africa. The government is also looking to use the Indian Coast Guard (ICG) more for its outreach to these island nations collectively known as Vanilla Islands (along with Seychelles, Mauritius and Mayotte). As a part of these efforts, an ICG ship, Vikram, arrived at Madagascar's port city Toamasina recently on a goodwill visit.

Both Madagascar and Comoros are often hit by cyclones and have expressed interest in involving the ICG more in humanitarian assistance and disaster relief operations. In the first high-level visit by an Indian leader to Comoros in October 2019 by Vice-President of India, Venkaiah Naidu. During this visit India and Comoros formally acknowledged the potential for enhancement and for expansion of defence ties, especially in the maritime domain to ensure "collaborative security and economic growth" for all littoral nations in the Indian Ocean region. Four Indian naval ships visited Madagascar in the year of 2019, followed by a defence MoU between India and Madagascar in 2018. The two countries are discussing several defence projects under the MoU for capacity building and training of Madagascar's defined personal is a welcome move in the strategic aspects of Indian Ocean Region security (Times of India, dt. 27-12-2019).

Project Mausam is considered the Modi government's most significant foreign policy initiative designed to counter China's Maritime Silk Route (MSR) Strategy launched in June 2014. The project Mausam is an initiative of Ministry of Culture, government of India to be implemented by the Archeological Survey of India (ASI) as a model agency through the Ministry of External Affairs. 39 Indian Ocean countries has been identified under Project Mausam as a multi-disciplinary, trans-national project that would reconnect and re-establish communications between countries of India and the Indian Ocean Region. The project Mausam would aim to understand the national culture of each Indian Ocean littoral in their regional maritime milieu, extending from East Africa, the Arabian Peninsula, the Indian sub-continent and Sri Lanka to the Southeast Asian archipelago coastal centres to their inter land. The project aims to enhance and multiply the movement of people, goods and ideas across the Indian Ocean enabling multi-cultural and multi-ethnic interaction and exchange and will also be useful in countering China in the Indian Ocean Region.

Though we claim India as a net security provider, India should rise to the occasion of this status and emerge as a net security provider in the region (Indian Ocean) to protect interests ranging from the straits of Hormuz to Malacca. Therefore, the Indian Navy should take up the onus of being the most formidable force in providing security in the region. The concept of net security provider can be viewed as (i) capacity building (ii) Military diplomacy (iii) Military Assistance (iv) Direct deployment of assets in the region. Although India has been active in capacity building and naval diplomacy, its track record in military assistance has been hesitant and on the other hand, due to internal capabilities and external posturing, its direct deployments have also been scratchy in comparison to other major powers, especially with

China. Hence, there is a need to overcome the deficiencies in the subject of net security providers, which needs a huge amount of allocation, as the existing budgetary provision is not sufficient as India wants to emerge as a net security provider and also to limit China's threat in the Indian Ocean Region.

Conclusion

India needs to realize that it not only has geopolitical advantage due to its location centrality but also has a huge benefit of connectivity with each one of the littoral states through its Diaspora. This must be achieved through cultural diplomacy. India needs to make special efforts to attract tourism from these countries in a big way as designed in Project Mausam. India may not be able to invest in these countries as China invests but can export affordable intermediate technologies for various infrastructure projects, IT connectivity and by helping them process their resources.

Indian companies-governmental or private need to further increase their presence in the Indian Ocean littoral states. With the fifth largest navy in the world, India needs to flex its naval muscle across the Indian Ocean by more port calls, offering training to the naval personnel from these countries and a play a pro-active role in fight against piracy, protecting SLOCs and frequently organize naval exercise with navy's of these countries. India must broaden and sharpen its look-east policy into 'Act East' to rope in the countries of Southeast Asia. India needs to build economic alliances involving Japan, the USA and Australia to counter China's growing economic might in the region, though these nations are undertaking naval exercises in the name of 'Malabar' is not enough. India has strong challenges ahead and needs to take a host of such measures to checkmate China's growing naval presence in the Indian Ocean Region. Towards this direction, India has to enhance its budgetary allocations from its existing levels of 13 percent to the Indian navy from the defence sector to rise to the level of net security provider to the Indian Ocean Region.

Notes and References

[1] Ahmad, S. Maqbul, ed. and translators (1960). India and neighbouring territories in the Kitab Nuzhat at Mushtaq al-afaq "of al-sharif al Idrisi, E.J. Brill; Ubayd Allah Ibn. Abd Allah Ibn Khurradabhbih *et al.* (1989). Arabic classical Account of India and China, Indian Institute of Adrmud Study in Association with Rddhi-India, Calcalla.

[2] Deng, Ganf (2005). Chinese maritime Activities and Sovio economic Development, C. 2100 BC – 1900 AD, Santa Barbara, Grenwood Press ISBN

No: 0-313-29212-4; Dreye, Edward L. (2007); Zhengtte: China and the Ocean in the Early Ming, 1405-1453, London, Longman ISBN no: 0-321-08443-8.

[3] Wang, Gungwu (2003). The Nanhai trade: Early Chinese Trade in the South China Sea, Hong Kong, Marshall Cavendish Internation. ISBN 978981 2102416.

[4] Milestones: 1866-1898, Office of the Historian, US State Department, 12th November 2014, at http://history.state.gov/milestone/1866-1898/mahan

[5] Mahan, A.T., The Influence of Sea Power Upon History:1660-1783, The Project Gutenberg E-Book, p. 25, at http://www.gutenberg.org/files/13529/13529-h/13529-h.htm#page 25.

[6] Sakhuja, Vijay, Asia maritime Power in the 2st Century: Strategic Transactions: China, India and Southeast Asia, Institute of Southeast Asian Studies, Singapore, 2011, p. 4.

[7] Ibid.

[8] Khalid, Irum, "Indian Ocean: Global and Regional strategies", *Journal of the Political Studies*, Vol. 20, Issue 2, November 2013, p. 22.

[9] Rais, Rasul Bux, Indian Ocean and the Super Powers: Economic, Political and Strategic Perspective, Rowman and Littlefield: USA, 1987, p. 22–23.

[10] Ibid, p. 22.

[11] Ibid, p. 22.

[12] Sakhuja, n. 3, p. 7.

[13] Juyurumu, P.S., "Indian Ocean as a Zone of Peace: Problems and Perspective", *The India Journal of Political Science*, Vol. 47, No. 2, November 6, 2014, p. 237.

[14] Indian Ocean: Memorandum from the Assistant Secretary of State for Near Eastern and South Asian Affairs to State Rogers, US Department of State Archive, November 6, 2014, p. 123.

[15] Soviet naval presence in the Indian Ocean, Central Intelligence Agency, November 8, 2014, p. 1 at http://www.foia.cia.gov/sites/default/files/document_converstions.

[16] Jayaramu, N. 11, p. 236.

[17] Roy-Chaudhury, Rahul, "US naval policy in the Indian Ocean" strategic Analysis, Vol. 22, No. 9, November 3, 2014, pp. 1314–1318.

[18] Kopp, Carlo, "Strategic Importance of the Indian Ocean", Defence Today, November 2, 2014, at http://www.ausair-power.net/PDF-A/DT-Indian Ocean-December2011.Pdf

[19] Kaplan, Robert D., "Centre Stage for the 21st Century" power plays in the Indian Ocean", Foreign Affairs, Vol. 88, No. 2, November 6, 2014, p. 17.

[20] Khurshid Salman, Salman: Bishop, Julie and Natalegawa, Marty," Putting Out to Sea a New Vision", The Hindu, November 11, 2014.

[21] World Oil Transit Choke-Points, US Energy Information Administration, November 4, 2014.

[22] Story, Ian, "China's Malacca Dilemma, "China brief, Jamestown Foundation, USA, 2006, Vol. 6, No. 8, November 3, 2014, at http://www.jamestown.org/single.

[23] Kaplan, n. 18, p. 21.

[24] Devichand, Mukul, Is Chittagong One of China's "String of Pearls", India Defence Forum; China offers to develop Chittagong Port," The Hindu March 15, 2010.

[25] "India's Lone Missile test-firing range Wheeler Island face sand erosion", Times of India, May 11, 2013.

[26] Geng, Lixim," Sino-Myanmar Relations: Analysis and Prospects," The Culture Mandala, Vol. 7, No. 2, December 2006; "Myanmar Shows India the Road to Southeast Asia", Ausia Times, February 21, 2001.

[27] Sirimane, Shirujiv, "Hambantota Port, Gateway to World" Sunday Observer, 21 February 2010.

[28] Bhutta, Zafer, Gwadar Port: Pakistan, "China all set to develop master plan", The Express Tribune, February 15, 2014; "China confirms takeover of Pakistan's Gwadar Port", Times of India, September 4, 2012.

[29] "With $11 bn Bagamoyo Port, Tanzania prepared to take on EA hub Mombasa", The East African, May 11, 2013, retrieved on 18/10/2014.

[30] "China-India rivalry in the Maldives", Jakarta Port, 17th June 2011.

[31] "China is a different kind of Global Power", available at, the diplomate.com/2014/china-is-a-different-kind-of-global-power

[32] Abhjit, Singh, "China's Maritime Silk Route: Implications for India", IDSA, posted on July 16, 2014.

[33] Rajan, D.S., "China in the Indian Ocean Region: Part of Larger PLAN", CSS Analysis in security Policy, No. 156, November 2, 2014 at www.css.ethz.ch/publication

[34] Ibid.

CHAPTER V

India's Maritime Security Strategy in the Indian Ocean Region

The Indian Ocean Region is witnessing unprecedented flux in its security complexion and recently there has been a flurry of events in the region, which has both regional and global implications. In the recent past, in spite of strong warning from India's national Security Advisor, a Chinese submarine, Changzheng-2 was docked at Colombo in 2014, along with warship Chang Xing Dao. This incident has geopolitical implications and portends to China's growing naval profile in the region. Similarly, several other incidents such as sinking of a naval vessel off Vishakhapatnam and the loss of life of naval personal, airports and seaports in Kolkata receiving series of intelligence warnings of serious threat of an attack exemplify the myriad complexities of maritime security. Coastal and maritime security assumed greater importance after Mumbai terrorist attacks of 2008. These events highlight the importance of maritime security challenges that needs to be addressed.

The Indian Ocean is of strategic significance to India as it covers about 20 percent of the water on the world's surface and it is the world's third largest ocean. The Indian Ocean Rim-Countries have a population of about 2.6 bn. The Indian Ocean accounts for 50 percent of the world's container traffic and Indian Ocean ports handle about 30 percent of global trade. Around 60 percent of the world's seaborne trade in oil transits the Indian Ocean. Roughly, 55 percent of known oil reserves and around 40 percent of gas reserves are in the Indian Ocean Region.[1]

Successive governments have underscored the strategic importance of securing the Indian Ocean and have given credence to the need for a maritime security agenda. Following the 26/11 terrorist attack on Mumbai policymakers in New Delhi realized that India needs a more focused maritime approach to national strategic planning—A robust maritime strategy is one which multi-dimensional, takes into consideration aspects of both traditional defence security issues and also covers non-traditional issues such as rising sea level, oil spill-overs, fishery depletion, piracy and management of living and non-living marine resources. Maritime security has an important bearing on a country's as the sea plays a pivotal role in maintaining the power and greatness of a nation. To an extent, it could be stated that a country's well-being is directly proportional to a strong navy and comprehensive infrastructure. Capabilities to utilize naval power to harness the strength of a state have lent a country the edge to military defend itself and strengthen maritime security. India, by virtue of having 7500 km long coastline which juts out in the Indian Ocean with two strategic outposts of Lakshadweep and Andaman, is a maritime power with naval ambitions and vulnerabilities.

This chapter argues central to Mahan's thesis that the greatness of a country is achieved through the control of the seas and its security issues. The Indian Ocean would become the epicenter of hard power projection as India, China and the US would each attempt to carve a sphere of influence. Taking into cognizance China's legitimate interests in the Indian Ocean, both India and China would face competition and security challenges from each other.

Several recent developments vindicate India's thrust towards the expansion of hard power and the protection of territorial waters and sea lanes. The expansion of hard power in the maritime domain has also become a necessity for India, as it is a major trade dependent on the import of energy resources by the sea. During Former External Affairs Minister Sushma Swaraj emphasized that maritime security is of vital significance for an island nation like Mauritius as well as a country that has a vast coastline like India. A large part of our trade passes through the vast expanse of the Indian Ocean. Safety and security of the sea lanes are thus indispensable for our territorial, economic and energy security. Therefore, the Indian navy is committed to ensuring continued smooth access of energy resources from the Persian Gulf to the Malacca Strait. To secure sea lanes of communication in the Indian Ocean, the government of India is also investing in the development of maritime infrastructure from time to time in the creation of world-class ports, shipbuilding capacity and maintaining Indian littoral interests in the Indian Ocean and as well as in the Pacific.[2]

Mahan Theory and Centrality of Indian Ocean

Assessing the 21st-century Indian Ocean through the prism of maritime thinkers like Mahan may appear quixotic but eminently fits the posture and power projection of India, the United States and China in the Indian Ocean. American naval strategist Alfred Thayer Mahan in his seminar work 'The Influence of Sea Power upon History' (1660–1783) a theoretical treatise argued that American national greatness could be achieved through control of the sea. The history of sea power largely, though by no means solely, a narrative of contests between nations, of mutual rivalries of violence frequently culminating in war.

Thayer offered intellectual argument, that if there is a profound shift of power in the Pacific, the US would stand to lose both economically and militarily. Mahan identified six elements of sea power-geographical positions, physical confirmation, the extent of territory, population, character of people and character of the government. And further argued that seas are a great means of communication between nations, the best defence is to crush the enemy by depriving enemy of the use of the sea.[3] In the struggle for sphere of influence and project power in the Indian Ocean, one can find a striking relevance between maritime strategy orientation and naval power reinforcement by India, China and the US in the Indian Ocean Region. Mahan's contribution strikes a chord among naval strategists and is relevant even today as his promulgated theory things on the idea that key to economic and military supremacy is not only a strong navy but also the promotion of commercial interests, protection of trade, and control of strategic choke points.

There has been a continuous discussions, debates and speculations about whether China would rise peacefully or will China flex its military muscle. While there is no single structural realist answer to these questions, some realist theorists predict that China's assent will lead to serious instability. The unchanging nature of geographical proximity that mandates two countries that inhabit a contested space would continue to be contracted with competition from each other. With China's forays into the Indian Ocean region, which India considers its strategic backyard, the Indian Ocean Region become one such contested space that has become a theatre of both competition for influence and power projection.

Chinese President Xi Jinping announced on September 7, 2013, in a speech at Kazakhstan's Nazarbayev University a new foreign policy initiative called "Silk Road Economic Belt" to intensify international cooperation and to undertake joint development through Eurasia. Elaborating on this new foreign policy initiative, Xi Jinping stated that, China with overall regional cooperation would strengthen economic collaboration improve road connectivity, promote trade, and investment, facilitate currency conversion and bolster people-to-people exchange. Following the communication of China's Silk Road Economic Belt, the Chinese president while addressing Indonesia's Parliament extended the Silk Road policy to the maritime domain. He called for a re-establishment of the old sea networks to create a 'Maritime Silk Road' for faster international connectivity. Scientific and environmental research fishery activities.[4] The idea of maritime Silk Road has evolved into a foreign and security policy of China as the country envisions constructing a maritime Silk Road that connects the waters of the Pacific and the Indian Ocean Region through a route of inter-state commercial activities.

The government of India also gearing up to undertake initiatives that restore strategic balance in the Indian Ocean Region. India has close defence ties with almost all important countries in the region, particularly Mauritius, Maldives, Seychelles, Sri Lanka, Singapore, Vietnam and Malaysia. India started maritime security cooperation in October 2011 with Sri Lanka and Maldives to intensify trilateral cooperation on Maritime security which included initiatives to enhance Maritime Domain Awareness (MDA) training and capacity building in the areas of MDA and Joint activities including trilateral exercises.[5] India cannot prevent the Maldives and Sri Lanka from joining Xi's Silk Road initiative, however, it could take another look at the existing cooperation agenda and improvise on the short to long-term agenda for the three countries in the Indian Ocean Region. India's External Affairs Minister traveled to these two key neighbours in the Indian Ocean Region, Mauritius, where three ships from the western fleet of the Indian Navy INS Mumbai, INS Deepak, and INS Talwar were docked, and to Maldives, to enhance and deepen security ties. This understood the importance of India's bilateral ties aimed at multifaceted cooperation in ensuring peace, stability, and maritime security with these countries. Along with regional neighbours, India has sought to deepen military ties with Vietnam. India has offered a $100 million concessional credit line to Vietnam for purchasing patrol boats and is focusing on enhancing naval cooperation through joint naval exercises to work on issues of maritime security.[6]

The element of trust deficit between India and China has created security dilemma leading to a gradual arms race in the region. Regarding frequent appearance of Chinese submarines and ships at Sri Lanka's ports, Indian strategic studies expert, C. Raja Mohan has stated that explanation often is worse than the presumed offence as statements from Colombo and Beijing are likely to worsen New Delhi's security concerns rather than blunt them.[7] China has been actively involved in building strategic ports, such as Chittagong, Sittwe and Cocos in Myanmar, Hambantota, Karachi and Gwadar in Pakistan. While many security experts worry about the Chinese presence in India Ocean Region, few see no reason for alarm. They point out that ports can't be quickly converted into naval facilities. Expert Bharat Karnad has noted that rising Chinese naval profile in the Indian Ocean Region is more of a shadow play. He cites reasons that during war or conflict time, no port in the Indian Ocean is going to be available to the Chinese navy because none of these countries can afford to alienate India. All of India's neighbours have relied heavily on Indian security for their protection, both in past and present.[8]

China's assertive stance in the south and East China Sea has met with apprehensions from neighbours of south and South-East Asian countries. Chinese project maritime Silk Road which aims to connect the waters of the Pacific and Indian Ocean has been accompanied by a profound shift in Chinese naval power's presence in the Indian Ocean Region. The fundamental problem with President Xi's enunciated MSR is the opaque nature of its proposal on the face of it, the project boosts the development of massive maritime and connectivity in the Indian Ocean and Western Pacific. Beijing has been smart enough to project the MSR as a purely commercial venture and has invited India to join the project. Significantly, China has not released any details specifically about the project and this forced India to object lack of specifics which added to its concern.

Mahan's thesis is a narrative of contests between nations to gain influence in Sea commerce, culminating in mutual rivalries and clashes of interests. Expansion of Chinese footprints in the Indian Ocean Region is likely to clash with Indian interests. The Indian government is also gearing up to undertake initiatives that restore strategic balance in the Indian Ocean region on the multi-lateral front. One of the key initiatives launched by the government of India to retain Indian influence in the Indian Ocean Region is "project Mausam", a multi-disciplinary trans-national project which would endeavor to position itself at two levels. At the macro-level, it would re-connect and re-establish communications between countries of the Indian Ocean, while at the micro-level, the focus would be to understand national cultures in their regional maritime milieu, which impacted ancient and historical trades, local economies, politics and cultural identities. Thus, along with re-kindling long lost ties across the Indian Ocean littoral and foreign, new avenues of cooperation and exchanges opened between India and states of the Indian Ocean. Project Mausam would also contribute to dissemination of culture and civilization along the Indian Ocean Region.[9]

Project Mausam: India's Answer to China's MSR?

The government of India, through Ministry of External Affairs, has enunciated a new foreign policy initiative 'Project Mausam' which is originated from Arabic word 'Mawsin.' The word refers to the season in ancient times when ships could sail safely. Project Mausam, launched by India, is a multi-disciplinary, trans-national project. The project would link cultural routes and maritime landscape across the multi-faceted Indian Ocean 'world'—extending from east-African, the Arabian Peninsula, the Indian Subcontinent and Sri Lanka to the Southeast Asian Archipelago coastal centre to their hinterland. This project aims to enhance and increase the movement of people, goods and ideas across the Indian Ocean, enabling multi-cultural and multi-ethnic interaction and exchange. Of particular interest is the utilization of the monsoon winds. India is leveraging its history, culture and geography to compete with China's maritime Silk Route.

The Project Mausam is considered the Modi government's most significant foreign policy initiative designed to counter China. It is inspired by India's historical role as the focal point for trade in the Indian Ocean. In pre-modern times, sailors used seasonal monsoons to make journey swiftly across the Indian Ocean. This trip usually involved starting from one of the edges of the ocean, around today's Indonesia or east Africa, sailing to India, stopping and allowing another crew to wait for another monsoon to sail to the other edge of the Indian Ocean, as different monsoon winds blew in different directions at different times of the year. Crew members would frequently winter for months in India or at one of the edges of the Ocean waiting for another season of monsoons. This allowed for significant cultural exchanges as diverse people from different places would often spend months at a time living in foreign countries.

Map 5.1: Mausam' Project

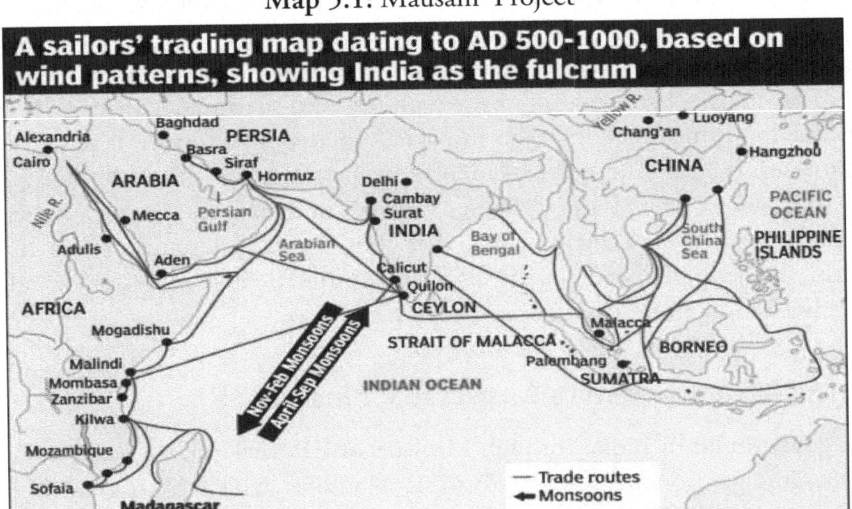

Source: www.googlemaps.com

Project Mausam would allow India to reestablish its ties with its ancient trade partners and re-establish an Indian Ocean world along with the littoral of the Indian Ocean. This would stretch from east Africa, along with the Arabian Peninsula, past Southern Iran to the major countries of South Asia and hence to Sri Lanka and Southeast Asia. Project Mausam is the initiative of the Ministry of Culture to be implemented by the Archeological Survey of India (ASI) as the nodal agency. The project Mausam was launched in June 2014, during the 38th session of the World Heritage Committee.

39 Indian Ocean countries have been identified under the project 1. Bahrain 2. Bangladesh 3. Cambodia 4. China 5. Comoros 6. Egypt 7. Eritrea 8. Reunion (French Dept.) 9. Iran 10. Jordan 11. Indonesia 12. Iraq 13. Kuwait 14. Kenya 15. Lebanan 16. Madagascar 17. Malaysia 18. Mozambique 19. Myanmar 20. Oman 21. Pakistan 22. Philippines 23. Qatar 24. Singapore 25. Saudi Arabia 26. Seychelles 27. Somalia 28. Africa 29. Sudan 30. Syria 31. Tanzania 32. Thailand 33. Turkey 34. UAE 35. Vietnam 36. Yemen 37. Maldives 38. Mauritius 39. Sri Lanka (Ministry of Culture & Tourism in a written reply to Sri Lanka, dt 4/7/2017).

Perhaps the Indian navy might have considered developing the Andaman Nicobar Islands as a bastion of trade and security. Towards this objective, Prime Minister Modi recently allocated more than ten thousand crores to develop in an integrated manner of Indian navy, Air force, and military under one command known as ANC. An interesting article titled 'From Outpost to Springboard' by an Economist reported that Andaman's islands are of strategic importance as the islands stretch 750 km-long above the entrance to the Malacca. The economist expressed in his article that the Andamans could not be treated as 'Chokepoints', a place to disrupt Chinese trade in the event of any future confrontation, as 80 percent of Chinese oil imports goes through the strait.[10]

Competition however, doesn't mean confrontation. Since India and China remain locked in the traditional security dilemmas, face similar security challenges and share common interests in the Indian Ocean Region, it is necessary that both countries compete to a reasonable extent while pushing forward functional cooperation. Robert Kaplan in his book Monsoon explained the civilization and political connections and players in the Indian Ocean Region focusing on the Indian-Chinese competition and the US interest in the region. He hopes as a solution, the US should act like a broker to mitigate the likelihood of conflict in the Indian Ocean Region. Robert Kaplan expects that with greater economic rise of India and China, the US power and influence in the region to counter balance will be welcomed. According to Kaplan, China and India will compete more with soft power than hard power since territorial expansion is an option for neither, and the US Navy can engineer an elegant decline from hegemony by fostering cooperation with navies to protect the maritime commons. It is to encourage that India and China resort to more liberal cooperative frameworks since both the countries are key players in Asia's maritime architecture and should combine efforts to constructively counter non-traditional security challenges such as piracy, and maritime terrorism. This would also offset the possibilities of an arms race in the Indian Ocean. The navies of India and China are operated together in the Gulf of Aden to tackle the threat of the Somalia pirates and their ships have escorted each other's commercial ships, as well as other flag vessels passing through the International Recommended Transit Corridor (IRTC).

The end of the Cold War marked a major shift in the world politics and fundamentally structured several relationships around the world, including that of India and the US. The post-1990 story of India-US relationship is one about discovering common political values, which also provided space for India and the US to explore the possibility of defence cooperation. The first military-to-military cooperation started between India and the US in 1991, which included Joint naval exercise, staff exchange and shared participation in United Nations (UN) peace-making operations. India's Army Chief visited the US in 1994 and held discussions with defence secretary, Chairman of Joint Chief Staff General and the Deputy Secretary of State. This show is symbolic of development of new military-to-military links between the two countries.

In October 2002, India and the US started the Joint military exercise known as the 'Geronimo Thrust', which took place in Alaska and was one more step towards enhancing 'inter-operability', between defence forces of the two sides. This was the first time that India was taking part in a military exercise in North America.[11] In February 2014, the Air Force of both the countries took part in Operation Cope India 04 at Gwalior. The navies conducted anti-submarine warfare in April 2004 and Malabar 04 exercises off Goa.

India-US defence relations in the recent past have witnessed a significant upward growth. The New Framework of defence for US-India Defence Relationships, signed in 2005 by the than Defence Minister, Pranab Mukherjee, set the tone for a new era, which transformed the complexion of India-US defence security ties.

Three clear and abiding US interests in the Indian Ocean that seems to remain the focus of US strategy are:

1. To maintain the Indian Ocean as a secure highway for international commerce, particularly between oil-rich gulf states and an economically dynamic East Asia.
2. To maintain freedom of navigation through the strategic choke points of Indian Ocean highway in the strait of Hormuz on one end and the Strait of Malacca and the South China Sea on the other.
3. To maintain a stable equilibrium in the region and partner with major maritime powers within the region that aligns sufficiently with the US' interests.[12]

As per the centre for strategic and international studies report, the US strategy focuses on supporting Indian pre-eminence in the Indian Ocean and closer US-India strategic cooperation. In addition, the US strategy should be encouraged and support closer alignment and enhanced strategic consultation among the major maritime democracies in the region, reviving the US-Japan, Australia and India 'Quad' concept.[13] It is highlighted that New Delhi intends to expand India's maritime presence culturally, strategically and psychologically in the region. Project Mausam is a positive step in that direction and has been generally well-received in the democratic world. However, the project Mausam requires huge amount of funds on par with Chinese MSR to maintain close relationship and help financially in the form of aid and investments etc. among the member countries.

India and Multilateralism

One of the fascinating developments of the post-World war period has been the growing recognition of the significance of multilateralism, though bilateralism continues to survive and remain a channel for achieving national goals. Global economic-political system is interdependent, no nation can remain alone and India is no exception. India therefore, embraced multilateralism and actively, enthusiastically associated itself with the formation and promotion of multilateral organizations, which serves eminently to advance its economic as well as security interests. As a country targeted particularly by state-supported terrorist outfits, India has to seek support from external powers and neighbourhood nations.[14] Transnational peace and security were regarded as global public goods—in the sense that no single state can deliver them on its own. Multilateral diplomacy also becomes imperative to India which seeks to demonstrate its military prowess by holding multilateral military exercises. Interests of Indians in multilateralism dates back to the pre-colonial period when an Indian delegation participated in the Bretton Woods Conference in 1944.

India, unwilling to compromise its cherished policy of non-alignment, showed little interest in multilateral engagements during the Cold War period. However, in post-cold war period, India began to evince interest in multilateral engagements. India hence actively participated with enthusiasm in quite a few multilateral institutions such as ASEAN,[15]-led forums like ARF (ASEAN-Regional Forum), EAS (East-Asia Summit), MGC (Mekong Ganga Cooperation), BBIN (Bangladesh, Bhutan, India and Nepal cooperation, NIB (Nepal, India and Bangladesh), RIC (Russia, India and China), BRICS (Brazil, Russia, India, China and South Africa), IORA (Indian Ocean Rim Association for Regional Cooperation), BIMSTEC (Bay of Bengal Initiative for Multi-Sectoral Technical and Economic Cooperation) and IBSA (India, Brazil and South Africa)

India also advocated reforming multilateral Financial Institutions including World Bank and IMF and the UN Security Council. India's engagement with multilateral organizations while contributing to global peace and prosperity and helping in addressing domestic issues of immediate and greater importance such as security, economic and infrastructure development. Given the growing importance of multilateralism and multilateral mechanisms, India joined as a full member of SCO (Shangai Cooperation Organization), the China-dominated security grouping. It is believed that as a member of SCO, India will have an opportunity to muster support in its crusade against the scourge of terrorism and also to discuss vital issues related to security and defence in the region.[16] Hence, China is wary about India's engagement with the US, Japan and Australia in a combined naval exercise under the name of 'Malabar' as the grouping can challenge China's dominance in the Indo-Pacific Region.

India's Security Concern in the Indian Ocean Region

India's Indian Ocean policy is centered on providing security and political stability to its maritime neighborhood, which includes the Maldives, Seychelles, and Sri Lanka in the face of China's expanding naval and strategic activities in the Indian Ocean Region. India has not learnt any lesson from the Mumbai terror attacks by way of undertaking efficacious measures to deal with future instances of maritime terrorism. So, India must craft a long-term strategy not only to modernize, update, and strengthen its naval resources, but also to plug loopholes in its decision-making on defence procurement and policy implication. Hence, India needs to reverse the perception of it as a regional hegemony through policy and actions that encourage the strategic cooperation of its neighbours and help balance China's increasing strategic influence in the Indian Ocean Region.

The Indian Ocean has always been, and will remain on the strategic radar of great power. Given its strategic location with abundant oil, mineral resources and fisheries and being a vast seaborne global trade and oil routes, it has turned out to be an arena of geo-political rivalry among world economic integration and complex given the persistent threats to the smooth flow of trade and commerce which demands freedom of navigation and security of sea lanes of communications.

In so far as India is concerned, as a resurgent maritime nation, it has myriad interests in the Indian Ocean, ranging from energy security, economic growth, the safety of sea lines to its maritime ambition to play a leading role in shaping security architecture in the Indian Ocean Region. With its growing military and economic capabilities, India is poised to develop its blue economy to ensure inclusive growth and job creation. Intertwined with national interests, its maritime stability is centered on providing security and political stability to its maritime.[17] India's Neighbors, such as Maldives, Mauritius, Seychelles and Sri Lanka, are increasingly concerned about China's expanding naval and strategic activities in the region. By this reasoning, China's presence entails a direct negative impact on India's energy and security interests and also undermines its role as a Prominent player in the region.

India's Act East Policy

PM Modi has attempted to redefine India's Indian Ocean Policy to articulate India's interests in a much broader framework of seeking a more integrated and cooperative future to ensure peace, security and sustainability development for all.[18] Towards that goal, the Modi government has launched a new approach to reach out to all friendly nations to renew and deepen strategic partnerships in the Indian Ocean Region. Modi is the 1st Indian PM to have undertaken such a record number of foreign visits which injected a new energy and dynamism into the wither to moribund maritime diplomacy of India. This resulted in the successful conclusion of the Logistics Exchange Memorandum of Agreement (LEMOA) agreement between Indian and the USA in 2016 permitting the use of each other bases, something quite unimaginable in the Cold War era.

Further, Modi gave a new nomenclature to the earlier Look East Policy into the Act East Policy. The choice of name was perhaps not without sarcasm and may imply that his predecessor UPA government suffered from passivity and policy paralysis, failing to address effectively the warnings from China about India's maritime engagement with South East Asia. He undertook a flurry of visits to ASEAN countries to convince their heads of State that India was committed to helping and maintaining peace and security in the Indian Ocean Region RIM states. He gave enough hints that India might be a solid hedge against China's increasing geopolitical influence in the region which was reflected in India's joint naval exercises with ASEAN member countries such as Singapore and Indonesia. In addition, India and Vietnam signed two MoUs on bilateral defence and coast guard cooperation in 2015. As part of the agreement, two warships visited Can Ranh Bay in the Philippines. Under the Act East Policy, the Modi government has boosted the morale of the Indian navy and expanded its strategic footprint beyond South Asia.

Undoubtedly, India's recent maritime policies towards Asian states impacted a new sense of confidence among the Indian people that their country was capable of defending its maritime security interests against potential threats from its adversaries. In particular, with the induction into the navy of the aircraft carrier INS Vikramaditya and ballistic missile submarines, India has recalibrated its maritime security policy to better safeguard its various security and economic interests in the Indian Ocean Region. Maritime security policy, under Modi government was articulated in 2015 document titled 'Ensuring Secure Seas: Indian maritime security strategy.'

More pertinently, PM Modi has endeavored as never before to inject new vigor and momentum into Indian neighbourhood maritime policy, by realizing the new geo-strategic reality that China was consolidating its maritime presence in the littoral states of the Indian Ocean. In response to that expansion, Modi visited Seychelles and Mauritius in March 2015 and stressed the imperative for comprehensive defence and maritime security cooperation with the Island States. During his call on the Seychelles, he concluded five agreements with the Seychelles government covering renewable energy, infrastructure, development and hydrographic surveys. More important was the agreement pertaining to the lease of Assumption Island for the development of its infrastructure. This will enable India to keep a close visit over any Chinese warships in the area. Apart from these agreements, Modi inaugurated the coastal surveillance Radar system to enhance India's maritime capabilities. Further, India has plans to set up more coastal surveillance Radar systems in Mauritius, Sri Lanka and the Maldives. Highlighting India's push for regional integration Modi has said that India also hopes that Seychelles will soon be a 'full partner' in the maritime security cooperation between India, the Maldives and Sri Lanka.

India's China Anxiety: Clash of Interests

In a new wave of Asian regionalism, China has emerged as an assertive and influential actor to reshape Asian economic and security architecture. Over the past one decade or so, China has emerged as India's archival in the Indian Ocean. Without exaggeration, China has already established its strategic bench head in the region. This is manifested from China's development of the Hambantota port in Sri Lanka, Marao in the Maldives, Chittagong port in Bangladesh and its operational control over Pakistan's Gwadar port, which will help China not only to encounter the Indian Navy directly, but also China's PLA-navy docked its nuclear submarines in Colombo in 2014, causing security anxiety to India. These instances reinforce China's intention to scuttle India's role and influence in the region. In Indian perceptions, China's objective is to jeopardize India's energy, security, economic and trade interests. It must be underlined that China has already established strong strategic ties with Sri Lanka and the Maldives with a focused motivation to dilute India's prominent role and influence over those countries. Towards the end, China launched the Maritime Silk Road project in India's backyard, of which the Maldives and Sri Lanka are the partners. Not only this, Chinese military elites are also reportedly engaged in working out a roadmap to set up a naval base in the Maldives, although that is denied by the Maldivian government.

In order to rejuvenate its ties with Sri Lanka and the Maldives, China conducted joint military exercises with Sri Lanka in June–July 2015, that was in addition to docking of two nuclear submarines at Colombo in 2014. India protested over the presence of the nuclear submarines in its backyard but it did not cut any ice with the Beijing leadership. In real political terms, China's game plan is centered on keeping a close surveillance over India's strategic assets and its naval activities offshore the Indian Ocean. It was also reported that Chinese nuclear submarines carried out patrols in the Bay of Bengal. The possible presence of Chinese nuclear missiles so close to its coastline was a matter of most concern to India's nuclear deterrence.[19] Undoubtedly, such sensitive strategic activities are seen as a serious threat to India's national security interests, further eroding India's role as a security stability provider in the region. Therefore, the Modi government, appears to be serious about helping the Indian Ocean states enhance their capabilities.

Future Requirements and Actions

In the face of the challenges to India's myriad interests, it is not sufficient just to conduct joint-naval exercises with various regional partners, including the US. India must realize that its naval capabilities are much weaker than those of China. The latter possesses four nuclear ballistic missile submarines while India has only one nuclear ballistic missile submarine, the Akula-Class INS Chakra. Moreover, INS Arihant India's nuclear ballistic missile submarine has still to undergo several more ballistic tests. Hence, the 2015 decision of the Modi government to upgrade the country's naval arm with the green light to the indigenous construction of six nuclear-powered submarines was a right move to bolster India's naval prowess. Moreover, India signed an agreement with a Russian ship builder at a cost of 5000 crore Rs. (1 bn USD) to refit its old kilo-class submarines, including leasing a world-class nuclear attack submarine from Russia to improve the depleted naval fleet. The Indian defence establishment has also given green light to the construction of 24 submarines by 2045. F India needs high-tech guardian drones from the US that were formally known as 'predator B' for maritime surveillance in the Indian Ocean. In a new dispensation from the Trump Administration, democrat senator Mark Warner and his Republican colleague Dan Sullivan supported the sale of Guardian drones to India.

However, the Modi government has made some big claims about India's defence preparedness, implying that India is fully capable of meeting any maritime challenges from any source. On the contrary, Modi's hyperbolic rhetoric and verbal assurances to the nation are a benefit of concrete policy actions. For instance, for a long, India has not undertaken appropriate measures to improve and strengthen its naval capabilities to counter maritime terrorism and piracy, in the light of Mumbai terror attack. A host of pragmatic measures are needed to undertake in the given terms.

First, India needs to further elevate, strengthen and deepen its security cooperation with regional partners such as Sri Lanka, the Maldives and Seychelles as well as the US, Japan and Australia to protect its core security interests in the Indian Ocean.

Second, India needs to develop hard and soft power resources to ensure its maritime security and to be able to deal with any contingent situation that might arise from any future Sino-US conflict in the South China Sea. Moreover, India must expand its strategic foothold in multilateral fora and organizations. Today, with the exponential development and modern weaponry unprecedented communications technology and vast intelligence resources, maritime threats have amplified. For India, the Indian Ocean Region is a nerve centre for its Sea Lanes of communications.

Third, any quadrilateral partnership of India, Japan, the US and Australia should not be exclusively focused on isolating China as some kind of Pariah state. Rather, China must engage as a cooperative partner in the process of negotiations to resolve mutual differences in the spirit of protecting the global commons.

Fourth, if it has to meet challenges, either real or perceived, posed by China to its maritime interests in the Indian Ocean Region, India will require to develop a multipronged strategy of maintaining an active and agile presence in the Indian Ocean Region by integrating its army, air force and its navy in fuller cooperation and coordination with the central-state governments.

Fifth, India's focus should be on the security of SLOC, and resources management. Finally, India will require to undertake defence infrastructure projects in the Indian Ocean as an effective counterweight to China's typed strategic encirclement of India through the so-called 'String of Pearls doctrine.'

Indian Naval Capabilities and Naval Exercises

The Indian Navy is the naval branch of the armed forces. The President of India is the supreme commander of the Indian navy. The Indian navy traces its origin back to the East India Company's marine, founded in 1612 to protect British merchant shipping in the region. In 1793, the British East Indian Company established its rule over the eastern part of the Indian subcontinent *i.e.* Bengal, but it was until 1830, that the colonial navy titled as his majesty's Indian Navy. When India became a republic in 1950, the Royal Indian Navy as it has been named since 1934, was renamed as 'Indian Navy'.[20] The primary objective of the navy is to safeguard the nations maritime borders and in conjunction with other Armed Forces of the union, act to deter or defeat any threats or aggression against the territory, people, or maritime interest of India. Through joint exercises, goodwill visits and humanitarian missions, including disaster reliefs, Indian navy promotes bilateral relations between nations. As of June 2019, Indian Navy has 67,252 personal[21] in service and has a fleet of 137 warships and 235 aircraft. As of March 2018, the operational fleet consists of one aircraft carrier, one amphibious transport dock, eight landing ship tanks, eleven destroyers, fourteen frigates, one nuclear-powered attack submarine, one ballistic missile submarine, fifteen conventionally-powered attack submarines, twenty-two corvettes, one mine counter measure vessel, four fleet tankers, and various other auxiliary vessels. Asymmetry in the force level between India and China is given in the below table.

Table 5.1: India-China Asymmetry in the Force Level

Particular	*China*	*India*
Defence budget	$ 224 billion	$ 72.6 billion
Troops	2.2 million	1.5 million
Big-size warships	110	37
Aircraft carriers	02	01
Destroyers	33	11
Frigates	54	14
Corvettes	42	11
Submarines	50	15
Nuclear powered subs	10	02
Aircrafts/helicopters	76 (only aircrafts)	235
Theatre commands	05	01
Tanks	7000	3300
Fighters & bombers	2100	500
Nuclear warheads	320	150
Large arsenal with long ranged dong Feng-31-A	11200 km	Agni III 3000 km & Agni V 5000 km
Missile arsenal, J L-2	7400 km	–

Source: Times of India 4th December 2019 and 19th June 2020 and 6th March 2023.

India often conducts naval exercises with other friendly countries designed to increase naval cooperation and also to strengthen cooperative security relationship. Some such exercises take place annually like the Varuna with the French Navy, Kankan with Royal Navy. Indira with Russian navy, Malabar with the US Navy and SIMBEX with Singapore (is an annual naval Exercise conducted by the Indian Navy and the Republic of Singapore Navy (RSN). The Exercise has been holding annually since 1994 with Republic of Singapore navy and IOSAMAR and with the Brazil and South African Navys. The Indian navy also conducted exercises with the People Liberation Army Navy (PLAN) in 2003, and sent ships to the South China Sea to participate in the fleet review apart from the Indian Ocean. India has steadily gained influence in the Pacific Ocean and signed an agreement with Japan in October 2008 for joint naval patrolling in the Asia Pacific region.

In 2007, India conducted naval exercise with Vietnam, Philippines and New Zealand also India and South Korea conducted annual naval exercise; alongside India participated in the South Korean International Fleet Review in 2008. Also in the same year, India held the first Indian Ocean Naval Symposium (IONS)[22] for all the littoral states of the Indian Ocean to cooperate on mutually agreed areas for better security in the region. Since the past decade, the Indian naval ships have made goodwill port calls to Israel, Turkey, Egypt, Thailand, Indonesia, Australia, New Zealand, Tonga, South Africa, Kenya, Qatar, Oman, UAE, Bahrain, Kuwait and other various countries.

The Chinese defence budget has up by 850 percentage in over a period of 20 years from 20 billion USD to 170 billion USD in 2018,[23] according to a top 'pentagon' official, who informed lawmakers recently, the US undersecretary of defence for policy John C Rood, in his testimony before the Senate Armed Services Committee noted that, the real figure was significantly higher than China's official budget of 170 bn. China possesses one of the largest militaries in the world. India continues to enhance its capabilities and has become increasingly pro-active in its activities in the South China Sea (SCS) and in Africa, where China established its first overseas base ever in Djibouti in 2017.

Whereas Chinese naval capabilities are in a different league altogether, with an overseas base at Djibouti in the Horn of Africa and naval turnaround facilities at Karachi, the fast-expanding Chinese navy already has two aircraft carriers (two more are being built), 33 destroyers, 54 frigates, 42 corvettes, 50 diesel-electric and 10 nuclear submarines among other warships.[24] In contrast, India is struggling with a fund crunch; the 140-warship Indian navy has just one aircraft carrier, as of now. Therefore, it has asked for an additional Rs. 16000 crore capital expenditure in the ongoing fiscal; may be forced to settle 175 warships, instead of the 212. India wanted to be a super naval power by 2027 according to Navy Chief Admiral Karambir Singh.[25]

Despite the India's navy's share of the defence budget declining from 18 percent in 2012 to around 13 percent in 2019–20, the Indian Navy has projected India's requirements to the government. These include countering China's expanding footprint in the Indian Ocean Region, deterring Pakistan, projecting power to guard strategic interests from the Persian Gulf to Malacca Strait and protecting the daily transit of sea trade worth $2 billion and offshore assets. To fulfill these, in anticipation of more funds to the navy in the defence budget, Indian Navy proposed a few projects (i) 41 warships worth $1.25 lakh crore have got acceptance of necessity (AON) includes, including 6 diesel electric submarines under projects—75 India ($ 50,000 crore) and 12 mine counter-measures vessels ($ 32,000 crores). Indian Navy also got AoN for more P-81 air-craft ($ 13000 crore), 10 kamov-31 helicopters (Rs. 3621 crore) and 24 multirole MH-60 Romeo helicopters (Rs. 13,5000 crores) separately. The Navy is pushing for a 65,000 tonne indigenous aircraft carrier II (INS vishal), which will cost Rs. 45,000 crore.

Indian Navy is concerned to safeguard the country's maritime interests and not to allow any action by any other player in the region to impact them adversely. Recently, Indian warships drove away a Chinese oceanic research vessel indulging in suspicious activity near the strategically located Andaman and Nicobar archipelago, amid the shadow-boxing between New Delhi and Beijing for some strategic space and influence in the Indian Ocean region. In view of this, the Indian navy is thoroughly convinced that the nation requires three aircraft carriers so that two are operational at any given time.

India currently has only one aircraft carrier in the 44,000 tonne INS Vikramaditya, while the second one—the 40,000-tonne Indigenous Aircraft Carrier (IAC-I) or INS Vikrant being built at Cochin Shipyard for over Rs. 20,000 crore-will become fully operational soon. The Navy's long-term plan is to have 'three' aircraft carriers so that two carrier battle groups are ready for deployment in the Indian Ocean Region round-the-clock. The Navy has been pitching for third aircraft carrier to deal with China's growing naval prowess and its growing influence over the Indian Ocean Region, a strategically key area for India.

The Indian Navy's P-81 long-range maritime reconnaissance aircraft had played an important role in gathering intelligence on Pakistan military deployments and keeping India's western seaboard safe after the Pulwama attack. The navy will be inducting more such aircraft, boosting its capabilities to conduct sustained surveillance and anti-ships and submarine preparedness in the Indian Ocean Region. According to Bipin Rawat, Chief of the Defence Staff (CDS) cost could be a major factor in deciding on the issue, as aircraft carrier are very expensive. Therefore, approval for 3rd Aircraft carrier may not come soon at the movement (Times of India dt 18-2-2020). However, it is on the agenda of the Indian Navy to have a third aircraft carrier. .

The Chinese navy has grown the fastest in the world over the past 20 years, said Admiral Sunil Lamba, the Indian navy chief speaking at the Raisina Dialogue. He further informed the audience that the Chinese had been present in the Indian Ocean since 2008, adding a phenomenal 80 ships to its navy in the past five years. Therefore, "they are a force that is here to stay." At any given time, there are six to eight Chinese navy ships deployed in the northern part of the Indian Ocean. Chinese naval presence in the Indian Ocean has been in the form of an anti-piracy escort force. However, concerns were raised over the actual nature of China's navy presence, as China declared that its base in Djibouti is for anti-piracy operations. It had deployed submarines for anti-piracy operations, which is most unlikely platform to be used for this role.

China seeks to expand its military reach in pursuit of its territorial and maritime expansion and claims the South China Sea and East China Sea as well as its land borders with India and Bhutan. The People's Liberation Army is expanding military might indicating that, China developed an inter-continental ballistic missile (ICBM) which represents a significant improvement in its nuclear-capable rocket forces, apart from its already large arsenal of cruise and ballistic missiles in order to project hard power and guard its multi-billion-dollar one Belt One Road (OBOR) infrastructure projects. China's expanding military capabilities are as of now mainly geared towards preventing any US military intervention in the Taiwan Strait, and South and East China Sea as well as to protect its energy supply routes in the Indian Ocean Region.

India, however, has no option but to keep a close watch on China's strategic moves in the Indian Ocean Region and along the 4057 km long line of actual control, stretching from eastern Ladakh to Arunachal Pradesh.[26] China is trying to encroach at Siliguri corridor and in Arunachal Pradesh. The BJP Member of Parliament Mr. Tapir Gao raised the issue of Chinese encroachment into Indian Territory in the Lok Sabha on 19th November 2019, urging the government to take action on such encroachments, failing which, Arunachal Pradesh will repeat another Doklam. The MP informed the house that China has already encroached on more than 50–60 km of Indian Territory (Time of India dt 20/11/2019).[27] Taking into cognizance of the 73-day troop face-off between India and China at Doklam is because of the encroachment of Chinese troops into Indian territory in 2017 and another confrontation at Demchok in 2018 shows clearly that Chinese leaders are adroit at employing shortage of armed conflicts to pursue Chinese strategic objective in dominating Indo-Pacific region.

Sino-Indian Border Disputes

The Sino-Indian border dispute is an ongoing territorial dispute over the sovereignty of two relatively large, and several smaller, separated pieces of territory between China and India. The first of which, Aksai Chin, is claimed by China as a part of the Xinjiang Uygur Autonomous Region and

Tibet Autonomous Region and claimed by India as a part of the union territory of Ladakh; it is virtually uninhabited high-altitude wasteland in the larger regions of Kashmir and Tibet and is crossed by the Xinjiang-Tibet Highway. The other disputed territory is south of the McMahan Line, formerly known as the North East Frontier Agency and now called Arunachal Pradesh. The McMohan Line was part of the 1914 Simla Convention signed between British India and Tibet, without China's agreement. As of 2020, India continues to maintain that the McMohan line is the legal border of the east. China has never accepted that border, stating that Tibet was never independent when it signed the Simla convention.

Map 5.2: India-China Border along LAC

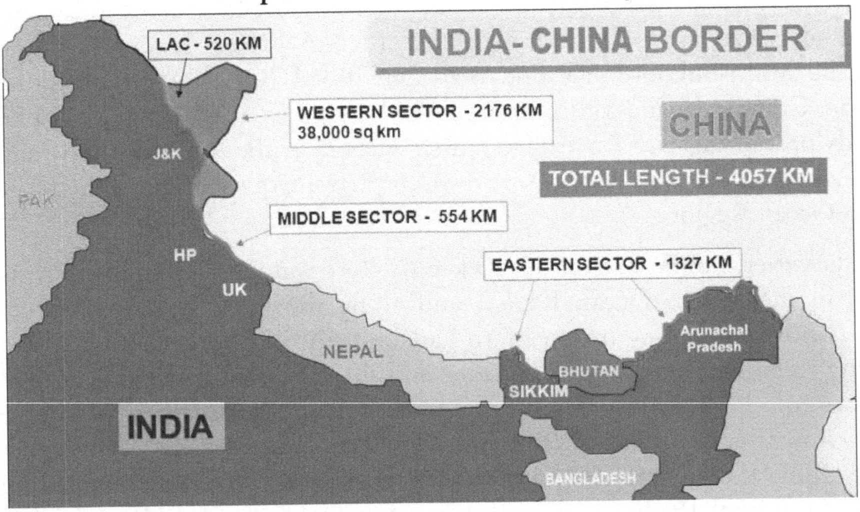

Source: www.googlemaps.com

Since Bhutan and Nepal belong to the Indian Ocean Region as land-locked states, it is very much relevant to discuss in brief here about the India- China border disputes along the Line of Actual Control (LAC), that has stood for the border between India and China. Actually, the border is not properly demarcated entity and hence has fuelled disputes among Indian and Chinese soldiers even as multiple rounds of talks have so far been unable to find a solution. The following are the key dates for understanding the Chinese ugly character:

- In 1962 China's aggression in India's northeast is followed by Beijing's call for a unilateral ceasefire .China withdrawn troops to 20 km behind LAC.
- In 1967 Clashes, Chinese troops are thwarted in an attempt to enter Indian territory along the Sikkim border.

- In 1975, the two sides—India and China exchanged fire along the LAC in Arunachal Pradesh in which four Indian soldiers were killed.
- In 1976, India and China agreed to resume diplomats after a 15-year gap.
- Chinese troops' presence in Arunachal Pradesh in 1986–87, met by Indian Army's 'Operation Falcon'. The stand-off ceased following negotiations:
- In 1988, India and China agreed to set up a joint working group on boundary issue.
- In 1993 an agreement was signed on Maintenance of Peace and Tranquility along the LAC, thus recognizing the Line of Actual Control.
- In 1999, amid the Kargil conflict with Pakistan, China built 5 km track right up to Pangong Tso's southern bank.
- In 2000, Chinese soldiers built permanent roads and set up bunkers inside the Indian part of LAC in Ladakh's Aksai Chin area.
- Again in 2013 Chinese troops intruded in- to Depsang Valley in Ladakh. The stand-off is resolved after negotiations. In October 2013, the two sides signed the Border Defence Cooperation Agreement.
- In 2014, Chinese soldiers attempted to build a road in the Chumar area of Ladakh. The face-off was resolved after Prime Minister Modi took up the matter with visiting Chinese President Xi Jinping.
- In 2017, Indian soldiers moved to prevent Chinese troops from building a road in the trijunction area of LAC near Bhutan border. The standoff ended after China's troops withdrew after a 73-day confrontation on Bhutanese territory of Doklam near the Sikkim-Bhutan-Tibet trijunction after Indian soldiers blocked Chinese troops from extending a road.
- In mid-May 2020, tensions arose at multiple areas again along LAC, Sikkim to Ladakh, seeing troop build-up before violent escalation occurs in Galwan Valley in Ladakh, the face-off has disengaging after 9th round of Commander's level talks agreement reached between two countries, India and China.

The 1962 Sino-Indian War was fought in both disputed areas. Chinese troops attacked Indian border posts in Ladakh in the west and crossed the McMohan line in the east, and there was a brief border clash in 1967 in the region of Sikkim. In 1987 and in 2013, potential conflicts over the two differing Lines of Actual Control were successfully de-escalated. A conflict involving a Bhutanese-controlled area on the border between Bhutan and China was successfully de-escalated in 2017, known as Doklam dispute following the injuries to both Indian and Chinese troops. Multiple brawls broke out in 2020, escalating to dozens of deaths both sides in June 2020 in the eastern Ladakh.

The agreement to resolve the dispute concluded in 1996, included "confidence-building measures" and the Line of Actual Control. In 2006, The Chinese Ambassador to India claimed that all of Arunachal Pradesh is Chinese territory amidst a military buildup. At that time, both countries claimed incursions as much as a kilometer at the northern tip of Sikkim. In 2014, India proposed China should acknowledge a "One India" policy to resolve the border dispute. Sino-Indian border dispute is seen as the territory-slicing components of China's salami slice strategy.

38 Chinese Soldiers died in Galwan Clash

China lost at least 38 soldiers during violent Galwan clashes with India in June 2020. The number is much more than the five casualties Beijing has officially announced and acknowledged till now, according to an Australian Website, the Klaxon, which was published recently in early February of 2022. Whereas, India had immediately announced that 20 of its soldiers led by Col. B. Santhosh Babu had laid down their lives while fighting the numerically superior Chinese troops armed with nail-studded rods and other sharp weapons.

India China troops' clash near LAC on 9th December 2022 is the first major clash between India-China since the Galwan Valley conflict which occurred in Eastern Ladakh on 15th June 2020. This time the face-off took place in Tawang of Arunachal Pradesh. Both sides sustained fractured limbs and other injuries. Nearly 300–400 soldiers from the PLA intruded across the LAC. Indian soldiers contested firmly and resolutely.

The latest skirmish again showed that China won't give up on salami-slicing Indian territory along the LAC. It clearly shows that China is determined to unilaterally change the status quo of the LAC westward and is no longer interested in engaging in serious dialogue to resolve the border issue. It is to understand that the recent physical scuffle at Tawang happened just days after India and the US held military exercises close to the LAC. Therefore, New Delhi needs to do more to buttress its infrastructure along the entire LAC Closing the border infrastructure gap with China is of paramount importance to secure India's territorial Sovereignty.

Water Wars by China

Fearing a Chinese threat of 'Water Wars', India has initiated its biggest hydroelectric project of 11,000 megawatt (MW) in Upper Subansiri in Arunachal Pradesh in response to Chinese dams coming up close to its borders in the north-east. According to government sources, a 60,000 MW Chinese project on the Yariung Zangbo (Brahmaputra) planned at Medog on Arunachal Pradesh's border could be a cause for concern for multiple reasons—scarcity of water if China decides to divert it, floods affecting lakhs in Arunachal Pradesh and Assam if China releases water, as well as environmental concerns. For India, the Brahmaputra accounts for nearly 30% of freshwater resources and 40% of total hydropower potential of the country. 50% of the basin of the Brahmaputra is in Chinese territory. This is not a north-east issue but a national issue. China is building dams with large storage capacities. According to analysts, China can also use the Medog dam as a political tool, which could be a matter of concern for India and Bangladesh. Fearing Water Wars by China, the Indian government puts dams in Arunachal Pradesh on fast track equipping itself to deal with the diversion of water or sudden release of Brahmaputra water. The project is also seen as significant for the people of Arunachal Pradesh in terms of livelihood and employment opportunities. When the dam is completed, India's capacity to store water will increase and the risk of floods will also reduce considerably. This is China's another form of creating problems to India, which is nothing, but a different form of war on India.

Line of Actual Control (LAC)

The Line of Actual Control (LAC) is a notional demarcation line that separates Indian-Controlled territory from Chinese-controlled territory in the Sino-Indian border. The term is said to have been used by Zhou Enlai in a letter to Jawaharlal Nehru. It subsequently refers to the line formed after the 1962 Sino-Indian war, which is a part of the Sino-Indian border dispute.

There are two common ways in which the term "Line of Actual Control" is used. In the narrow sense, it refers only to the line of control in the western sector of the borderland between the Indian union territory of Ladakh and Chinese Tibet Autonomous Region. In that sense, the LAC, together with a disputed border in the east (the McMohan Line for India and a line close to the McMohan Line for China) and a small disputed section in between, forms the effective border between the two countries. In the wider sense, it is the effective border between India and the People's Republic of China (PRC).

The entire Sino-Indian border, including the western LAC, the small undisputed section in the centre, and the McMohan Line in the east is 4056 km long and traverses five Indian states/territories: Ladakh, Uttarakhand, Himachal Pradesh, Sikkim and Arunachal Pradesh. On the Chinese side, the line traverses the Tibet Autonomous Region.

Ladakh Stand-off 2020

The relationship between India and China has never been comfortable since the unprovoked attack by China in 1962. The root cause of the problem at that time was the boundary issue, but now many new issues got added over the years. The Ladakh incursion is an outcome of Beijing's ambitions and insecurities and lack of clarity on Line of Actual Control.

In the present day, China is ambitious to emerge as the number one power in the world and is involved in a bitter economic and boundary conflicts with neighbours and power struggle with the US. China feels that India is getting close to the US and is emerging as an obstacle to China's ambitious expansion plan. Hence, they must shut India down. The nexus between China and Pakistan serves their purpose and further enhances their threat to India. The Galwan clashes, the bloodiest India and China had experienced since 1975, which shows the rising ferocity of the India China engagement on the borders. Post-1962, the bloodiest clashes took place at Nathu La in 1967 in which 80 Indian soldiers died, while around 400 soldiers of Chinese were estimated to have been killed.

The Ladakh stand-off, in the Galwan Valley, is due to the skirmish was triggered by Chinese soldiers, who, after initially pulling back a little, came back to 'erect a temporary post' near patrolling point 14 (pp. 14) on the Indian side of the Galwan region along the LAC. The PLA soldiers suddenly attacked a small contingent of Indian troops led by Colonel B. Santosh Babu after they were challenged for flouting the phased disengagement agreement thrashed out by the rival Commanders of China on the ground. China has begun the hostilities, starting preparations in April 2020 itself. Hostilities began in May when India started to counter-deploy rapidly in response to China's substantial build-up at several points on the LAC.

China's immediate goal is to dominate the recently built 255 km long road by India, called Darbuk Shyok-Doulat Beg Oldie (DBO) that connects Leh to DBO at the base of Karakoram Pass. The Darbuk-Shyok-DBO road is seen as a threat to China—to the east is Aksai Chin, which India claims and China holds and north is Shaksgan Valley which was illegally ceded to China in the 1960's by Pakistan. By appropriating all of Galwan Valley, China seeks to threaten India. The stand-off between India and China is continuing since May 2020. Both the countries agreed to disengage to return pre-April 2020 positions after the 16th round of Corps Commander level talks which began on 24th January 2021. The talks went on for 16 hours according to The Hindu report published on 11th February 2021. But the problem will not go away. The Chinese will be back, because they are pushing for more than a boundary claims with India. Chinese are trying to secure the key routes of communication and trade, the flagship project of Chinese President Xi Jinping's Belt and Road Initiative (BRI).

India's Security Concern at Siliguri Corridor

Adhir Ranjan Chaudary, leader of Congress party in Lok Sabha raised the issue of threat from China in the backdrop of a Chinese naval ship being found off the Andaman coast. Mr Chaudary has also referred to Chinese incursions into Arunachal Pradesh, as the issue has also been raised by the BJP member Tapir Gao recently.[28] At this juncture, China has objected to the visit of Defence Minister Rajnath Singh saying that the Chinese government never acknowledged the northeast Indian state, which it claims to be part of south Tibet. The Indian Defence Minister visited Tawang on the occasion of 'Maitree Divas' celebrations to boost civil-military friendship in the region bordering China. The objection by China to visits by Indian government officials to Arunachal Pradesh is highly condemnable. Arunachal Pradesh is an integral and inalienable part of India, and hence Indian leaders have every right to visit the state as they do other parts of the country. The activities conducted by the Chinese in this area, along with their objections, undermine India's sovereignty and territorial integrity. It is essential for the international community to recognize and respect the established borders and the rights of nations to govern and visit all parts of their territory without external interference.

Map 5.3: Chicken Neck Corridor/Siliguri Corridor

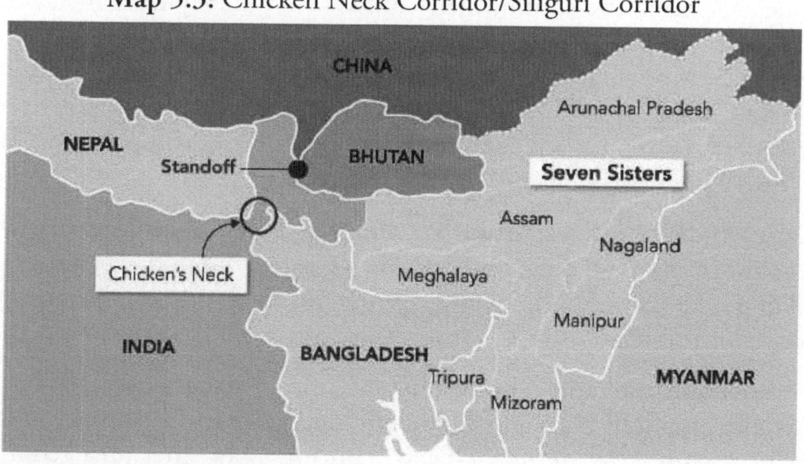

Source: www.googlemaps.com

The Siliguri corridor, a narrow passage to India's eight north-eastern (NE) states, is a perennial threat to our security. Strategically, it is the Achilles heel in the defence of almost 2000 km of borders in the northeast states with China and Myanmar. This piece of land is about 60 km in length, but a meagre 22 km in width at its narrowest point. With plain terrain not interspersed with any natural or manmade obstacle, this patch makes defence a real challenge to India. Undoubtedly, this 2000 sq km stretch of land will be the prime, strategically significant from the Indian side and an early target of the enemy during any confrontation. Therefore, naturally, the road corridor passing through this narrow corridor becomes a vital piece of ground which must be defended at all costs, failing which China wrings India's 'Chicken's Neck' –Siliguri corridor.

Hence, India had deployed the Navy's Poseidon-81 long-range maritime patrol aircraft, which is packed with weapons and sensors for anti-submarine warfare aircraft, to keep tabs on Chinese troops during the 73-day troop face-off at Doklam near the Sikkim-Bhutan-Tibet tri-junction in 2017[29]. Chief of the Defence Staff Gen Bipin Rawat had confirmed on 17th February 2020 the use of naval aircraft. The P-81 was also deployed to keep an eye on the movement of Pakistani troops after the Pulwama attack, according to Bipin Rawat, CDS. Hence, acquiring more P-81 maritime patrol aircraft is needed to identify the threat from enemies.

In 2003, India and China came to an unwritten agreement whereby China agreed to Sikkim's addition to India and gave up all claims to the state and in return, India should recognize China's sovereignty over Taiwan as China's integral part. This is known as a quid pro quo understanding. Both the countries respected the commitment and China publicly did not say Sikkim did not belong to India. Secondly, China also doesn't dispute the tripartite agreement between India-China and Sikkim border agreement. Thirdly, the then Prime Minister of India, A.B. Vajpayee and Chinese President signed an agreement to allow trade between the two countries through the 'Nathula Pass', the old trade route between Sikkim and China.

Similarly, India respected China's claim on Taiwan. However, whenever both countries have bilateral tensions, they tend to dilute their commitments on Sikkim and Taiwan. Diplomatic agreements are becoming hostages to the spirit of political relationships.

The escalation in the India-Bhutan-China tri-junction region was significantly reduced through diplomatic and military measures. However, China's attempts to seize de-facto control over the area continued, culminating in the Doklam standoff between India and China during June–

August 2017. The threat to the Siliguri corridor, also known as the 'Chicken Neck' corridor, remains perennial. China has continued its road and airstrip construction activities on its side of the border, potentially facilitating rapid mobilization and deployment of troops into Indian territory. This ongoing construction poses a strategic threat to the Siliguri Corridor. Therefore, the deployment of artillery, missiles or anti- aircrafts weaponry could easily jeopardies India's efforts to resupply the region in time of war. In view of that there is only a single railway line through the region to NE states.

India has to undertake some measures to overcome the constraints imposed by geography and improve its position in all respects with China. In this connection, widening and strengthening this corridor is essential. The first option for India is to enter into a treaty with Bangladesh permitting not only transit of military equipment during times of conflict, but also civilian traffic and trade activities. This would add a layer of strategic depth in the region and alleviate concerns about the possible severance of the north-east with the mainland. The treaty can cover multi-model transport including road and rail. With the revival of Bimstec, India's relationship with Bangladesh has seen a fillip. India and Bangladesh have already mooted a proposal to facilitate transit with India's landlocked north-east and PMs of both countries have issued Joint statements in this regard in 2010 and 2016.

The second option is to strengthen connectivity to the tri-junction area at Doklam so that our response as well as surveillance capability are augmented. The third option is to make alternative transport arrangements which are safe and secure within the country itself. The development of multi-model transport corridor through Siliguri itself can be undertaken by India. As part of this initiative, we can even build underground road tunnels which are less likely to be susceptible to air and artillery attack in a time of military conflict. This would also enhance trade and tourism in the NE region manifold during peacetime. With some of these said measures, India can look to overcome the constraints imposed by geography and face any laid of threat or troop conflict from China. Also, these measures can help in improving the position with regard to China as China set up '5' theatre commands in early 2016, "to boost offence capabilities and to establish better command control structures.

Western Theatre Command (WTC) is responsible for conflict with India and managing terrorism in western China. The WTC includes '2' 'Groupe armies' (each with 6 combined-arms brigades & 6 combat support brigades) 3 air force bases, 1 rocket force base and a whole host of other forces. China has also built 14 air bases, an extensive rail network and over 58,000 km of roads in Tibet. So, PLA can swiftly induct and sustain 30–32 divisions (each with over 12000 troops) along the LOC. However, with no Theatre command, India has 4 armies & 3 IAF commands for northern borders with China. Therefore, India has to improve its capabilities along with China, but has plans to counter the latter's expanding strategic footprint in the Indian Ocean Region, while allocating thousands of crores of Rupees towards military infrastructure development at the strategically located Andaman and Nicobar archipelago so that India can check-mate China's any misadventurism with India, either in the encirclement of India in the Indian Ocean Region or at the India-China border. India can give fitting reply and jeopardize Chinese energy supply from the Arab world at 8°Channel in the Andaman Sea.

China Slams US over Tibet Bill

The US has passed a bill with new moves from Washington marking the start of the last month of President Donald Trump in office, the Tibetan Policy and Support Act (TPSA) fuelling fresh tensions in an already fraught relationship. It is a landmark legislation that calls for the opening of a US consulate in Lhasa and undermines US banking for the Dalai Lama to determine his successor. The act stated that decisions regarding the succession of the Dalai Lama should be made by the appropriate religious authorities, aligning with the wishes of the 14th Dalai Lama. It emphasized the determinative role of these authorities and condemned interference by China in the succession process as a clear violation of the fundamental religious freedom of Tibetan Buddhists and the Tibetan people.

However, China hit out at the US for passing the TPSA bill and said it 'resolutely opposes' the adaption of the bills containing such ill contents on China issues related to Tibet, Taiwan and Hong Kong concern China's sovereignty and territorial integrity. They are Chinese affairs that do not allow foreign interference, according to a report published in The Hindu on December 23, 2020.

In contrast, the passing of the bill TPSA, which will have to be signed into law by Mr. Trump, was welcomed by the government in Exile in Dharmasala and its leader Lobsang Sangay, who described it as a momentum landmark for the Tibetan people. By passing the TPSA, Congress has sent its message loud and clear that Tibet remains a priority for the US. Lobsang Sangay termed this as a "Victory for the Tibetan Freedom Struggle" (Times of India Dt. 29/12/2020).

India, like the US, must have a clear Tibet policy to counter China in the Indian Ocean Region, as Tibet is a most sensitive issue to China. So far, India has taken r tentative steps with the US and other allies to balance China, but these have not generated any deterrence. Following the stand-off in the eastern Ladakh, including the clash in Galwan which marked the most precipitous decline in India-China bi-lateral relationship in the last 40 years, India has not been able to develop a strategy to offset Beijing's periodic coercion along the LAC. Therefore, India should also pass a bill in the Indian Parliament for the protection of a Tibetan autonomous and independent state on par with the US, to teach a lesson to the China.

India's Vibrant Village Programme

A major decision has been taken by the Modi government in Delhi on 15th February 2023, which aimed at enhancing security along the Indian-China border by granting Rs. 4800 crores for Vibrant Village Programme (VVP) for an all-round development of civilian settlements adjoining the northern land borders. The purpose of VVP is the comprehensive development of 2966 border villages spread over 19 districts and 46 border blocks of four states—Himachal Pradesh, Uttarakand, Arunachal Pradesh and Sikkim and the UT of Ladakh by 2025–26, on par with China's dual-use villages along inside LAC. China has planned to construct 628 dual-use villages along LAC. The new initiative of the Modi government will improve quality of life for residents of the identified border villages, encouraging them to stay back and reverse the outmigration trend. The permanent border settlements under the VVP scheme will benefit people through tourism, skill development and other initiatives, which will enhance border security along the LAC.

Eye on China, Indian Army Mulls Course on Tibet

India, under the leadership of PM Modi, is contemplating undertaking a rebalance of military forces and fire power to the northern borders with China amid the continuing troops' confrontation in the eastern Ladakh through Tibetology. The army is now fine-tuning a proposal for its officers to study Tibetan history, culture and language on' both sides' of the Line of Actual Control and the international boundary as part of the measures being discussed to counter the spread of influence by China.

Indian army officers are generally well-versed with Pakistan in all respects. But, a similar expertise on China and Chinese psyche is lacking. Officers who really understand China are very few in number. Tibetology fares even worse. These deficiencies need to be plugged. So, Indian army needs to assiduously build expertise in both China and Tibet in terms of linguistic, cultural and behavioural patterns. This will require language and sector specializations, with selected officers being posted for longer tenure along LAC instead of the western front with Pakistan. Of course, just two-year course will not make an officer a China expert, but definitely will read and understand their behaviour and conduct.

Chief Defence Services and Theatre Commands: Momentous Reforms in India

In a significant initiative, Prime Minister Modi created Department of military affairs and institutionalization of post of Chief of Defence Staff, which is a comprehensive reform that will help India face the ever-changing challenges of modern warfare. The Chief Defence Services (CDS) is facilitating to integrate the three services of Army, Air Force and Navy so as to enhance their capabilities through team work. The government of India has appointed Gen Bipin Rawat as Director of the CDS, who was an outstanding officer and served with great zeal. Under the leadership of Gen Bipin Rawat, India desires to establish a few Theatre Commands taking into consideration threat perception from our neighbouring countries and taking into consideration India's geo-graphical area. Till date, India has established only one Theatre Command in Andaman & Nicobar in 2001. A Theatre Command is an integration of Army, Navy, Air Force and other military assets/manpower under one operational commander in a particular geographical region.[31]

Now, the government of India intends to create and establish 5–8 theatre commands under the leadership of Modi to face the challenges from neighbouring countries. This move is indeed a welcome step to face terrorism and infiltration. With this India stood along with China and US. China re-organized its 2.3 million PLA into 5 theatre commands in early 2016. The Western Theatre command handles the entire line of actual control with India, from eastern Ladakh to Arunachal Pradesh. In a similar way, the United States of America has established 11 unified combatant commands with its Armed forces. Six geographic commands meant to handle different parts of the globe (Indo-Pacific Command covers, the entire Asia-Pacific including India); five commands as 'functional' to handle nuclear arsenal, special operations, space, cyberspace and transport/mobility. The creation of commands like these is cost-effective, saves resources and prepares forces for integrated land-air-sea-operations.

Therefore, the government of India, through the Department of Chief of Defence Services contemplating to create 5–8 Theatre Commands shortly is a significant move by PM Modi, despite the ongoing fund crunch for military modernization and despite IAF opposition on the ground that it would be operationally unwise to divide the country's "limited air assets" among different Theatre Commands. Till date, the force has just 30 fighter squadrons, when at least 42 are needed for requisite deterrence against any collusive threat from Pakistan and China. It is similar in the case of other critical platforms like AWACS—airborne warning and control systems and mid-air refueling aircraft.

In order to acquire the required extent of defence capabilities, recently India and the US has linked $3 billion worth of helicopters during Trump's visit to India on 24th February 2020, which includes 24 MH-60 Romeo helicopters for Rs. 15,157 crores and six additional 'Apache' attack choppers for Rs. 5691 crores worth. The MH-60, the multi-mission helicopter will be the most useful to plug the navy's critical operational gap in detecting, tracking and destroying enemy submarines. The $ 3 billion of advanced American military equipment including Apache and MH-60 Romeo helicopters are finest in the world, and the deal between the US and India with enhance joint defence capabilities as both the countries' military continue to train and operate side-by-side as part of expanded defence cooperation.[32]

Northern Command that will be responsible for the India-China border from the Karakoram passes to the west of Nepal and Eastern Command will guard the border from east of Nepal. There is a plan to create Jammu and Kashmir into one Theatre Command and have Punjab, Rajasthan and Gujarat that border Pakistan in another command. A peninsular command will be responsible for India's Exclusive Economic Zone (EEZ) also to be created. This will also lead to having 'seamless integration' between the navy's eastern and western commands with coordination being done by the naval headquarters in Delhi. There will also be an Air defence Command, besides ones on joint training and logistics. Some of these commands such as Air Defence will come under a particular service such as the Air Force.

A Theatre Command is a military structure wherein all the assets of the army, air force and navy in particular theatre of war are under the operational control of a three-star general. Currently, some of these areas that are planned under new theatre commands are under existing military commands.[33]

The institution of CDS carries tremendous responsibility for modernizing over military forces. It would also reflect the hopes and aspirations of 1.4 billion Indians and New India. A key mandate of the CDS will be to facilitate the re-structuring of military commands for optional utilization of resources by bridging about jointness in operations through the establishment of joint and Theatre commands. The entire world's attention is focused on the Indian Ocean Region, where our navy is increasingly expected as a net security provider. Our maritime security strategy is aimed at providing a maritime environment *i.e.* free from all forms of traditional and non-traditional threats to our national development, according to the Indian navy chief.

However, India has to enhance its budget allocation defence department substantially, as of now only 13.5% of resources from defence budget are spent on navy, which is insufficient, in view of global expectations as India being a net security provider. In the light of the government of India's proposal through chief defence, a service is planning to create theatre commands. It needs more funds to acquire assets in three services.

India allocated 4.6 lakh crore (approximately $ 66.5 billion) to defence sector—a quarter of China's allocation of $ 250 billion in 2018, according to SIPRI. In comparison, the US spent $ 649 billion, making it the highest spender on defence in the world, with a military expenditure almost equal to the next eight countries combined. There is a huge gap in the required capacity and capability of the Indian Navy, if it is to perform effectively and face the crucial tasks ahead in the Indian Ocean Region. Currently, there is a shortage of modern submarines (both conventional and nuclear), fighter planes, integral helicopters, modern weapons and sensors.

Military Gets Funds to Counter China

There is a marginal hike in the capital outlay for military modernisation in 2021–22 budget and in 2023 budget, amid troop confrontation between India and China since May 2020 in eastern Ladakh along the LAC. But, hardly any increase in the overall defence budget due to a reduction in the defence pensions. Overall defence expenditure for 2021-22 has been increased marginally to Rs. 4,78,196 crore from 4,71,378 crores, an increase of 6,818 crores only. This is the highest increase in capital outlay for defence in the last 15 years, after repeated requests for hike by several defence experts in the light of China's growing influence in the Indian Ocean Region. India had also spent an additional unbudgeted amount of Rs. 20,776 crore on emergency armed procurements last year in the face of Chinese belligerence on the northern borders. This increase in revised estimates of capital expenditure for 2021–22 shows the flurry of emergency procurements from countries like the US, France, Russia and Israel to bolster military preparedness.

The Rs. 4.78 lakh crore defence budget includes Rs. 1.15 lakh crore as pensions, which has declined from the Rs. 1.33 lakh crore allocation in the last year. Overall, the defence expenditure works out to just 1.63 per cent of the projected GDP for 2021–22. Military experts have been demanding an allocation of over 2.5% out of India's GDP for the defence sector in view of the collusive threat from China-Pakistan in the mind. In spite of the requirements India's defence budget for 2023–2024 amounted to Rs. 5.9 lakh crore, which is 72.6 bn only.

India's New Project to Tackle Maritime Threats

The Government of India has approved a major National Maritime Domain Awareness (NMDA) project even as the Indian Navy keeps an eagle eye on the expanding Chinese naval activities in the Indian Ocean Region, while cranking up cooperation with littoral nations in the neighborhood. According to the Indian Navy chief, the long-standing plan for a third aircraft carrier of a much larger size has been, 'put on hold', with the force now examining whether to go in for a "repeat order" of the recently commissioned 45,000ton INS Vikrant which is in the future. The NMDA project will provide actionable intelligence for tackling Maritime threats in the Indian Ocean Region.

The Rs. 250 crore NMDA project, which was recently cleared by the Prime Minister-led Cabinet Committee on Security will be an integrated intelligence grid that can detect and thwart threats emanating from the sea in real-time. The NMDA project will subsume the naval Information Management and Analysis Centre (IMAC) which located at Gurgaon and, in turn takes feeds from multiple sources ranging from coastal radars to satellites to assess threats in the IOR.

Together with the Information Fusion Centre-Indian Ocean Region (IFC-IOR), a collaborative naval venture with like-minded nations that has currently 11 foreign Liaison Officers, the NMDA will bolster India's overall Maritime Security. The threat from China, of course, is clear and present in the IOR. China is also fast building two more aircraft carriers. There are a lot of Chinese ships operating in the Indian Ocean Region. As a resident Maritime Power, India needs to keep a close watch on them, as the Indian Navy's job is to ensure India's Maritime interests are protected.

Conclusion

India and China will remain strategic rivals due to their competing energy and security interests in the Indian Ocean Region. By logic and extension, India will need to improve its maritime infrastructure and upgrade its naval capabilities. Mere drum beating under the Act East Policy will not be enough to deliver the goods since India is facing with divergent maritime threats and challenges of a vast scale, magnitude and intensity to its maritime borders. It can't protect those maritime borders and ensure its energy security without the cooperation of and intelligence sharing with, regional partners. However, cooperative security mechanisms cannot be developed unless there is the convergence of perceptions on common regional security interests among regional and extra-regional powers.

The time has come for India to build sturdy and stable partnerships with other liberal democratic states particularly, the US, Japan and Australia. At the same time, it must be kept in mind that any partnership is not exclusively directed against China, for the latter is already a global power with a global reach in every domain. It would thus be a chimera to contain China, rather, China needs to be more fully coopted into the evolving global and regional security architecture. Achieving that will better serve the common interests of all states including China in a cooperative security mechanism. More importantly, India needs to shed off the dominant dependent psyche that it suffers from. It must treat its South Asian neighbours on an oral footing with due respect to each partner in a cooperative security order. The fact is that India is still perceived as a regional hegemony. Unless this perception is reversed through policy behavior and action, India will not be able to seek the strategic cooperation of its neighbours to balance China's increasing strategic influence in the Indian Ocean Region.

Notes and References

[1] Khurshid, Salman, http://www.thehindu.com/opinion/op-ed/puttion-out-to-sea-a-new-vision

[2] Mishra, Sylia, India's Maritime security: Strategy, Choices and Imperatives; India writes, December 1 2004, at http://www.indiawrites.org/diplomacy/india's-maritime.security-strategy-choices-and-imperatives

[3] Mahan, Alfred Thayer, the influence of sea power upon history 1660–1783.

[4] President Xi gives speech to Indonesia's parliament', China Daily, October 2, 2013.

[5] NSA Level Meeting on Trilateral maritime security cooperation between India, Sri Lanka and Maldives, Ministry of external Affairs, March 6, 2014.

[6] 'India to supply naval vessels to Vietnam', wall street journal, October 28, 2014.

[7] Mohan C. Raja, 'Lanka pit-stop', Indian Express, November 5, 2014, available at http://indianexpress.com/article/opinion/columns/chinese-takeaway-lankapit-stop

[8] 'India consumed about Chinese subs at Sri Lankan port', voice of America, November 5, 2014.

[9] Mukherjee, Ambassador Bhaswati, "International Recognition of India world Heritage; New Exciting Projects on the Anvil", Ministry of External Affairs July 10, 2014.

[10] 'From outpost to springboard', the Economist, September 13, 2014, available at http://www.economist.com/news/asia/21617000-india-eyes-startegic-oppor tunity-bay-bengal-outpost-springboard

[11] 'India-US Joint Military Exercise Begins', Times of India, October 4, 2002.

[12] 'Green, Michael J. and Shearer, Andrew, defining US Indian Ocean Strategy', centre for strategic and international studies, March 19, 2012.

[13] Ibid.

[14] Jayaprakash, N.D. (2005). India and Asian Leadership, The Diplomat, http://www.thediplomat.com/2015/05/india-and-asian-leadership

[15] Ankit, Panda (2015). ASEAN-India and East Asian Summits: India's oppurtunities to 'Act East', the Diplomat, November 21, 2015.

[16] What's in SCO for India, 29 May 2017, http://www.rediff.com/news/column/whats-in-sco-for-india/20170529.htm

[17] For details visit official website of Indian Ocean Region Association (IORA) at http://www.iora.net

[18] Jayachandra, Reddy, India's multilateral engagement: opportunities and challenges, p. 8&9, 2017, ISBN 978-81-926904-9-0

[19] Mohammed Khalid, Somalia and its law-less Coast: India's growing security Responsibility in the Indian Ocean; *Journal of Indian Ocean Studies,* Vol. 18, No. 1, April 2010, p. 67–80.

[20] Rao, S.V. Seshagiri, India's Ocean neighbourhood—Narendra Modi's strategy initiatives, 2 November, 2018.

[21] India to have its own model of Theatre Commands: CDS Rawat, Times of India, dt. 2/1/2020.

[22] Sundaran, Shankari, 'India extends Malacca Strait Reach', Asia Times, 8 August 2012.

[23] Times of India, dt 7 December 2019.

[24] China seeking to expand military reach, warm's US; Times of India dt. 4 May 2019.

[25] China-Wary govt clears plan for 56 ships, 6 subs, Times of India, dt 4th December 2018.

[26] Eye on China, South gets 1st Sukhoi squad with Brahmos, Times of India; 20 January 2020.

[27] Times of India, 20 November 2019.

[28] Times of India, 16 November 2019.

[29] Air Defence Command within a year, Times of India, 18th February 2020.

[30] India to have its own model of Theatre Commands: CDS Rawat, Times of India, dt. 2/1/2020.

[31] Ibid.

[32] The Economic Times, 5th February 2020, works on Theatre Commands to begin Next Year.

[33] $ 3 bn defence deal done, sharing of advanced satellite data nest, Times of India, 26th February 2020.

CHAPTER VI

Suggestions and Policy Recommendations

The following are the suggestions and policy Recommendations:

1. India badly needs to undertake major reforms in the army to face the challenges from China and to protect any threats from it both the 3,480 km border and the Indian Ocean Region. The present capabilities of India are not sufficient for modern warfare. The last military reform was planned in the late 1970s and were executed in the 80s and the Indian army today still based on those reforms.
2. In order to face wars in the future, the army would be based on high technology. So, a strategic review is the need of the hour and it should be done by the government. The national security strategy and defence planning is the government's responsibility, which requires and it should come from the Indian government. But, India's defence budget has decreased to the lowest in the last 58 years from 18.5 per cent to 13.5 per cent in 2019–20. With these reduced allocations, building military power in the long run is difficult, making it challenging for India to counter threats from China.

   India should have long-run planning and strategic intent taking into cognizant of contemporary situations. However, India appears to have an ad-hoc attitude towards defence planning, and that to reactionary responding to threats as and when they arise. Hence, keeping in view of the collusive threats from China and Pakistan India should initiate steps to undertake reforms in the defence sector by allocating enough funds for modernisation and for up-gradation of Indian army.
3. To counter the Chinese increasing presence in the Indian Ocean Region, India should concentrate on the military up-gradation of its Island territories in the airstrip at INS Kohassu Shibpur in the north Andamans and the Compbell strip at Nicobar has to up-grade into a full-fledged fighter base. Also, the airstrip at Agatti in Lakshadweep will be upgraded for military operations to secure both the Bay of Bengal up to Malacca and the Arabia Sea up to the Gulf of Aden. The two Island territories will be useful like the new aircraft carriers for India extending the Navy's reach in the region, which is far from the mainland and both the islands are on the busiest sea lanes of the world with more than half of the world trade going through this route. China is seriously working

out to bypass the Malacca Strait through Thai Canal (also known as Kra Canal) that would connect the Gulf of Thailand with the Andaman Sea to solve its Malacca problem anticipating India's threat in the Andaman Sea.

4. India has to think seriously about building a military on fast track for basing additional military forces in the strategically located Andaman & Nicobar archipelago, along with the requisite development of infrastructure as an effective counter to China's expanding strategic presence in the Indian Ocean Region. Many of the Indian navy officers felt that the Andaman Archipelago, remains at risk from People's Liberation Army, as surveillance established by China and the Chinese navy has been very active in the region, as most Chinese vessels including submarines have lurked close to India's territorial waters.

   As the Andaman & Nicobar Islands [ANC] was only one Theatre Command with land, sea, and air force under one operational Commander which has long suffered from general apathy, funds crunch and lack of environmental clearance in order to build infrastructure. Hence, the ANC needs military build-up to counter growing Chinese influence quickly. In India out of the $ 66 billion allocation to defence sector 25 per cent of the funds going to pay Pensions to defence personnel who served in the past. The 2/3rd of the budget goes for day-to-day running costs, such as salaries and for maintaining almost 15 lakhs of strong armed forces. So, this leaves only 1/4th of the funds available for military modernisation and purchasing new weapons.

   According to a report by Pentagon to the US Congress very recently in September 2020, China is actively looking at setting up military logistics facilities in Myanmar, Thailand, Singapore, Indonesia, Pakistan, Sri Lanka, UAE, Kenya, Seychelles, Tanzania, Angola and Tajikistan. China with an overall force of around 350 warships and submarines, including over 130 'major surface combatants', China even overtaken The US Navy's force level of 293 warships according to the Pentagon report. In this connection the US warned India it also needs to worry about the fast-emerging collusive China-Pakistan threat in the Indian Ocean Region, with Beijing set to supply eight Yaan-class diesel electrical submarines, 4-type-054 multi-role stealth frigates and other naval platforms and weapons, those may use Pakistan against India in the Indian Ocean Region.

   India has a huge advantage in the IOR due to the tyranny of logistics faced by China, and can if required exploit its 'Malacca Dilemma'. But the Indian Navy force level of having only one aircraft carrier, 10 destroyers,14 frigates, 11 corvettes, and as well as 15 diesel-electric and two nuclear power submarines in terms of major combatants at present disposal of India, which is not sufficient to counter China.

5. India urgently has to go for a third aircraft carrier on an immediate basis, as the Indian economy goal is to grow towards $ 5 trillion target. The third aircraft carrier is absolutely necessary, any air power is critically required an immediate priority to protect its strategic interests in the Indian Ocean Region from growing Chinese presence. India needs a third aircraft carrier with 'reach and substances'. Presently, India has only one aircraft carrier in the 44,000-tonne INS Vikramaditya, while the long-delayed indigenous carrier 40,000-tonne INS Vikrant may be ready for commissioning end of next year, 2021.In the given situation where China's growing influence in the IOR, a third aircraft is seriously necessary to replace readily in the Indian Ocean Region.
6. Though, India keeping an eye on China and its aggressions both at borders and in the Indian Ocean, the virtual allocation exclusively made Rs 5650 crores to the military infrastructure development plan to spend in 10 years by Modi government is also insufficient for the strategically located Andaman & Nicobar archipelago which, unable to stationing of additional warships, aircraft, drones, Millet batteries and infantry soldiers in the backdrop of China's rapidly expanding footprints in the Indian Ocean Region. Therefore, the Indian defence sector badly needs higher allocations to bring some reforms in the army and to implement new technology and modernisation of equipment to face the challenges. To counter Beijing's moves requires India to prepare for a long multi-dimensional contest. For instance, Beijing is building advanced naval warships for Pakistan, which will surely use them against India and to counter India. Therefore, India needs to be smart and coordinate with like-minded countries that are equally concerned about China's belligerence.
7. India should allocate more funds to create infrastructure and Roads along the border to reach the Indian Army at the earliest possible to give a fitting reply to Chinese soldiers. However, after Modi came to power substantial amounts of funds were given to the Border Road Organisation (BRO) for the construction of Roads and Infrastructure, which is not sufficient in the light of China's recent aggression in the Galwan Valley.

   China immediate goal is to dominate the recently built 255 km long DBO road by India that connects Leh to DBO at the base of Karakoram Pass. The Darbuk-Shyok-DBO road is seen as a threat to China's game plan, as this road gives India greater ability to protect itself in inhospitable terrain and also, gives India connectivity to China's restive Xinjiang Province with an actual physical link. Therefore, India will be continuously pushed by China in this sector in future also, as it wants to appropriate all of the Galwan Valley to threaten this Darbuk-Shyok-DBO road. So, India should go ahead DBO road which spoils China's game plan.

8. India should consolidate its position among the small Islands of the Indian Ocean Region, which includes Sri Lanka, the Maldives, Mauritius, and Seychelles, extending to other countries like Madagascar, Comoros and the French Reunion in the Western Indian Ocean, a region where China continuously expanding its presence both economically and militarily, as China emerging as a major player in the region, which it considers as its bridge to Africa. India also needs to concentrate on this region by adopting bilateral engagements and supporting the small Island nations in all respects.
9. India should recognise every island in the neighbourhood is as important as a large nation from the strategic point of view, as the Cuban island example, irrespective of those island nations, lie close to the strategic sea lanes or are close to the mainland, have its own important strategic and commercial significance. India only confined its relationships with a few larger nations of the Oceania Region like, Australia, New Zealand, Fiji, and Papua New Guinea, leaving several small island nations of this region, as the region consists of 14 countries and 19 island nations are external dependencies and internal dependencies islands are 8. In the Indian foreign policy and strategic discourse island nations have found a special reference. Narendra Modi after becoming Prime Minister gave more importance to the small island nations in the Indian Ocean Region. From today onwards India should extend relationships with the entire Oceanic Region, as this region has huge natural resources, apart from this, the region has a large number of UN members that will help in fulfilling India's aspirations for permanent membership in the Security Council of the UN General Assembly.
10. The root cause of the problem for the border tensions between India and China is the LAC has not been jointly demarcated by India and China and there is no consensus on where it lies. In some parts of this mountainous geography, each side's perception of the LAC is different from the others and hence, there are pockets where these perceptions overlap.
11. It is exactly these pockets in which close proximity situations occur, where troops come face to face each other, because each side believes

that it is merely patrolling up to the LAC and that the other side has transgressed it. Poor map-making by the British was also the reason for this trouble in the border as there is no agreed border. Despite the name, in practice the Line of Actual Control has functioned more like a frontier—a vague zone liable to shift depending on the ability to occupy and control it. China has taken advantage of that continued lack of clarity in the demarcation of borders, therefore, the absence of an accepted border is largely the fault of the British Empire. Despite McMahon Line there is no agreed border between India and China, as the line is the demarcation line between Tibet and the northeast region of India proposed by British colonial administrator Sir Henry McMahon at Simla Convention in 1914 signed between British and Tibetan representatives. It is currently the generally recognised boundary between China and India, although its legal status is disputed by the Chinese government. India regards its interpretation of the McMahon Line as a legal national border, but China rejected the Simla Accord and the McMahon Line, contending that Tibet was not a Sovereign State and therefore, did not have the power to conclude treaties. China does recognise a Line of Actual Control which closely approximates most of the McMahon Line in the eastern parts of its border with India, according to a 1959 'diplomatic note' by Prime Minister of China Zhou Enlai to the then Indian Prime Minister Nehru. Therefore, India should focus on the demarcation of the border with China to avoid periodical aggressions, incursions, and face-off by China. Towards this, India sought the help of world bodies to settle the border issue permanently.

12. According to IANS (Indo-Asian News Service) C-Voter poll survey conducted recently, 73.7 per cent of Indians want Tibet's status as buffer-zone to be restored to pre-1959 status to prevent conflicts with China along the China-India border. With anti-China emotions running high in India after China's recent aggressions in the Galwan Valley at eastern Ladakh more people are willing to back Tibet and its cause, which requires a clear understanding of the ground situation and more people need to be educated about India's historic ties with Tibet.
13. India should raise the Tibet issue in bilateral talks with China amid the Sino-Indian stand-off in eastern Ladakh as well as in the international forums, more specifically in the UNO. Tibet has always acted as a buffer zone between the two of the most populated countries in the world until China occupied Tibet in 1959. Tibet has been become one of the factors for tension between China and India after the occupation of Tibet by China and India paid a huge price for it, as there were aggressions/face-offs and stand-offs by China along the Indian border

more than 16 times since 1962, due to there was no properly demarcated border between India and China. And since last two decades, China launched and developed its 'Great Western Development Initiative' in Tibet, whereby created a huge infrastructure including roads for dual purposes for civilian welfare and more for building a robust civil-military infrastructure. Today in Tibet China has built more than a lakh km of highways, particularly near Tibet's' Nagari' Prefecture' which borders India, Nepal and Xinjiang has seen a massive expansion of road network in the last few years. The recent Galwan military face-off in eastern Ladakh was an instance, as China used these roads to indicate how 'easy it has became for China for its incursions. To check-mate China in the border, not to repeat any further incursions India should raise the Tibet issue and see that Tibet get Independent and Autonomous.

14. India should also pass a bill in the Parliament in support of Tibetans on par with the USA, which has upped the ante against China, legislating new policy aimed at challenging Beijing's efforts—acquiesced for years by Washington to bully Tibet and Taiwan into submission. The US President Donald Trump in the last fag of his tenure signed into law regarding the Tibet Policy and Support Act (TPSA), which bolsters support for the autonomous conduct of Tibetan affairs and calls for establishment of a US consulate in Lhasa, and also the Taiwan Assurance Act (TAA) which strengthens military ties with Taiwan. So, similarly India also should pass a bill in support of Tibetan autonomy to conduct their religious affairs independently without interference from China.
15. China trying to limit India not to rise hegemony in its neighbourhood and Asia under PM Modi's strong leadership, hence willfully again and again creating problems in the borders while incursion into Indian territory and claiming India's territory based on the so-called historical basis from eastern Ladakh to Arunachal Pradesh to divert India's attention from growth trajectory which led to diverting India's funds earmarked for development purpose in general and in particular to Army. India has spent an additional unbudgeted amount of Rs. 20,776 crores on emergency arms procurement in the last year, 2020–21 to face China's belligerence on the northern borders from countries like the US, France, Russia and Israel to bolster military readiness.
16. India should invoke United Nations [UN] to intervene and see that China vacate Tibet. The history of Tibet shows that it had never been a part of China and Chinese government and was an independent State with its own spiritual rule. After China gained freedom in 1949, under the People's Republic of China, the People's Liberation Army crossed

into Tibet and after defeating a small Tibetan army occupied half of the country and imposed the so-called 17-point agreement for the peaceful liberation of Tibet in May 1951. Because it was signed under duress, the agreement lacked validity under international law of the land. The presence of 40,000 Chinese troops in Tibet, the threat of an immediate occupation of Lhasa and the prospect of total obliteration of the Tibetan state left Tibetan's little choice.

In view of the above, United Nation's must take action against China to vacate Tibet and let them have a peaceful spiritual Tibetan monarchy. Tibet never had any boundary problems with India, China, and Nepal, Bhutan or any adjoining countries. China which had no boundary with most of these countries is now trying to create boundary problems through Tibet and unnecessarily creating tension with not only India but with most of the countries in the South China Sea. Therefore, India should see that The UN must intervene in such a way that China withdraws its troops from Tibet, as China should not be allowed to make Tibet as its military base to deal.

17. India should win not just Galwan but India needs to overcome 5-more areas too. China is the 2nd largest economy today and proclaims itself a superpower. But just 40 years ago it was almost equal level with India in terms of several parameters, such as GDP, per capita income, life expectation, transport including railways etc., and other economic social indicators. The 'Deng' reforms of the 1980s helped China's surge past on almost all economic and social indicators, but it is not too late for India to show that we can also do better under the Modi government Atmanirbhar policy of self-reliance. India certainly has the capabilities, numbers, resources and willpower to overcome in 5-areas within a few years with sustained effort, as mentioned below:

    (a) In 1980, China's GDP was just $191 billion, a shade ahead of India's GDP of $186 billion and China's per capita income was $195 and India's was $ 267 per person due to huge population in China its per capita income was less than India. By 2018, its per capita income had grown 50 times to $ 9771, while India's had grown moderately to just over $ 2000. As far as GDP is concerned, China has touched $ 13.6 trillion, but whereas India's GDP grown to just about $ 3 trillion. China's bigger success lies in taming poverty from 66 per cent of its population to only o.5 per cent, whereas India's poverty level's reduced from 49% to about 20 per cent

    (b) India has slipped behind China both in Education and in Urbanisation. At present 60 per cent of Chinese lives in cities, while

Indians living about only 35%. Around the time when both countries got freedom, only 12% of Chinese lived in cities and Indians with 17 per cent. In the case of literacy, China had the advantage of literacy even in the 80's. 2/3rd of China's population was literate as against 2/5th of Indians. Since then, literacy has increased faster in India to touch 74%, but China's head start has taken it to 97% of the population.

(c) As far as industrial sector is concerned, India had more industrial centres than China at the time of independence, but today, China is the factory of the world. Data from the International Organisation of Motor Vehicle Manufacturers reveals that in the year 2019, India made 36.2 lakh cars, whereas China had produced 2.10 crores of cars.

(d) India had a very high infant mortality rate [IMR], of 1000 babies born 145 died. China's IMR was 48 at that time. Since then, India has sharply reduced its IMR to 30 with investment in institutional deliveries and maternal health, but China's prosperity has enabled it to reduce its IMR to 07 only, which is at the level of advanced countries like the US that had an IMR of 5.6 in 2018. China's prosperity is also reflected in its higher life expectancy of 77.6 years, as against India's 69.2 years, which means an average Chinese lives 7 years more than the average.

(e) Transport an area where the Chinese have made serious progress. In 1974 their planes flew only 0.7 million passengers when compared with 3 million on Indian planes. Now, Chinese carry by roughly four times more than Indian's. In 2018, the number was 611.4 million for China and 164 million for India. The Chinese were also behind India in term's rail network. In 1980's India's network was 61,240 km to China's 51,700 km. By 2018, India's network had grown to 68,442 km, while China's had more than doubled to 1.27 lakh km.

India needs to overcome the above said areas shortly under PM Modi leadership with Atmanirbhar initiation and emerge as self-reliant, by which India will face and counter China in the Indian Ocean Region with the help of likeminded countries in the region who are opposing China's hegemony. Towards this, inking military pacts with its neighbourhood in the region to enhance its strategic reach to counter China's expanding footprints in the IOR and beyond.

Recently, in the first week of September 2020 India and Japan inked a military pact, with this, Japan has now become the sixth country after the US, France, Australia, South Korea and Singapore, with which India had such an agreement to enable military forces to share logistics to support each other's warships and aircraft. In an another development, the US and Maldives signed defence agreement in the same month of September 2020 amid China's growing presence in the Indian Ocean Region to support maintaining peace and security in the strategic Indian Ocean is a welcome step forward which can check-mate China in the IOR.

18. India should raise the Chinese vulnerable issues like, China's 'One China Policy' at every forum and at every opportunity to give a fitting reply to China. As China condones and protects Pakistan's State sponsorship of terrorism in J&K. For India to remain ambivalent on the one-China policy is no longer tenable. If the government of India wants to safeguard India's national security and national interest in the long run, the PM must bite the bullet on both Tibet and Taiwan issues. Tibet is China's second most sensitive issue and the Taiwan is the first sensitive issue. China has managed India into silence over the One-China Policy which accepts Taiwan as an inseparable part of China. Does China reciprocate by accepting the One-Indian Policy including POK and China-occupied Aksai Chin? Now, India needs urgently to increase trade with Taiwan and maintain relations including that of diplomatic and drop its 60-year-old policy of appeasing China.
19. Similarly, the Xinjiang issue is also vulnerable to China. So that India should utilise the situation by involving directly or indirectly to create headache to China. The Xinjiang conflict more popularly known as the Uyghur-Chinese conflict—is a conflict in China's north-west autonomous region of Xinjiang centered on the Uyghurs—a Turkic minority ethnic group, is the largest group in the region facing suffering and harassment from the Chinese.

    In the 18th Century, the area was conquered by the Chinese Qing dynasty. In 1884, after the Dungan Revolt [1862–77], the area was renamed as Xinjiang. It is now a part of the People's Republic of China, despite resistance from the local population. Xinjiang since 1949 has been part of the PRC, following the Chinese civil war. In 1955 Xinjiang was turned into an autonomous region from a province. Xinjiang borders the countries of Mongolia, Russia, Kazakhstan, Kyrghyzstan, Afghanistan, Pakistan and India, also borders Tibet Autonomous Region.

    Though the conflict is traced in 1931, factors such as the massive state sponsored migration of Han. Chinese from the 1950s to the 1970s, government policies promoting Chinese cultural unity and punishing certain expressions have contributed to tension between Uyghur's and state police and Han Chinese. In view of this, India should consider interfering in the Xinjiang conflict in support of one sect, mostly Uyghur, the largest minority ethnic against Chinese, in the light of the tension along the border. India should re-strategies and use Tibet, Taiwan, Xinjiang and Hong Kong' cards' as retaliation against China's growing belligerence, as China is more sensitive and vulnerable to the issues of Taiwan, Tibet, Xinjiang, so that India can create trouble for China and to disturb China.

20. India should send a tough message to China while avoiding the risk of war for which it may be ill-prepared at this movement of post-pandemic corona virus. Therefore, India declared a formal ban on 'Huawei' providing 5th generation equipment [5G] and its services in India, which poses a serious threat to India's digital security. The UK and the US have already shut out the company over similar concerns. India's ban on 5G will have a cascading effect hurting Chinese plans for erecting the 'Digital Silk Road', to fortify its Belt and Road Initiative.
21. India needs to strengthen Cyber Security, because the Coronavirus Pandemic has pushed many sectors through unprecedented digital transformation. For this, International Collaboration is necessary and urgent to share intelligence with the like-minded countries to neutralize cyber-attacks. The Chinese armed forces are as prepared in cyber warfare as they are fighting in pitched battles on the ground. But the Indian government is grappling with after the Galwan Valley clash last year, as the Chinese hackers had attacked India's power grid immediately after the Galwan clash which shows the nature of war has changed. Recently, the Telangana State government in India and some other states were alerted by Central Agency in the first week of March 2021. After that the Telangana government removed all malware in 40 Sub-Stations in SLDC and strengthened firewall. So, there is a need to ward off Chinese Cyber-attacks from foreign countries, especially, from China and Pakistan in view of the coronavirus-induced Lock-down with measures to ensure safety and work from home. In this connection robust Cyber security mechanisms are imperative for the effective implementation of the Digital India program.
22. India under the leadership of Prime Minister Modi should stop China's expansionism designs in the region not only in borders but also in oceans, particularly in the South China Sea. 31% of China's land was occupied by neighboring countries/Regions/provinces. China has forcefully occupied Xinjiang in 1949. The Xinjiang Uyghur Autonomous Region has an area of 1.66 million. sq. km. that is equal to 17.68% of the total of China, i.e. 93,88,210 sq. km as per the World Bank

Databank. China had also forcefully occupied Tibet land in 1950. The Tibet Autonomous Region [TAR] has an area of 1.22 million sq. km, that is 13% of the total area of China. That makes up a total of 31%, of the present China's geography. China also occupied two pieces of Indian territories, it includes Aksai Chin, a 38,000 sq. km border area in Ladakh that China occupied in 1962 India-China war, while Pakistan ceded to China 5,180 sq. km of occupied Indian territory in 1963, under Sino-Pakistan Boundary agreement. It clearly shows that about the expansionist designs of Chinese government. China is currently involved in territorial disputes with over 20 countries including, India, Nepal, Bhutan etc., apart from in the South China Sea.

23. India needs to utilize the opportunities of the new construction of the Indo-Pacific doctrine to balance and to counter China in the Indian Ocean Region. The US-led Indo-Pacific a 24 countries framework aimed to free, open navigation in the region. China is not on the list of Indo-Pacific countries, as China's behavior with its neighborhood countries, especially with India in the Indian Ocean Region for its increasing influence and amid China's aggressiveness in the Eastern Ladakh along the Sino-Indian border. In view of this background, India should utilize the opportunity arising from the Indo-Pacific framework to check-mate China.
24. India needs to take steps to counter China's capabilities to launch devastating cyber-attacks through risk mitigation strategies, building firewall and recovery systems by integrating cyber security resources of the Army, Navy and IAF. Though India is working on 'offensive' cyber capabilities, the fact is that India is way behind China in this domain of warfare as of now. As India knows China is capable of launching cyber-attacks on us that can disturb a large number of our systems.
25. India's Arctic policy must address double standards of rich countries. The Arctic is essentially for the stability of the earth's climate. The Arctic is warming more rapidly than global average and its ice decreased dramatically since the late 1970s. India is an observer state at the Arctic Council and has recently released its draft Arctic policy, which terms the Arctic as a common heritage of mankind and calls for sustainable responsible and transparent human activity. The world's wealthiest people living in the already wealthy Arctic states, will gain the most by exploiting the resources, however, the cost will be borne by the world's poorest, living in the coastal areas of the global south. China's major stake in Russia's Yamal Liquefied Natural gas project which is expected to supply China 4 million tonnes of LNG a year. India will not gain

economically but is likely to lose massively due to coastal flooding, monsoon disruptions and changes in the ecosystems.

26. There is a need to create an extended bloc to safeguard the interests of countries in the Indo-Pacific, against China's belligerence which spoiling the stability and freedom of navigation in the region. Towards this Quad plus countries should be involved in the group like France etc. Recently, the European Union a 27-member countries bloc declared their firm interest to step up its influence in the Indo-Pacific region to counter China's growing power in the Indo-Pacific region is an important development especially from Indian point of view. The 27-member bloc considering that EU is going to reinforce its strategic focus, presence, and actions in the Indo-Pacific region based on the rule of law. So, the decision of the EU will certainly be useful in responding to the challenges posed by China from time to time to international security, maritime security, freedom of navigation and its aggression into its neighbors along the borders which China shares, like recently in Ladakh in the Indian border. Therefore, India should initiate efforts to coordinate among multilateral groups of Quad, Indo-Pacific and now with 27-member countries bloc to counter China in the Indian Ocean, and Indo-Pacific Region, which includes the South China Sea.

Conclusion

The Andaman Nicobar Islands [ANI] is a huge force multiplier for India due to its geographic location as it connects with South Asia and with Southeast Asia. The Northernmost point of the Island Chain is nearly 22 nautical miles from Myanmar, while the southernmost point is only 90 nautical miles away from Indonesia. All vessels passing through the Strait of Malacca must pass through the 6 Degree Channel located to the south of the Andaman Nicobar Islands. India has started militarising its greatest geopolitical asset. With this development, the world at large wondering what makes India emerge so powerful as a centre of the Indo-Pacific and why it is being billed as an alternative to China. The answer lies in the Andaman Nicobar Islands—an archipelago located at the juncture of the Bay of Bengal and the Andaman Sea. Running in a North-South configuration, the archipelago is situated north-west of the Strait of Malacca giving India the option of single handily blocking Malacca's western point so that India can block Chinese ships and save its Himalayas and protect border along the Line of Actual Control from Eastern Ladakh to Arunachal Pradesh. Therefore, the ANI needs further budgetary provisions to face and counter China in the Indian Ocean Region.

CHAPTER VII

Executive Summary and Conclusions

This chapter is an attempt to summarise the study of the project report and analyse the emerging geo-strategic environment of the Indian Ocean Region with reference to complex interactions between three key players in the Region, India, China and the United States of America. As China dominates Eurasia physically, India bisects Indian Ocean. It was Sardar K.M. Panikkar, who way back in 1945, was one of the Indian analysts to highlight the geo-strategic importance of the Indian Ocean for India.

According to Panikkar, India's peninsular geography, characterised by an extensive and open coastline and a fertile, resource-rich littoral has historically made the country heavily reliant on the Indian Ocean. This reliance is due to the fact that a significant portion of India's vast trade has traditionally been conducted via this maritime route, connecting it to global markets throughout history.

Pannikar had also cautioned India against a resurgent China trying to establish its dominance in the Indian Ocean and against the US, which guided by its long-term economic and strategic concerns would inevitably attempt to enter these waters as a major naval power in the future. In fact, much of Pannikar's dire predictions regarding the geo-strategic importance of the Indian Ocean vis-a-vis the key stakeholders in the region [India China and the US] seems to be translating into reality in the present century. The imperative of India safeguarding the Indian Ocean Region emerges from its extensive coastline of over 7516 km, an Exclusive Economic Zone [EEZ] of 2.172 million sq. km. and a continental shelf of more than 1 million sq.km beyond the EEZ. In view of these considerations, the modern vision of the country's responsible power profile in the Indian Ocean was outlined by the Indian Naval Doctrine in 2004 and modified subsequently in 2009, which constitutes an important edifice of India's Look East policy and the present 'Act East' policy under Prime Minister Modi's vision.

Geography of the Indian Ocean

Geographically, the Indian Ocean is the world's third largest Ocean and it has an area of 26,469,900 sq. miles. It spans the coasts of India, Pakistan,

Iran, the Arabian Peninsula and Antarctica, East Africa, Australia, certain Islands of Indonesia, the Malay Peninsula and Antarctica. This region contains 25 per cent of the world's landmass, 40 per cent of the world's oil and gas reserves and 30 per cent world's trade. It constitutes between a quarter and a third of the world's population, which makes it a massive market. The Indian Ocean is rich in strategic and precious minerals and metals and other natural resources ranging from food, fisheries to raw materials and energy for industry. It has abundant agricultural wealth in terms of the variety and mass of arable land and has significant human resources and technological capabilities. Many countries of the RIM are becoming globally competitive and are developing new capacities, which can be jointly harnessed through the Ocean. They have carved out many strategic island locations, viz., St. Paul. Rodrignez, Chagos Island group, Seychelles, Mauritius, Reunion, Christmas Island, Cocos, Prince Edward islands and so on. Indian Ocean is also the locus of important international Sea Lanes of Communications [SLOC]. Also, significant is the location of maritime chock points in the ocean. These include the Suez Canal, Bab-el Mandab and the Strait of Hormuz in the north-west, Mozambique Channel in the south-west, and Malacca Strait, Sunda Strait and Lombok Strait is the south-east of the ocean. These chock-points typically have the potential to to control the entry and exit of the flow of maritime traffic in the Indian Ocean.

Indian Ocean Region: Sino-Indian Rivalry

The geo-strategic significance of the Indian Ocean region has been the principal factor responsible for transforming it into an arena of rivalry. Beijing's attempts at expanding its footprints in the region have been borne out by the increasing frequency of anti-piracy deployments, naval exercises and the growing investment in maritime infrastructure projects including docking of two Chinese naval vessels at Colombo South Container terminal, a deep-water facility built controlled and built by Chinese company, succeeded by the docking of a Chinese submarine at Colombo, have strengthened Indian concerns that the PLAN assets are being allowed privileged access to Sri Lankan ports funded by Chinese investments. The issue has received greater attention since November 2014, when reports came about China's plan to construct 18 strategic overseas bases in the Indian Ocean Region, stretching from the Seychelles through Pakistan to Djibouti. In this background, the rationale behind China's Maritime Silk Route, an umbrella term referring to maritime infrastructure projects in the Indo-Pacific region may be viewed seriously as a supplement to the 'String of Pearls' strategy aimed at encircling India and challenging the Indian Navy's role and stature in the region.

In addition to these hard power calculations, both India and China are dependent on energy resources transported through the Indian Ocean sea lanes, accounting for approximately 80 and 84 per cent of their energy imports respectively. Over the period of last 20 years, the number of oil tankers navigating these waterways is projected to increase three-fold. Therefore, the Indian Ocean Region has gained importance in the context of Sino-Indian rivalry, primarily over energy resources, strategic facilities and the competitive degree of naval deployment as both the countries have embarked on their' blue water' naval status. India has been working hard to evolve from 'brown water' guarding its coastlines to enhance its maritime domain of interest and outreach for forging pragmatic naval cooperation linkages with regional maritime neighbours is a priority. The strategy outlined in the Maritime Doctrine of 2004 and its revised version in 2009 highlights various ways in which the Indian Navy could serve as a catalyst for peace, security, and stability in the Indian Ocean Region. The revised Maritime Doctrine 2009 clearly states that the Indian navy has a key role to play in addressing the maritime components of challenges that have grown both in scale and scope in recent years.

Therefore, the dimensions of the maritime collaboration have evoked a greater strategic significance, within the framework of which, the Indian navy has sent warships, tankers and submarines to Japan, South Korea, Thailand, New Zealand, Indonesia and Vietnam for joint exercises and to raise the goodwill quotient, through regional confidence-building and cooperative mechanisms like regular participation in institutions of regional governance like the ASEAN—Regional Forum [ARF], EAS, ASEAN Defence Ministers meeting +8[ADMM+8], Indian Ocean Naval Symposium [IONS], meeting and singing of agreements like the Regional Cooperation Agreement on Combating Piracy and Armed Robbery against ships in the Asia [ReCAAP]. Further, India's significant naval build-up in the Andaman and Nicobar Islands and the establishment of the Far Eastern Naval Command (FENC) based in these islands have manifested more strategically pragmatic and vision-oriented Look East & Act East policies.

China's Maritime Silk Road (MSR) appears to be part of its overall maritime strategy to consolidate its influence and neutralise the dominance of the US in the Indian Ocean Region. Even before the MSR initiative, China addressed its energy interests through investments along the littorals of the Indian Ocean, including Pakistan, Myanmar, Sri Lanka, Bangladesh and the

Maldives etc., as part of a grand strategy. In addition to these investments, under the MSR initiative, China has initiated several corridors in order to connect to the Indian Ocean Region as alternative routes for its energy supplies, such as CPEC, CMEC, BCIM, Kra Canal and OBOR initiative. These initiatives aim to bolster China's influence in the region, secure its oil supplies and expand its markets. In this context, a brief discussion has been provided on China's 21st century initiative of the Maritime Silk Road and other initiatives/corridors and how these are impacting India's sovereignty and security in the Indian Ocean Region.

China's New Silk Road concept is rooted in history as there existed an overland silk route and an MSR that connected China to countries across Asia, Africa and Europe drawing from past experience, China in recent years has built a network of highways and railroads from north to south and from east to western regions. With its achievements at the domestic level, China sees it as an opportunity to link the hinterland with South Asia, Europe, and Africa and even to the US.

The declaration of the MSR in 2013 by Xi Jinping opened up new vistas for expanding the footprint of China in the Indian Ocean and beyond to protect its seaborne interests which simultaneously provides leverages for increasing the influence in the target countries in South and Southeast Asia and Africa. The developing cash-starved countries in India's maritime neighbourhood would welcome any investment on easy terms that would improve the livelihood and employment opportunities for its citizens. From the Chinese point of view, it has found new avenues in which to invest surplus reserves expected to be around three trillion, using AIIB and other banking sectors to facilitate the process. This enables China to closely interact with destination countries by employing its technology, manpower and other resources.

The One Belt One Road [OBOR] initiative has caused ripples in Economic, Strategic, and political spheres not just in the neighbouring countries but around the world. The ingredients, such as surplus funds, utilisation of surplus capacity and providing connectivity to find new markets, are the success mantras of this century and beyond, both on land and on sea routes. These strategies would provide China with opportunities to raise the bar in terms of becoming a superpower. The OBOR/BRI is the game changer in the region and India has serious concerns about the possible impact of the OBOR in its neighbourhood. Except for some half-hearted efforts on projects such as 'Mausam' or spice route by India, there is no concrete proposal to respond to the growing influence of China which will alter the strategic balance in the region.

India is apprehensive about the possible impact of China's MSR policy initiatives implemented through the CPEC, BCIM, CMEC and the proposed Thai canal project. These initiatives are the arteries that will carry goods through the Central Asian Republic States and through Bangladesh, India and Myanmar. The China-Myanmar Economic Corridor will provide an exit to the Bay of Bengal and will largely serve the markets of the world. The developments in the Maldives have been worrisome for Indian establishments, as the Chinese are now moving in a big way with investments and assistance that will create strong bonds, making it difficult to ignore from a security point of view.

Enhancing the Indian Navy's Footprint in the Indian Ocean Region

Within the evolving framework of the Indian Navy's initiatives for expanding its sphere of influence and cooperation in the Indian Ocean Region is the most recent operational blueprint in the form of a maritime guidance document christened ensuring secure seas: Indian Maritime Security Strategy [IMSS] 2015. In keeping with the principles and concepts of national security and maritime power incorporated in the joint Doctrine, it builds upon the Indian Navy's vision statement and guiding principles formulated in 2014. The significance of the Indian Navy as the primary instrument to secure the oceanic neighbourhood for economic purposes is underscored by India's centrality in the Indian Ocean Region. Towards this end, the IMSS has recommended a four-pronged approach for the Indian Navy under the present and emerging situations in 2015.

1. Steady increase in the Indian navy's operational footprints across India's area of maritime interest with a growing cooperative framework and to contribute as a net security provider, Non-combatant Evacuations [NEO] and Humanitarian Assistance and Disaster Relief [HADR] operations.
2. An expansion in maritime operational engagements with increased number and complexity of exercises with foreign navies, coordinated mechanisms for maritime security operations and enhanced training, technical and hydrographic cooperation with friendly maritime forces.
3. Continued development of regional cooperative approach for enhancing maritime security in the Indian Ocean Region including MILAN, IONS and the emergence of maritime security cooperation as a priority area for the Indian Ocean Regional Association [IORA] and
4. The growth and development of the Indian navy force levels and maritime capabilities with a steady focus on indigenization.

- The renewed emphasis of the Indian navy in securing the Indian Ocean, while acknowledging the navy's central role as a 'net security provider' may be viewed in the backdrop of the Indian Prime Minister, Narendra Modi's visit to Seychelles, Mauritius and Sri Lanka in March 2015 within the preview of which he demonstrated in the region's niche at the top of New Delhi's policy priorities while endorsing the vision for the Indian Ocean Region, rooted in advancing regional cooperation as well as using our capabilities for the benefit of all in our common maritime home. Prime Minister Modi advocated as,
- Firstly, the deepening of regional economic and security cooperations, particularly with the maritime neighbours and island states,
- Secondly, undertaking collective action and cooperation to best advance peace and security in the maritime region for ensuring better preparedness to respond to emergencies and challenges ranging from piracy, terrorism, natural disasters, etc.
- Thirdly, to achieve this, PM Modi acknowledged India's existing maritime security cooperation with the Maldives, and Sri Lanka [trilateral Initiative] and hoped that Mauritius and Seychelles and other littoral nations would join the initiative.
- Finally, the need to promote a more integrated and cooperative future in the region that enhances the prospects for sustainable development facilitating greater collaboration in trade, tourism, investment, infrastructural development, marine science and technology, sustainable fisheries, protection of the marine environment and overall development of the blue economy.

World Engages in Covid-19 Battle, China Expands in Indo-Pacific

Even as the world remains distracted by the novel Corona virus pandemic, China has ramped up its aggressive expansion issue in the South China Sea causing concern not only among smaller neighbours but also to India and the US. Recently China has renamed 80 geographical features in the South China Sea-Standard names for 23 islands and reefs and 55 underwater geographic entities, signalling its intention of establishing sovereignty over parts of the sea covered by the 9-dash line that is deemed illegal according to an international tribunal order.

The pandemic here monitoring these days has not stopped China from pursuing its long-term strategic goals in the region. According to the Indian security establishment, Chinese doubled standards with regard to its aggressive postures towards smaller and weaker neighbours and the insistence that other countries remain sensitive to its concerns is becoming more evident. According to Abhijit Singh of ORF, the bottleneck for New Delhi is, once China firms its grip over SCS, it will use islands as an outpost to power in the eastern Indian Ocean.

India has a bigger worry than LAC, as China is now expanding its military footprints in the Indian Ocean. According to a recent media report rounds in the news on 12th June 2020, China is growing its military presence in the Indian Ocean too. Satellite pictures in May 2020 this year suggested that the China military base at Djibouti is being modernised and upgraded into a full-fledged base with a 1120-foot pier that can berth Chinese warships including the Liaoning aircraft carrier. This follows Chinese expansion of an artificial island in the Maldives a development with seemingly strategic overtones, raising concerns that China is encroaching on India's sphere of influence.

One way to deter China is through a sea-denial complex in the Andaman Islands. The Indian navy has been deploying in the Andaman &Nicobar as strategic outposts to monitor rival naval activities. The government of India, under PM Modi, has enhanced budgetary provisions to develop an integrated surveillance network. Thus, India, with the help of the US Navy, which is deployed at the Singapore naval base, can deter China's over-activism with vested interest in the Indian Ocean Region.

Keeping in view China's threat perception in the Indian Ocean Region both at Ocean and at border, the maritime strategy of India is ever-changing, particularly after Modi took over as Prime Minister of India in response to myriad geostrategic demands to suit its ambition in the wider global order to substantial competition. In the contemporary time, the Indian PM Modi is all set to reclaim India's stance here as a leading power reshaping its renewed outlook to a small country like Seychelles and islands in the western Indian Ocean. The last three years have been particularly eventful for the India-Seychelles bi-lateral partnership, which was established in 1997. This partnership can enable further strengthening of Indian Maritime diplomacy in the south-western Indian Ocean. Since 2018, India has been moving forward with the establishment of a military base on Assumption Island in Seychelles to monitor the Mozambique Channel. However, this initiative is being closely observed by China.

The inclusion of Madagascar and Comoros as a part of the Indian Ocean vision by PM Modi clearly shows the growing importance of the Indian Ocean

Region in India's foreign policy. This is the first time a single assistance mission is covering all island countries of the western Indian Ocean, which will reflect the contiguity of the Indian government's Indian Ocean policy.

Quadrilateral Security Dialogue [Quad]

The USA, Japan, Australia and India declared in Manila on November 11th 2017 that they had agreed to create a coalition that would patrol and exert influence on waterways from the Indian Ocean to the Pacific to the East and South China Sea. The grouping of four nations is also called as Quadrilateral Security Dialogue, which was first rooted in 2007 by Japan. That the Quad nations were committed to ensuring a free and open region with respect for international law, and the rule-based order in the Indo-Pacific.

The emergence of the Quad as an expression of concern against China's flouting of territorial, maritime and trade norms, including Beijing's rejection of an international tribunal's ruling in its South China Sea dispute with Philippines. The series of joint military exercises by India, Japan and the US, titled 'Malabar' exercises, have seen Japan as a regular participant in the high-voltage Malabar naval combat exercises between India and the US since 2015. Japan's participation reflects its concerns about China's aggressive actions in the Indo-Pacific region. China had strongly objected the Indo-US Malabar exercises in the Bay of Bengal in 2007, when the event was extended to include Japan, Australia and Singapore. India had then restricted the Malabar to a bilateral one in the north-western Pacific in 2009 and in 2014 might be, to avoid antagonizing with China in view of the UPA II government in Delhi.

'Quad' Summit October 2020

The latest meeting of the 'Quad' foreign ministers, which took place in Tokyo, Japan on October 6, 2020 once again reaffirmed a "Collective Vision" of maintaining a free, open and inclusive Indo-Pacific in the face of growing Chinese assertiveness and the ongoing India-China border face-off.

The US called in the meeting for collaboration against Chinese "exploitation, corruption and Coercion", as witnessed among other places, in' the Himalayas'. The US State Secretary Mike Pompeo also brought to the notice of the members of the Quad about the Chinese adventurism in the South China Sea, East China Sea, the Nekong and the Taiwan Straits apart from mentioning the Himalayas as he alluded to the India-China Line of Actual Control stand-off. The Quad declared that it committed to upholding the rule-based international order, underpinned by the rule of law, transparency, freedom of navigation in the international seas, respect for territorial integrity and sovereignty and peaceful resolution of disputes. The meeting has also reiterated their firm support for ASEAN Centrality.

Foreign Ministers from four Indo-Pacific nations—India, the US, Japan and Australia—held discussions in Tokyo. The discussion aimed at countering China's growing assertiveness in the region, amid the stand-off between India and China at the border since mid-May 2020. The meeting focused on planning to contain China in the region. Upping the ante against China amid the ongoing military confrontation in eastern Ladakh, India finally invited Australia to take part in its top-notch trilateral Malabar naval exercises with the US and Japan in the Bay of Bengal and Arabian Sea in two phases in the first and third weeks of November 2020 According to the Times of India dated 20 October20, 2020, this will mark the first time in 13 years that the Quad countries will come for combat manoeuvres on the high seas. The four-nation war-game will clearly signal their intent against China's expansionist behaviour in the entire Indo-Pacific.

Tension between the US and China have escalated over issues like the COVID-19, trade, technology, Hong Kong, Taiwan and human rights. India-China are locked in a tense military stand-off in eastern Ladakh without any signs of easing tension despite several rounds of talks. Relationship between China and Australia have also deteriorated in recent months, particularly, after spread of Corona virus in Wuhan of China and its spread to the entire globe. Also, Japan meanwhile is concerned a lot about China's claim to the Japanese-controlled Senkaku Island, called, Diaoyu in China, in the East China Sea. Japan also considers China's growing military activity to be a security threat. The meeting of four nations was also sought cooperation in the 5G and 5G plus technologies given the Chinese dominance in the segment. The US has made it very clear in the meeting that the focus will be on China as its "tactics, aggression and coercions increasing in the region".

The Chinese focus was also underlined in the meeting by the US Secretary of State, as he accused Beijing of "threatening the world's economy and jeopardizing the global environment". Meanwhile, Canada is willing to become a part of the Quad to promote a free and open Indo-Pacific region", according to Times of India report on October 7, 2020. Canada, which has increased its interaction with India in recent months, also sent a warship in the first week of October'20, through the Strait of Taiwan, from South China Sea—a move intended to send a clear message to China about territorial rights over both Taiwan and the South China Sea.

Malabar Exercise-2020

The 'Quad' is back after a 13-year gap, with an expansionist China firmly in its cross-hairs. Another likeminded country—Germany has also declared that it will too deploy warships to patrol the Indo-Pacific to safeguard the international rule-based order in the critical region from next year onwards is a welcome step in the direction which will strengthen the Quad plus group in the near future. Recently Canada has also announced in a similar way.

Warships of Quad nations—The US, Japan, India and Australia— kicked off the four-day phase-I of the 24th Malabar naval exercise in the Bay of Bengal, with the focus being on complex anti-submarine warfare and other combat manoeuvres on the high seas. Phase-II of the war games in the Arabian Sea from November 17–20 will be "more power packed", with the US deploying a nuclear-powered aircraft carrier.

"The strategic show intent to China is unambiguous", suggests the high voltage exercise, which comes amidst India's ongoing military confrontation with China in eastern Ladakh, where disengagement has not yet been completed. Australia has promptly backtracked to participate in the Malabar exercise. China now has the world's largest navy, surpassing even the US in the number of warships, not to speak of technology and began to aggressively flex its muscles from South China Sea to the Indian Ocean Region. Like "Quad", many other countries, like Germany and the UK, are obviously troubled with China's strong-arm tactics in the region. India again reiterated during the Malabar exercise that the Malabar will" showcase the high-levels of synergy and coordination between the friendly navies, which is based on their shared values and commitment to an open, inclusive Indo-Pacific and rules-based international order"

The Australian Defence Minister Linda Reynolds emphasised that the imperative to cooperate closely with the regional defence partners on shared challenges was stronger than ever before. The Australian defence minister further added that participation in sophisticated exercises like Malabar not only highlights the strategic trust among the members but also strengthens our collective ability to contribute to regional security. "Malabar-2020 will witness complex and advanced naval exercises including surface, anti-submarine and anti-air warfare operations, across-deck flying, seamanship evolutions and weapon firing exercises".

Amid India-China being locked in a major troop confrontation in eastern Ladakh, India and Japanese warships held a small exercise towards the Malacca Strait in the Indian Ocean Region on June 29 2020. It definitely amounts to some strategic signalling for China in this movement. Incidentally, three American Aircraft Carriers, USS Ronald Reagan, USS Theodore Roosevelt and USS Nimitz are also deployed at the same time in the Indo-Pacific region for the first time in the recent past in a move that has not gone down well with China. The present tense situation prevailed in the Sino-Indian border since June 15, 2020. The Malabar exercise was held in the Bay of Bengal in November 2020 successfully without any consideration to China.

India is fast in inking reciprocal military logistical pacts with like-minded countries to extend its strategic and naval operational reach in the entire Indian Ocean Region and beyond, with an eye firmly on China's expansionist behaviour in the Indo-Pacific. After similar agreements with the US, France, South Korea and Singapore, it was India's turn to ink Mutual Logistics Support Arrangement [MLSA]. This arrangement will enable India's warships to get refuelling from Australian tankers on the high seas. It will also avail berthing, maintenance and storage facilities at Australian naval bases. It will, of course, be on a similar reciprocal basis to Australian ships. India inked a military logistics pact with Japan in September 2020 and also similar arrangements were proposed with Russia and the UK.

The Logistic Exchange Memorandum of Agreement [LEMOA] inked with The US in 2016 similarly gives India refuelling facilities and access to American bases in Djibouti, Diego Garcia, Guam and the Subic Bay. The agreement inked with France in 2008, in turn also extends the Indian navy's reach in South-Western Indian Ocean Region due to French bases in Reunion islands near Madagascar and Djibouti on the Horn of Africa. The MLSA with Australia will help us to extend the reach of our warships in the Southern Indian Ocean Region as well as the western Pacific region. This region, south of the Indonesian Strait is also important for India.

With this, an Indian military base in Coco's [Keeping] island could become a reality. This should 'plug' all loopholes in India's presence and situational awareness in the vast Indian Ocean Region. This small base could prove critical in India's ambition of monitoring a credible presence in the vast Indian Ocean. The Coco's Islands, an Australian Indian Ocean territory which is almost mid-way from India's maritime neighbour *i.e.* Sri Lanka and mainland Australia, fall right in the middle of the things.

The 'virtual summit' between PM Modi of India and his Australian counterpart Scott Morrison could prove to be a fruitful watershed movement in maritime cooperation between India and Australia. A development that could boost Maritime Domain Awareness [MDA] for the two countries with an inkling of an agreement through a virtual meeting could lay the foundation for mutual use of two strategically located islands—India's Andamans & Nicobar Islands for a mutual military purposes.

The recent India-China stand-off in Galwan valley and the Chinese build-up along various parts of 3480 km Line of Actual Control [LAC] have got senior navy officers worried about the Andamans, as the archipelago, nearly 700 nautical miles from the mainland remains at risk from PLAN. Surveillance has established that the Chinese navy has been active in the region and close to Indian territory waters. The Galwan face-off is not just a border conflict, but there is much more to it. China is trying to secure a key communication and trade route-the flag-ship project of Chinese President Xi Jinping's Belt and Road Initiative [BRI], which was conceptualised in an audaciously, ambitiously designed to stamp China's centrality in re-ordered global economic, eco-system. The project seeks to cover 65 countries, touching the lives of 62 per cent of the global population. While more than 120 countries lined up for 2ndBRI summits, India remains the most significant naysayer to BRI. The China-Pakistan Economic Corridor is the part of the flagship project of the Belt & Road Initiative, which connects China's province of Xinjiang and Gwadar port in Pakistan, which goes through Gilgit-Baltistan and Pakistan-occupied Kashmir [POK], violating dejure sovereignty. Therefore, India since its inception objecting to China from timetotime at various diplomatic summits. Not only this, India also has not given consent to another Chinese project/corridor, Bangladesh, China, India and Myanmar [BCIM]—a 2800 km rail/road corridor from Kunming of China to Kolkata via Myanmar and Bangladesh. India has reservations about China's Maritime Silk Road projects like—CPEC, BCIM and 741 km rail corridor project from Lhasa in Tibet to Kathmandu to Patna in Bihar, India. Hence, India wants to go with its own Maritime scheme called the Mausam project instead of joining China's Maritime Silk Road/Belt and Road Initiative.

The reason to present face-off at Galwan valley is, China immediately wants to dominate the recently built 255 km road by India in its territory from Darbuk-Shyok-Doulat Beg Oldie [DBO] that connects Leh to DBO at the base of Karakoram pass. The DBO road is seen as a threat to China to the east by Aksim Chin which India claims and presently holds and to the north is Shaksgam valley that was illegally ceded to China in 1960s by Pakistan. China seeks to threaten this road [DBO] as China wants to preserve this route from Xinjiang, crossing the Karakoram pass to the Siachen glacier and into Pakistan, ending at Gwadar in order to safe running of China's CPEC, which is the engine of Pakistan's growth as a part of China's BRI. Hence, the Chinese will push against India in the near future time and again to safeguard its interests in its corridor. The face-off along LAC will continue for a long as

Galwan valley conflict is not just a border dispute only between India and China, but there is much more behind it.

China has emerged as the world's second-largest economy surpassing Japan. This position naturally leads to huge outputs in the countries and the energy consumption of China exceeds the US levels. So, China has emerged as an export-centric economy, therefore, adopting the same old imperialistic methods as China desires to emerge as global power even surpassing the US. The so-called Belt and Road Initiative and other corridors of its are only a ploy to lure, subjugate and loot the resources of vulnerable countries of the Indian Ocean Region and to push them into a debt-trap under the grab of developing infrastructure facilities through Maritime Silk Road. Therefore, in view of this, India has been objecting since a long Chinese various initiatives/corridors implemented under MSR programme, as these initiatives are likely to impact India's security and sovereignty in future by encircling India.

Further, China is also planning to construct a few other corridors/canals, etc. in the Indian Ocean up and around Russia to solve China's Malacca Dilemma and to lure resources into the Arctic states. India is spoked by China's push to expedite work on the Thai Canal across the Kra Isthmus—the narrowest part of the Malay Peninsula in Southern Thailand. The Thai Canal, also known as Kra Canal would connect the Gulf of Thailand with the Andaman Sea across the Isthmus in Southern Thailand. The canal would provide an alternative to transit through the Strait of Malacca and shorten transit for shipments of oil to China and Japan also by 1200 km. China refers it as a part of its 21st Century MSR, which measures 120 km length, which is itself a key constituent of China's ambitious OBOR project. The canal is China's attempt at solving its Malacca problem, as India is thinking of checking China's trade at the Strait of Malacca. With this canal, China can directly enter the Andaman Sea, providing an alternative route for Chinese transportation

After OBOR, China pushed 'Polar Silk Road', as China outlined its ambitions to extend President Xi Jinping's ambitious Belt &Road Initiative to the Arctic by developing shipping lanes opened up by global warming. China has released its first Arctic policy, 'white paper', indicating that it would encourage enterprises to build infrastructure and conduct commercial voyages. This initiative aims to pave the way for Arctic shipping routes, forming a 'Polar Silk Road', up and around Russia.

China, despite being a non-Arctic state is increasingly active in the polar region. It became an observer member of the Arctic Council in 2013. Among its increasing interests in the region is its major stake in Russia's Yamal liquefied natural gas project which is expected to supply China with 4 million tonnes of LNG a year. China's increasing prominence in the region has prompted concerns from Arctic states over its long-term strategic objectives, including possible military deployment as China is doing in the Indian Ocean Region in the form of the 'String of Pearl's strategy.

Therefore, India needs to think of new forms, approaches and initiatives to face Chinese challenges, both in the IOR and at the India-China 3488 km long border. India has potential assets in its waters such as the Eight and Nine Degree Channels in the Lakshadweep Sea and the Six Degree Channel in the Andaman Sea so that India can deter and check-mate China's trade at Malacca Strait. It is to be mentioned here that, International Sea Routes connecting Europe, Gulf with Southeast Asia will pass through these channels. The government of India, under Modi, has already initiated significant steps in this direction by allocating more funds to strengthen Andaman & Nicobar Islands and deploying more naval forces to be more assertive in the Indian Ocean Region.

China Views India as a Rising Power

China perceives India as a rising power, hence seeks to limit in all aspects including with the US ties, and wants to constrain its strategic partnership with the United States of America. The relationship between India and the US, its allies, and other democracies has been growing rapidly since Modi became Prime Minister of India. Beijing intends to displace America as the world's foremost power.

China is undermining the security, autonomy, and economic interests of many nations in the Region, according to the US report published in Times of India on November 20, 2020. China perceives 'rising India 'under Modi leadership as a 'rival and seeks to impel it to accommodate Beijing's ambitions by engaging economically while construing New Delhi's strategic partnership with the US, Japan, and Australia and its relationship with other democracies. The report further reveals that awareness has been growing in the US and in other nations that the ruling Chinese Communist Party (CCP) has triggered a new era of great-power competition.

The CCP under Xi Jinping aims not merely at pre-eminence within the established world order but to revise the world order serving Beijing's hegemony ambitions. China is trying to diminish US influence by fostering a sense in the region nations that China's dominance is inevitable and by limiting US ties with allies. The recent Chinese incursions in the India-China border at Galwan Valley in the Ladakh region is China's game plan to warn India to limit relations with the US.

Also, the recent visit of the Tibetan leader to the White House in November 2020, after a gap of six decades enraged China. The head of the Tibetan government in exile, Los Angeles Sanjay visited the White House and met the newly appointed senior official on Tibetan issues and discussed on wide range between the two. China has accused the US that it is trying to interfere in its internal affairs. China has also objected very recently to India-Taiwan trade relations, which shows that China is worried about India's growing power in the world.

China has objected to the India-US ongoing military exercises near the LAC in Uttarakhand stating that it violates the spirit of bilateral agreements for border peace.

The 18th edition of the India-US military exercise "Yudh Abbyas" was conducted in the first week of December 2022 in Uttarakhand, about 100 km away from the LAC. Yudh Abbiyas is a bilateral exercise held annually since 2004, which aims to improve the interoperability of the Indian and US armies for future contingency throughout the Indo-Pacific region. The joint military exercise conducted inside the Indian border towards India away from 100 km as per the relevant agreements signed by China and India in 1993 and 1996.

India in reply to China hit out for claiming that the ongoing India-US 'Yudh Abbyas' military exercise violates Sino-Indian bilateral agreements for border peace and asked Beijing to reflect on its own breach of pacts in the form of Chinese transgressions in the eastern Ladakh. India further said candidly that India has not given a 'Veto' to any third country on whom to conduct military exercises. So, the Yudh Abbyas military exercises have nothing to do with the bilateral agreements. Therefore, it is none of the business of China to object to the military exercises.

China Recognised India's Rise in the Indian Ocean Region

The ruling Chinese Communist Party has accepted grudgingly that India has a unique geographical advantage in the Indian Ocean. Hence, New Delhi has been able to leverage the advantage with more and more countries joining Indian-led initiatives. In fact, with the Indo-Pacific construct, India is connecting the Indian and Pacific Oceans from the east coast of Africa to the west coast of the Americas.

In an article on December 17, 2020, titled 'India changes attitude towards multilateral mechanisms for global ambitions', published in its mouthpiece,

Global Times, by Hu Shisheng, Director, Institute of Contemporary International Relations, India has also taken the lead in planning small-scale multilateral cooperation mechanisms in the Indian Ocean.

India has expanded its role in the Indian Ocean Region in the last few years, from Humanitarian Assistance and Disaster Relief to supplying food and medical aid amidst the COVID-19 Pandemic to five counties of the Indian Ocean, namely, the Maldives, Mauritius, Madagascar, Comoros and Seychelles.

Earlier in 2019, Prime Minister Modi had proposed the Indo-Pacific Oceans Initiative (IPOI), under which countries like Australia, Japan and ASEAN grouping have expressed willingness to work with India on issues like maritime security to transport. In fact, in what looks like a taunt, but is more a reminder for itself, that "India wants to be the net security provider of the Indian Ocean." While New Delhi has not said so, it is seen as a preferred Security Partner.

India's Information Fusion Centre at Gurugram which keeps an eye on the movement of ships in the Indian Ocean is emerging as the nodal centre for real-time information in the region. The US and France have sent their liaison officers already, with more countries joining in. Under its defence training programme, India has provided mobile teams to eleven countries from Vietnam to South Africa, as well as Sri Lanka, Bangladesh and Myanmar.

The Chinese Communist Party's indignation via its mouthpiece about India's 'Sinophobic', pro-west diplomacy, comes as no surprise. While Beijing seems India drifting away, it forgets how it opposed New Delhi's bid for Nuclear Supplies at the UN Security Council. The year 2020 witnessed an increasingly aggressive China, which not only violated agreements on buildings at the Line of Actual Control (LAC) but also indulged in actions such as Galwan Valley where 20 Indian soldiers were killed in action.

Beijing is already perturbed by the 'Quad' meeting and Australia's invitation to the Malabar exercises. The country seems to have failed to understand or recall New Delhi's outreach through informal summits in Wuhan and then the Chennai connect. However, the past is past, and the world has woken up to a new, more aggressive China amidst the Corona virus outbreak.

India Trains IOR Diplomats

In a first of its kind, India had conducted a special training course for Diplomats of six Indian Ocean Region countries, four of them from the strategically important Western Indian Ocean, where India has been struggling to catch up with China. Thirty-five Diplomats from Madagascar, Comoros Seychelles, Mauritius Sri Lanka and Maldives participated in the 2-week special course, the training was held at Sushma Swaraj Institute of Foreign Services. Comoros and Madagascar are in the Western Indian Ocean Region where bureaucratic Red Tapism has threatened to undermine the Indian Ocean outreach. The fact that countries like Comoros and Madagascar, the largest Islands in the Indian Ocean, have shown keen interest in the program, is a good sign for India. China has recently consolidated its naval presence in the region with the appointment of defence attaché in Madagascar. The course involved India's polity, foreign policy, contemporary Maritime issues, Humanitarian Assistance, disaster relief, international framework under UNCLOS, multilateral & Economic diplomacy Diplomatic protocol, health diplomacy and Climate change challenges. The training course has designed to keep an eye on China which substantially increased its presence in a strategically important area that may adversely affect India's Security if India does not improve its footprints in the western Indian Ocean Region.

Project Mausam

Project Mausam is a parallel programme to the Chinese Maritime Silk Road. India must use its history, culture and geography to compete with China's Maritime Silk Road. The project is considered the government's most significant foreign policy initiative designed to counter China. It is inspired by India's historical role as the focal point for trade in the Indian Ocean.

The Project Mausam would allow India to re-establish its ties with its ancient trade partners and re-establish an Indian Ocean world along the littoral of the Indian Ocean. This world would stretch from east Africa, along the Arabian Peninsula, past southern Iran to the major countries of South Asia and then to Sri Lanka and Southeast Asia. The project is supposed to have both a cultural and serious strategic dimension. It is clear that the Indian government intended to expand its maritime presence, culturally, strategically, and psychologically.

The Mausam Project initiative coined in 2004 seems so far to have had nowhere to go. The initial energy displayed in an effort to list the Indian Ocean with UNESCO, as a world cultural heritage site remained what it was, an initial effort. A well-meaning decision to list 39 countries around the Indian Ocean littoral as probable partners in the initiative has not realized so far and support in the region not yet been received as expected.

If the Mausam initiative is to take off, its protagonists must be clear about its direction and evolve equal partnerships with states that have a stake in the history and culture of the Indian Ocean world. The history of cosmopolitanism in the Indian Ocean world must resonate with contemporary concerns about the region.

Though the Project Mausam aims to rebuild maritime and economic connections with the 39 countries bordering the Indian Ocean. The project also aims to bring together historical and archaeological researchers to record the diversity of economic, cultural and religious interactions between countries. There are two visions for Project Mausam (1) to understand national cultures between countries and the (2) to rebuild communications between countries.

So, the government of India will have to take strong measures to effectively implement the project by minimizing overlapping governing bodies with a single dominating agency. Once the project is implemented, it will provide more opportunities for India's economy and trade, as well as build international contacts, in accordance with the 'Look East' and "Link West Policies".

Significance of Small Islands in the Indian Ocean Region

Small Islands have played a very significant geo-strategic role in the Indian Ocean Region historically. From the ancient Persians and Arab's links with Pemba and Zanzibar on the Eastern African coasts to the more recent American military presence on Diego Garcia, several small islands have been viewed with interests used by regional and foreign powers for military purposes. Their location at sea and isolation from the continental land masses can provide a very advantageous position to armed forces for a wide range of activities, such as defence, surveillance, support and power projection from sea to land.

The military forces' interests in these islands have been greatly renewed since the beginning of the 21st century, given the growing importance of the Indian Ocean Region in global geopolitics and the world economy. This is evident in the case of the United States with Diego Garcia in the Chagos Archipelago (BIOT), as well as for India and its island territories, Andaman & Nicobar, Lakshadweep and for France with its Indian Ocean Islands, Reunion and Mayotte. Many other small islands that are already in use for ongoing military operations, are now integrated into strategic planning. These include Seychelles, Mauritius, the Maldives, Oman's Masriah Islands,

Yemen's Socotra island, Australia's Cocos (Keeling) Islands and Burma's Coco Islands. Therefore, Prime Minister of India Narendra Modi initiated a strategic approach towards small island nations as a part of his (India's) vision by using small islands for military forward presence in the Indian Ocean Region to face the challenges in future in the Indian Ocean Region by China and Pakistan jointly.

Oceania Region

In Indian foreign policy and strategic discourse, island nations have gained special attention. While India did not pay much attention to them till 2014, Prime Minister Narendra Modi has now recognized the significance of Small Island Nations in India's foreign policy. With China increasing increases its presence day-by-day in the Indian Ocean Region, the Modi government acknowledges that small island nations, regardless of their proximity to strategic sea lanes or the mainland, hold important strategic and commercial significance. This does not diminish the importance of other island nations to India.

Oceania is a Region made up of thousands of islands throughout the Central & South Pacific Ocean. It includes Australia, the smallest continent in terms of total land area. Oceania Region consists of 14 countries, 2 associated countries and 14 Dependencies.

Oceania is one of the regions where India's approach is dependent on information from larger neighbours, such as Australia and New Zealand. One of the severe limitations has been the lack of diplomatic missions and commercial liaison offices in many of the Oceania countries, such as Fiji, Australia, New Zealand and Papua New Guinea (PNG). Indian mindset needs to change as any island nation can be a strategic asset, both in terms of monitoring as well as using that island nation as a refuelling base or transit point. The Cuban missile crisis is one case in history when a small island nation became too important for both the Super powers that time, the US and former USSR.

The entry of China into this geostrategic theatre has forced countries, like Australia, the US and other major powers to recalibrate their strategy towards this region. Aid assistance, development and infrastructure projects have become the new currency, which has been utilized by these nations. The superiority of the US and its allied partners in the region has been challenged. China's inroads into Timor-Leste and constantly improving relations with Fiji, PNG and Vanuatu have created decision-makers in countries like Australia and New Zealand.

As India aims to be a global player and pursue its aspiration to become a UN Security Council member, the votes from these island nations become crucial. India's offering such as low-cost education, particularly in distance education, healthcare and agricultural equipment exports, can create a positive influence in the region. Therefore, India needs to prioritize its engagement with these island nations in line with Prime Minister Modi's foreign policy objectives.

Prime Minster Modi's strategic initiatives are not only useful in securing the Indian Ocean maritime domain against traditional and non-traditional challenges but also to enhance means of ensuring sustainable and balanced development, establishing and maintaining a climate of mutual trust and confidence among the countries while respecting international maritime rules and norms. Furthermore, in addition to boosting bilateral engagement between India's littoral states of the Indian Ocean Region, it is the contingent of the multi-lateral institutions like the Indian Ocean Rim Association, Indian Ocean Naval Symposium and, ARF, etc. to forge a focussed collaborative endeavour for carving a secure, sustainable and prosperous future of the region, in keeping the letter and spirit of 'SAGAR'—Security and Growth for All in the Region.

Results of the Hypothesis

1. The first hypothesis of the study-India holds a strategic position in the Indian Ocean Region and has been proved positively on the given grounds.

The geographic proximity of the Indian Ocean with resource-rich regions and its periphery has enhanced its strategic importance and eminence. The Indian Ocean is the third largest Ocean of the world that covers 14 per cent of the earth's surface touching the coastline of 37 independent countries and the Indian Ocean Region has been described as a centre stage for 21st Century, according to Robert Kaplan in 2009 which never lost its strategic Sheen since ancient times.

It has an area of 26,469,900 sq. miles and it spans the coasts of India, Pakistan, Iran, The Arabia Peninsula, East Africa, Australia, Antarctica and certain Islands Indonesia, and The Malaya Peninsula. This region contains 25 per cent of world's land mass, and 40 per cent of world's oil and gas reserves and handles 30 per cent world's trade. The Indian Ocean Region constitutes between a quarter and a third of the world's population, making it a massive market. This region is also rich in strategic and precious minerals, metals and other natural resources ranging from food and fisheries to raw materials and energy for industry.

The Indian Ocean is also the locus of important international Sea Lanes of Communication (SLOCs) and is significant in the location of maritime Choke–points in the Ocean. These include the Suez Canal, Bab-el-Mandab, Strait of Hormuz, Mozambique Channel in the south-west, Malacca Strait and Sunda, and Lombok Strait in the South-east of the Ocean. These choke points typically have the potential to control the entry and exit of the flow of maritime traffic in the Indian Ocean.

Because of the narrow land outlets to other continents, the significance of the SLOCs and choke points belonging to the Indian Ocean became prominent in the region. This character distinguishes the Indian Ocean Region from that of the Atlantic and Pacific Oceans. Indian Ocean has nine major choke-points. Of these, five routes are frequented by the energy resources carrying ships-1/10th of the global trade oil is transported through the Gulf of Aden and about 40 per cent of the global oil commerce passes through the Strait of Hormuz (15.5 million's barrels of oil) as compared to 11 million barrels through the Strait of Malacca. Over and above, 70,000 ships passes through the Strait of Malacca every year.

Given the profile of the region, many countries of the world have attempted to influence it through unilateral, bilateral and multi-lateral efforts. Foremost of these, is the US which has a major base in the Indian Ocean Region with Diego Garcia. So, the significance of the Indian Ocean Region is loud and clear to the international community in several aspects, especially, the emerging context for power between the US and rising resource China, as reflected in the Obama Administration rebalance strategy and the idea of Indo-Pacific and Xi Jinping's Maritime Silk Road Initiative, with China deploying 7–8 warships in the Indian Ocean at any given time. In view of these facts mentioned above, the Hypothesis of significance of the Indian Ocean Region was established positively.

2. The second Hypothesis of the study is India followed weak security policy in the Indian Ocean is established positively based on the following grounds.

Enough importance was not given to the study of geography in general and the Indian Ocean in particular in the post-independence period including maritime strategy was also not given any prominence. Until 1958, the Indian Navy headed by British Officers showed the situation of Indian security perceptions and vision of the Indian Navy was just confined to coastal waters only. The College of Naval Warfare was established only after 40 years of Independence, which shows negligence on the part of the then government under congress, and in addition, government deliberately deprived India of any strategic role in its Ocean Neighbourhood. The government at Delhi never paid any attention to its strategic advantages due to the country's two-long coasts protruding into the Indian Ocean, Lakshadweep and Andaman & Nicobar Islands. Even the advantage of the UN Law of Sea enacted in 1982 and the vast Exclusive Economic Zone did not mean anything to the then government of India, which forgot the policies with regard to Small Islands of the Indian Ocean.

The ambitious Maritime Military Strategy of 2007 envisages exploiting the geo-graphical advantages available to India by adopting an oceanic approach, rather than the coastal one. Either the grand plan of strategy of Force Building or the imperative diplomatic initiatives for achieving the goals of the 'Maritime Strategy of 2007' remained on the paper until Narendra Modi government took it seriously. In 2015, PM Modi sanctioned $ 1.5 billion infrastructure package for the Andamans. This move is a significant step to provide security and to counter China's increasing presence in the Indian Ocean.

The budgetary allocations to Indian defence sector, specifically to the Indian Navy is insufficient, when compared with China whose allocations are 'four' times higher than India. China's defence sector allocation in 2019–20 is $ 170 billion, whereas India's allocation is 45 billion only, according to a Times of India report dated June 19, 2020. Out of which most of the expenditure goes to maintenance of cantonments, salaries, and pensions, instead of purchasing critical arms, ammunition and leaving very less for modernisation.

Prime Minister Modi has visited several Island nations to strengthen relations in the region. Modi visited Mauritius in 2015 and signed an MOU for the improvement of sea and air transportation facilities in Agalela. PM was also able to convince Seychelles to India's Naval base in Assumption Island during his visit in 2015. In the same year, India and Mozambique agreed to broaden training beyond the navy. In 2016, India and Iran signed 12 MOUs, centered around the port of Chabahar, the tri-lateral transit agreement between India, Iran and Afghanistan, which allows Indian goods to reach Afghanistan through Iran.

India had also entered a Quadrilateral Security Dialogue with the US and Japan and Australia in Manila in 2017, which would enable Patrolling and exerting influence on waterways from the Indian Ocean to Pacific to East and South China Sea. In an another move, India and Singapore signed a bilateral agreement under Modi that will facilitate logistical support to Indian Navy ships. In 2018, a logistical agreement was signed with Oman which facilitates the use of Port Duqm by the Indian Navy and Omini air bases by Indian Air Forces. Also, in 2018 India and France entered the Logistic Support Agreement. In a similar way, India and Australia signed a Mutual Logistical Support agreement by virtual method recently in 2020.

India and the US signed on geospatial cooperation under PM Modi recently in November 2020 which is the fourth and final 'foundational military pact', called the Basic Exchange and Cooperation Agreement for Geospatial Cooperation to further tighten the strategic clinch between the two countries. India has already signed the General Security of Military Information agreement with the US in 2002, which was followed by the Logistics Exchange Memorandum of Agreement in 2016 and then the Communications, Compatibility and Security Agreement in 2018 with the US.

The above fact proves that India's security policy was very weak and neglected for a long. It is only after Modi became Prime Minister of India and initiated steps to strengthen relationship with Indian Ocean Neighbourhood and several Island nations that it became evident that India's security policy had been neglected for a long after Independence. Hence, the Hypothesis has been established positively.

3. That China is a threat to India in the Indian Ocean has been proved positively on the following bases.

Since last one and a half decades China has been seriously working to encircle India, which is a fast-growing economy. As China's interests in the Indian Ocean region are geo-strategic and geo-economic, to realise its objective China has initiated several corridors, apart from its Maritime Silk Road. China plans to sell its excess capacity to the poor and under-developed countries while undertaking various infrastructure facilities and indirectly luring the resources from these countries.

The geo-strategic interest has been fulfilled through adopting its 'String of Pearls' strategy in the Indian Ocean Region by getting access to its strategically located ports—Chittagong and Mongla on the Bay of Bengal. China also got access to deep water ports in Sri Lanka, Myanmar, Gwadar in Pakistan and Djibouti in the Indian Ocean Region. China has also initiated a few corridors for this purpose like CPEC, CMEC, Kra Canal Project, BCIM, Polar Silk Road and digital Silk Road etc. According to a survey conducted by the Australia India Institute, University of Melbourne in May 2013, India sees China as the biggest threat to the nation, because of its high GDP rate, its bigger economy, strong military, constant military support to Pakistan, its nuclear capabilities, etc. As per a survey report, 84 per cent of the respondents expressed that China is a threat and 60 per cent felt that, China and Pakistan together can pose a major threat to India in the future. Further 70 per cent of respondents agreed that China aims to dominate Asia and 65 per cent of respondents felt that to counter China, India should join hands with like-minded countries in the region, as China possesses one of the largest militaries in the world.

China's defence budget up by 850 per cent over a period of 20 years from $ 20 billion in 2002, increased to $ 170 billion in 2018, whereas India's defence budget increased to only $ 45 billion (as of 19/6/2020 Times of India Report) which is 1/4th of China's allocation, the lowest allocation since 1962 war with China. In fact, the allocation to the Indian navy has decreased 13.5 per cent in 2018 from 18 per cent allocated in 2013–14, which is insufficient to modernise India's capabilities and difficulties in facing China's threat in the Indian Ocean Region. The survey report of the Australia India Institute findings reveals the way that 84 per cent of respondents agreed that India has to face threat from both the countries China and Pakistan, called a' collusive threat' as has been evident by the aggression of China's military into the Galwan valley of Ladakh. In view of the above, it has been proved that the hypothesis of China is a serious threat to India in the Indian Ocean Region.

4. The fourth and final Hypothesis of the study is India, being in a strategic position in the Indian Ocean Region, needs to enhance its Security Capabilities to counter China's increasing presence in the area. This hypothesis is also established positively, as the following facts reveal the same.

In the present situation, India alone can't counter China due to its size of the economy, China possessing high GDP, huge military power, huge defence capabilities, etc. According to a survey report of the Australia India Institute (2013), 65% of respondents expressed that India should join hands with other countries to limit China's growing influence in the region. The world today witnessing the way China has been interfering in 10 nation groups of ASEAN in the South China Sea, Hong Kong, Taiwan, Xinjiang and China's recent incursion into India's territory in the Eastern Ladakh against all agreements made till date between India and China. Till date, the stand-off is continuing since mid-May 2020.

China possesses 2.2 million troops with huge military capabilities, while India's military strength is 1.5 million troops. China has at its disposal Large Missile Arsenal with Long Ranges Missiles—Land based Dong Feng-31A (11200 km) and submarines launched JL-(7400 km)—whereas India has only Small Missile Arsenal-Agni-III (3000 km), Agni V (over 5000 km). China also possesses 320 Nuclear Warheads, whereas India has only 150. Additionally, China has over 2100 Fighters and Bombers, while India possesses only 500. Furthermore, China holds over 7,000 Tanks, whereas India has 3300, less than half of China.

China has over 110 Big Warships (2 Aircraft Carriers) & 33 destroyers, whereas India has only 37 Big Warships. India has only one aircraft carrier at its disposal and 11 destroyers. Therefore, it badly needs at least three aircraft carriers. Finally, China has over 60 Submarines, out of 10 are nuclear powered, but India has 17 submarines, out of which only 2 are nuclear powered. China has 5 Theatre Commands to deal with the crisis, but India holds only one *i.e.*, in Andaman Nicobar Island. The force-levels and capabilities mentioned exist as on June 19, 2020.

So, in view of the above fact, the level available with India and China-India needs to emerge as powerful blue-water navy to protect & guard strategic interest from the Persian Gulf to Malacca Strait and to counter China's expanding footprint in the Indian Ocean Region and also to deter Pakistan. India badly needs to protect its daily sea trade transit worth $ 2 billion and off-shore assets. This requires naval modernisation and up-gradation, despite budgetary constraints, to enhance India's security in the Indian Ocean Region.

China's PLA has a significant numerical advantage over the Indian Army. But India will have to mainly deal Chinese Western Theatre Command which handles the entire LAC with 3488 km, WTC, which is the largest of '5' in China. In addition, China has built 14 air bases, rail network and 58,000 km of roads in Tibet. So, the PLA can swiftly induct and sustain 30–32 divisions along LAC, each division with over 12 K troops.

China is using Tibet's water against India for supremacy to further its territorial ambitions. The announcement to build a major hydropower project, also known as 'super dam' on the Brahmaputra river in Tibet, on the lower reaches of the Yarlung Zangbo river (name of the river in Tibet), came amid ongoing border tensions between India and China since mid-May 2020. This tension is rooted in China's refusal to acknowledge the McMahon Line. Originating in the so-called Tibet Autonomous Region (TAR), the trans-border river flows into Arunachal Pradesh, where it is called 'Siang', and then to Assam as the Brahmaputra river before flowing into Bangladesh and draining into the Bay of Bengal.

The super hydropower station is being planned with an (one) aim to equip China with strategic leverage over India. Such a huge water storage capacity could be used as a tool for consolidating supremacy in the disputed territories. India should be aware and cautious that the Yarlung Zangbo Brahmaputra dam issue is not just about resource management. China is using Tibet's water to further consolidate its territorial ambitions and achieve supremacy.

China is Emerging as Bigger Threat than Pakistan

China has been emerging as the biggest threat to India if we analyze its actions, both in the Indian Ocean Region and in its neighbourhood, particularly its aggression along with India-China border. The Chief Defence Staff of India late Gen. Rawat also echoed a similar statement recently in the month of November 2021, saying that India is facing the biggest threat, much bigger than Pakistan and the country is preparing to face any eventuality on the borders or on the high seas and he further elaborated that the threat on the northern borders is much bigger.

China recently delivered the largest, the most advanced warship to Pakistan to boost China's presence in the Indian Ocean and in the Arabian Sea, where it has increased its own naval presence in recent years. Designed and built by China State Ship Building Corporation Limited, the frigate was delivered to Pakistan Navy. Besides, the advanced naval ships, China also partners with Pakistan Air Force to build JP-17 Thunder fighter aircraft.

In view of the seriousness of the threat from China, echoed in Xi Jinping's speech delivered at the 20th Congress of the Communist Party of China in October, 2022 where he stated that China has the capabilities to 'win local wars', India must recognize the increasing intensity of security threats from the PLA, which will likely become more sophisticated in and multifaceted. Although India has significantly reduced the huge infrastructure gap with China along with LAC in the recent years under PM Modi, including roads, tunnels, bridges, troop, habitats, permanent defences, helipads, and airfields, Indian and Chinese troops have remained forward deployed for the third consecutive winter in the 30-month-old military confrontation in Eastern Ladakh. Several more infrastructure projects by the Indian Army's Corps of Engineers and the Border Roads Organization are currently underway to further address the asymmetry with China.

To deal with Xi's China, the answer is to improve India's strength in all aspects. In other words, the asymmetry between India and China will have to be reduced. The economic asymmetry also signifies differentials in military preparedness, technological prowess, and comprehensive national power. So, to decrease this asymmetry, India will have to enhance its economic size over the coming years and quickly grow towards a minimum of $ 6-7 trillion economy. At present, India's economy is around $ 3 trillion. And this is the reason why Prime Minister Modi is visualizing to grow India's economy to $ 5 trillion. However, due to Covid-19 Pandemic, India is facing complex problems. In order to defend her territorial integrity on her own, India needs to obtain high-technology equipment and weaponry.

From the above facts, to enhance India's security in the region and protect itself from China's threat, India needs to increase its budgetary allocations to the defence sector. Furthermore, India should collaborate with neighbouring countries through bilateral and multi-lateral groups with like-minded countries, such as the 'Quad.' The present security arrangements and capabilities of India are insufficient to counter China. From this, it is established that the fourth and final hypothesis is established positively.

Conclusions

China's Security Challenges are not only confined to the Indian Ocean Region, but India is also facing security challenges with China in a few other less-visible areas, such as trade, border disputes, water disputes, Digital Technology, and Cyber Attacks, etc. A brief note on these issues is as follows:

The bilateral trade between India and China amidst the military standoff along the borders since 2020 went up to $ 103.63 billion, an increase of 14.6% in the last year. China has been enjoying a favorable trade balance with India since bilateral commerce began in early 2000, which has cumulatively exceeded more than $ 1 trillion. The trade gap has been widened in the past decade. In 2021, the annual two-way trade crossed $ 100 billion for the first time reaching $ 126.6 billion with India's imports accounting for $ 97.7 billion pegging the imbalance close to $ 70 billion. The huge gap is due to China not allowing Indian products into its markets in spite of negotiations and agreements reaching at diplomatic levels several times between India and China.

The Line of Actual Control (LAC) has not been jointly demarcated by India-China and there is no mutually agreed consensus on where it lies. In some parts of this mountainous geography each side's perceptions of LAC is different from other side, hence there are pockets where these perceptions are overlapping which leads to disputes on the India-China border. Since 1962 Fourteen times aggressions, face-offs, and incursions have taken place. Recently, China's troops clashed with Indian soldiers on December 9, 2022 in Tawang of Arunachal Pradesh where on both sides, soldiers sustained fractured limbs and other injuries.

China has been planning to construct 60,000 MW project on the Yariung Zangbo (Brahmaputra) at Medog on Arunachal Pradesh's border would be a cause of concern to India for multiple reasons. China has been building dams with large storage capacities which is going to use the Medog dam as a political tool which could be a matter of concern for India and Bangladesh and may lead to water wars between India and China in the future.

Ever since the Silk Road was launched in 2017, China has been building up an information expressway of fiber optic network links to several countries around the world. Less visible than the ports and railways of BRI projects, China's expanding control over the world's digital communication networks gives Beijing unparalleled influence. Major BRI partners don't have even an option; they are supposed to use only Chinese 5G (fifth generation) suppliers, which may lead to security challenges in their respective countries.

Additionally, Chinese company ZTE is a global leader in Telecommunications and Information Technology, setting its products and services in more than 160 countries. In June, 2020 the Federal Communications Commission of the US formally designated China's Huawei Technologies Co. and ZTE Corporation as threats to the US and the world. Since Galwan tussle, Cyber threats to Indian infrastructure have escalated. Chinese hostilities along its border are not the only incursions, India faces, so it needs to stay alert. Despite the US continuing to issue warnings about the espionage risks of using Chinese 5G network equipment, infrastructure projects keep growing day by day.

Cyber attacks are usually aimed at accessing, changing, destroying sensitive information, extorting money from users, or interrupting normal business processes. So, cyber security is the practice of protecting systems, networks, and programs from digital attacks. Implementing cyber security mechanisms is a particularly challenging task today as there are more devices than people and attackers are becoming innovative.

Therefore, India will need to improve its maritime infrastructure, upgrade its naval capabilities while enhancing budgetary allocations to the defense sector to meet the *growing* challenges from China. Mere drum beatings will not be enough to deliver the goods since India is facing divergent threat challenges, not only in the Indian Ocean, but also in other less visible areas as explained above.

Bibliography

Books

1. Abraham, Saji (2015). China's Role in Indian Ocean—its Implications on India's National Security, New Delhi: Vijay Books Publishers.
2. Athwal, Amardeep (2008). India-China Relations: Contemporary Dynamics, New York: Routledge.
3. Chaudhury, Rahul Roy (2000). India's Maritime Security, New Delhi: Institute for Defence Studies and Analysis.
4. Chellaney, Brahma (1999). Securing India's Future in the New Millennium, New Delhi: Orient Longman.
5. Cohen, Stephan (2001). India: Emerging Power, Washington D.C.: Brookings Institution Press.
6. Garver, John W. (2000). Protracted Contest: Sino-Indian Rivalry in the Twentieth Century, London: University of Washington (House Trade Paperbacks).
7. Guruswamy, Mohan and Zorawar Daulet Singh (2009). India China Relations: The Border Issue and Beyond, New Delhi: Viva Books.
8. Kaplan, Robert D. (2010). Monsoon: The Indian Ocean and Future of American Power, New York: Random House.
9. Lanteigne, Marc (2009). Chinese Foreign Policy: An Introduction, Abingdon: Routledge.
10. Lintner, Bertil (2012). Great Game East: India, China and the Struggle for Asia's most volatile frontier, New Delhi: Harper Collins publication.
11. Liu, Xuecheng (1994). The Sino-Indian Border Dispute and Sino-Indian Relations, USA: University Press of America.
12. Mohan, Raja (2013). Samudra Manthan: Sino-Indian Rivalry in Indo-Pacific, New Delhi: Oxford University Press India.
13. Pant, Harsh V. (2012). Rise of China: Implications for India, New Delhi: Cambridge University Press.
14. Patel, Bimal N. *et al.* (2016). Indian Ocean and Maritime Security: Competition, Cooperation and Threat, India: Routledge.
15. Ramesh, Jairam (2005). Making Sense of Chindia: Reflections on China and India, New Delhi: India Research Press.
16. Sen, Tansen (2015). Buddhism, Diplomacy, and Trade: The Realignment of India-China Relations, 600–1400, Maryland: Rowman and Littlefield.
17. Surei, M. and S. Prasai (2015). Strengthening Transparency and Access to Information on Transboundary Rivers in South Asia, New Delhi: The Asia Foundation.

18. Swamy, Subramanian (2001). India's China Perspective, New Delhi: Konrak Publishers.
19. Tripathi, D.P. and B.R. Deepak (2012). India China Relation: Future Perspectives, New Delhi: Vij Books.
20. Tzou, Byron N. (1990). China and International Law: The Boundary Disputes, New York: Praeger Publication.
21. Vertzberger, Yaacov (1983). The Enduring Entente: Sino-Pakistan Relations (1960– 80). New York: Praeger Publication.
22. Wu, Shicun and Zou Keyuan (2009). Maritime Security in the South China Sea: Regional Implications and International Cooperation, UK: Ashgate Publishing.
23. Zhu, Cuiping (2018). India's Ocean: Can China and India Coexist? Singapore: Springer.

Articles in Journals

1. Acharya, Alka (2008). "India-China Relations: Towards a Shared Vision", *Economic and Political Weekly*, 43(4): 10–13.
2. Cohen Stephen P. (1998). "The United States and India: Recovering Lost Ground", *SAIS Review of International Affairs,* 18(1): 93–107.
3. Cordner, Lee G. (2010). "Rethinking maritime security in the Indian Ocean Region", *Journal of the Indian Ocean Region,* Australian National Centre for Ocean Resources and Security.
4. Bercovitch, Jacob (2014). "Conflict and Conflict Management in Organizations: A Framework for Analysis", *Hong Kong Journal of Public Administration,* 5(2): 104–123.
5. Bueger, Christian (2014). "What is maritime security", *Marine Policy,* 53: 159–164.
6. David, M. Malone and Rohan, Mukherjee (2010). "India and China: Conflict and Cooperation", *Survival,* 52(1): 137–158.
7. Garver, John W. (1996). "Sino-Indian Rapprochement and the Sino-Pakistan Entente," *Political Science Quarterly*, 111(2): 323–347.
8. Garver, John W. (2002). "The China-India-U.S. Triangle Strategic Relations in the Post-Cold War Era", *The National Bureau of Asian Research,* 13(5): 1–61.
9. Granados, Ulises (2018) "India's Approaches to the South China Sea: Priorities and Balances", *Asia & the Pacific Policy Studies*, 5: 122–137.
10. Holslag, Jonathan (2009). "The Persistent Military Security Dilemma between China and India", *The Journal of Strategic Studies* 32(6): 811–840.
11. Hong, Nong (2012). "Charting a Maritime Security Cooperation Mechanism in the Indian Ocean: Sharing Responsibilities among Littoral States and User States", *Strategic Analysis*, 36(3): 400–412.

12. Holmes, James and Toshi Yoshihara (2008). "China's Naval Ambitions in the Indian Ocean", *The Journal of Strategic Studies,* 31(3): 367–394.
13. Ho, Joshua (2006). "The Security of Sea Lanes in Southeast Asia", *Asian Survey,* 46 (4): 558–574.
14. Kaplan, Robert D. (2009). "Centre Stage for the 21st Century: Power Plays in the Indian Ocean", *Foreign Affairs,* 88 (2): 16–29.
15. Khalid, N. (2012). "The Sea lanes under strain", *IUP Journal of International Relations,* 6(2): 57–66.
16. Kumar, Anand (2012). "Chinese Engagement with the Maldives: Impact on Security Environment in the Indian Ocean Region", *Strategic Analysis,* 36(2): 276–289.
17. Lanteigne, Marc (2008). "China's Maritime Security and the 'Malacca Dilemma", *Asian Security,* 4(2): 143–161.
18. Malik, V.P. (2012). "Reflections on Indio-Myanmar Relations", *Scholar Warrior,* Autumn: 2–13.
19. Mizo, R. (2016). "India, China and Climate Cooperation", *Indian Council of World Affairs, Sage Publications,* 72(4): 1–20.
20. Parmar, Sarabjeet Singh (2014). "Maritime Security in the Indian Ocean an Indian Perspective", *Journal of Defence Studies,* 8(1): 49–63.
21. Price, G. (2007). "India and China: Cooperation and Competition", Asia *Programme Briefing Paper, Chatham House,* 07(01): 01–11.
22. Rana, Waheeda (2015). "Theory of Complex Interdependence: A Comparative Analysis of Realist and Neoliberal Thoughts", *International Journal of Business and Social Science,* 6 (2): 290–297.
23. Scott, David (2012). "Conflict Irresolution in the South China Sea", *Asian Survey,* University of California, 52(6): 1019–1042.
24. Scott, David (2008). "The Great Power 'Great Game' between India and China: 'The Logic of Geography", *Geopolitics,* 13(1): 1–26.
25. Shah, Dhara P. (2017). "China's Maritime Security Strategy: An Assessment of The White Paper on Asia-Pacific Security Cooperation", *Maritime Affairs,* 13(1).
26. Sidhu, Waheguru Pal Singh and Yuan, Jing-dong (2001). "Resolving the Sino-Indian Border Dispute," *Asian Survey,* 41(2), 351–376.
27. Siddiqi, Farhan Hanif (2012). "India-China Relations in the 21st Century: Impact on Regional and Global Politics", *Pakistan Horizon,* 65(2): 59–72.
28. Till, Geoffrey (2008). "A Cooperative Strategy for 21st Century Sea power: What's New? What's Next? A View From Outside", *Defence Studies,* 8(2): 240–257.
29. Villaruel, Jemimah J.C. (2015). "India's Interests in the South China Sea", *Centre for International relations and Strategic Studies,* 2(8).

30. Wang, Vincent Wei-cheng (2011). "Chindia" or Rivalry? Rising China, Rising India, and Contending Perspectives on India China Relations", *Asian Perspective*, 35(3): 437–469.
31. Yong, Tan Tai & See Chak Mun (2009). "The Evolution of India-ASEAN Relations", *India Review*, 8(1): 20–42.

Chapters in Edited Books

1. Acharya, A. (1998). "Beyond Anarchy: Third World Instability and International Order after the Cold War" in Stephanie Neumann (eds.) *International Theory and the Third World,* London: Macmillan.
2. Ashley, J.T. (2012). "Asia Responds to Its Rising Powers: China and India", in Ashley J. Tellis, Travis Tanner, Jessica Keough (eds.), *Strategic Asia 2011–12,* Washington D.C.: The National Bureau of Asian Research.
3. Bajpai, K. (2000). "India-China and Asian Security", in Bajpai, K. and Mattoo (eds.) *The Peacock and the Dragon,* in India-China relations in the 21st Century, New Delhi: Haran and Publication Private Ltd.
4. Brar, Ateetmani (2015). "India-China Maritime Cooperation," in Gurpreet S. Khurana and Antara Ghosal Singh (eds.) *India and China: Exploring Convergences in Asia,* New Delhi: National Maritime Foundation.
5. Fraver, M. Taylor (2011). "China Views India's Rise: Deepening Co-operation, Managing Differences," in Ashley Tellis, Travis Tanner, and Jessica.
6. Keogh (eds.) *Asia Responds to its Rising Powers: China and India,* Seattle, WA: National Bureau of Asian Research.
7. Ganguly, Sumit (2004). "India and China: Border Issues, Domestic Integration, and International Security," in Francine Frankel and Harry Harding (eds.) *The India-China Relationship*. New York: Columbia University Press.
8. Hue, T. (2012). "China's 21st Century Status and Challenges, in Sudhir S. Devare, Swaran Singh and Reena Marwah (eds.) *Emerging China: Prospects for Partnership in Asia,* New Delhi: Routledge.
9. Kusaka, Sumio (2016). "Indo-Pacific Maritime Security: Challenges and Cooperation", in David Brewster (ed.) *Indo-Pacific maritime security: Challenges and cooperation,* Commonwealth Government and The Australian National University.
10. Li, L. and Srinath Raghavan, (2013). "Stability in Southern Asia", in Ashley J. Tellis and Sean Mirski (eds.) *Crux of Asia: China, India, and the Emerging Global Order,* Washington, DC: Carnegie Endowment for International Peace.
11. Mattoo, Amitabh (2000). "Imagining China", in Bajpai, K. and Mattoo (eds.) *The Peacock and the Dragon,* India-China relations in 21st Century, New Delhi: Haranand Publication Private Ltd.

12. Malik, Aruna Kumar and William Nunes, (2016). "Revisiting maritime security in the Indian Ocean: A note on current scenario", in Patel, N. Malik, Aruna and William Nunes, (eds.) *Indian Ocean and Maritime Security: Competition, Cooperation and Threat,* New York: Routledge.
13. Mishra, Sylvia (2015). "Great Game in the Indian Ocean Region: Revisiting the Legacy of Mahan", in Sidda Goud, Manisha Mookherjee (eds.), *China in Indian Ocean Region,* Allied Publishers.
14. Shie, Tamara Renee (2006). "Maritime Piracy in Southeast Asia: The Evolution and Progress of Intra-ASEAN Cooperation", in Graham Gerard Ong-Webb (ed.) *Piracy, Maritime Terrorism and Securing the Malacca Straits,* Singapore: Institute of Southeast Asian Studies.
15. Susan, L.S. (2004). "One-Sided Rivalry: China's Perceptions and Policies Toward India," in Francine R. Frankel and Harry Harding, (eds.) The *IndiaChina Relationship: What the United States Needs to Know,* New York: Columbia University Press.
16. Ye Zhang (2015). "The Current Situation and Prospects for Sino-Indian Maritime Security Cooperation", in Gurpreet S Khurana and Antara Ghosal Singh (eds.) *India and China: Exploring Convergences in Asia,* New Delhi: National Maritime Foundation.

Articles in a Newspaper/Magazine/Web-Portal

1. Aroor, Shiv (2013). "Myanmar Army intrudes into Manipur border village, tries to set up base camp", *India Today,* New Delhi, August 28, 2013.
2. Banerjee, Ajay (2017). Indian Navy looks to dominate Malacca Straits, *The Tribune,* New Delhi, 11th June 2017.
3. Dahiya, O. (2015). "Maritime Security of India: Challenges and Opportunities", *Employment News Weekly,* New Delhi, 42 (1): 32.
4. Dikshit, Sandeep (2013). "One river, two countries, too many dams", *The Hindu,* New Delhi, 02 April 2013
5. Dikshit, Sandeep (2012). "India, China move to maritime cooperation", *The Hindu,* New Delhi, 2 March 2012.
6. Kasturi, C.S. (2017). "China holds back data on water", *The Telegraph,* New Delhi, 19 August 2017.
7. Krishnan, Ananth (2013). "China details Indian Ocean strategy and interest", *The Hindu,* Chennai, 09 June 2013.
8. Parsai, Gargi (2013). "India, China renew flood data pact on Brahmaputra", *The Hindu, New Delhi,* 20 May 20 2013.
9. Suryanarayana, P.S. (2003). "Sino-Indian naval exercise", *The Hindu,* New Delhi, 7 November 2003.

Internet Sources (Magazine & Newspaper)

1. Chaudhary, Rahul (2015). "Five Reasons the World needs to Pay Heed to India's New Maritime Security Strategy", *The Wire,* New Delhi, 22 December 2015, (Online: Web). Accessed on 5 January 2016, URL: https://thewire.in/17741/five-reasons-the-world-needs-to-pay-heed-toindias-new-maritime-security-strategy/
2. Browne, Ryan and Brad Lendon (2017). "US destroyer sails close to disputed island in the South China Sea", CNN, 2 July 2017 (Online: Web) Accessed on 8 Sept. 2017 URL: https://edition.cnn.com/2017/07/02/politics/usnavy-south-china-sea/index.html
3. "India Sends Three Major Warships for Joint Naval Exercises", *People's Daily,* 12 November 2003 (Online: Web) Accessed on 4 April 2016 URL: http://sars.china.com.cn/english/international/79854.htm
4. "Killing of Sea Bird not a Big Blow to LTTE Shipping Operations", *The Sunday Times,* 18 February 1996 (Online: Web) Accessed on 4 April 2016 URL: http://www.sundaytimes.lk/960218/oped/mil.html
5. Lendon, Brad and Steve George (2017). "China sends troops to Djibouti, establishes first overseas military base", *CNN.* 13 July 2017 (Online: Web) Accessed on 4 April 2016 URL: https://edition.cnn.com/2017/07/12/asia/china-djibouti-militarybase/index.html
6. Mohan, C. Raja (2015). "Revealed: India's Master Plan for the Indian Ocean", *The National Interest,* [Online: web] Accessed 14 March 2016 URL: http://nationalinterest.org/blog/the-buzz/revealed-indias-master-planthe-indian-ocean-13198?page=2
7. Parameswaran, Prashanth (2015). "Japan to Join US, India in Military Exercises this Year", *The Diplomat,* 1 July 2015 (Online: Web) Accessed on 5 April 2016 URL: https://thediplomat.com/2015/07/japan-to-join-us-india-inmilitary-exercises-this-year/
8. Pillai, M.G.G. (2001). "Archipelago of Dreams", *Outlook India,* 12 February 2001 (Online: Web) Accessed on 14 August 2016 URL: https://www.outlookindia.com/magazine/story/archipelago-of-dreams/210846
9. Roy, Shubhajit (2012). China to start 'maritime dialogue", *Indian Express,* New Delhi, 2 Mar 2012 (Online: Web) Accessed on 24 Sept. 2016URL: http://archive.indianexpress.com/news/india-china-to-start--maritimedialogue-/918922/.
10. Samaranayake, Nilanthi (2014). "The Indian Ocean: A Great-Game Danger Zone", *The National Interest,* 30 May 2014 (Online: Web) Accessed on 19 Oct. 2016 URL: http://nationalinterest.org/feature/the-indian-oceangreat-power-danger-zone-10568
11. Singh, Abhijit (2014). "The Developing India-China Maritime Dynamic", *The Diplomat,* 1 May 2014 (Online: Web) Accessed on 19 Oct. 2016 URL:

https://thediplomat.com/2014/05/the-developing-india-china-maritimedy namic/

12. Singh, N. (2017). "China and India water 'dispute' after border stand-off", *Khadka Environment Correspondent*, BBC World Service [Online: web] Accessed 18 September 2017, URL: http://www.bbc.com/news/worldasia-41303082.
13. Tharoor, Ishaan (2013). "After Fighting over Mountains, India and China Lock Horns in the Indian Ocean", *Time,* 16 May 2013 (Online: Web) Accessed on 19 Oct. 2016 URL: http://world.time.com/2013/05/16/after-fightingover-mountains-india-and-china-lock-horns-in-the-indian-ocean/print
14. Woody, Christopher (2017). "China is not Father Christmas': India's concern about Beijing's expansion grows after a new port deal", *Business Insider,* 14 August 2017 (Online: Web) Accessed on 19 Oct. 2016, URL: https://www.businessinsider.in/china-is-not-father-christmas-indiasconcern-about-beijings-expansion-grows-after-a-new-portdeal/articleshow/60062895.cms
15. Yoshihara, T. and Holmes, J. (2011). "The Meaning of Sea Power", *The Diplomat,* New Delhi, 10 December 2011 (Online: Web) Accessed on 19th Oct. 2016 URL: http://thediplomat.com/2011/12/the-meaning-of-seapower/ on 15 August 2015).

Other Internet Sources (Including Web-Portal)

1. Baruah, D.M. (2015). "India's Evolving Maritime Strategy India shifts its focus from 'using' to 'securing' maritime security in the Indo-Pacific", [Online: web] Accessed on 12 January 2016 URL: https://thediplomat.com/2015/12/indias-evolving-maritime-strategy
2. Chang, C. (2016). "Sino-India Strategic Rivalry: Misperception or Reality", *Centre for International Maritime Security,* [Online: web] Accessed on 21st August 2017 URL: http://cimsec.org/sino-india-strategic-rivalrymis perception-reality/24499
3. Chandrashekhara (2014). "Piracy on the rise in Malacca straits again", *Sand Prints,* 8 January 2014 (Online: Web) Accessed on 19th Oct. 2016 URL: https://chandrashekharasandprints.wordpress.com/2014/01/08/piracyon-the-rise-in-malacca-straits-again/
4. Chunhao, Lou (2017). "China-India Maritime Security: Competition or Cooperation?" *China Policy Institute: Analysis.* [Online: web] Accessed 21st September 2017 URL: https://cpianalysis.org/2017/10/16/china-indiamari time-security-competition-or-cooperation/
5. Fallingham, Z. (2013). "China-India Relations: Cooperation and Conflict", *Geopolitical Monitor,* [Online: web] Accessed 15th June 2016 URL

https://www.geopoliticalmonitor.com/china-india-relationscooperation-and-conflict-4798/.

6. George, Steve and Manveena Suri (2018). "India looks to build military presence in Seychelles", 18th February 2018 (Online: Web) Accessed on 19th January 2018 URL: http://www.localnews8.com/news/national-world/aschina-concerns-grow-india-looks-to-build-military-presence-in seychelles/703846354
7. "Global Opposition to U.S. Surveillance and Drones, but Limited Harm to America's Image," *Pew Research Center*, 14th July 2014 (Online: Web) Accessed on 19th Oct. 2016 URL: http://www.pewglobal.org/files/2014/07/201407-14-Balance-of-Power.pdf.
8. Herberg, Mikkal E. (2016). "The Role of Energy in Disputes over the South China Sea", *Maritime Awareness Project Analysis*, 28th June 2016 (Online: Web) Accessed on 19 Oct. 2016 URL:http://maritimeawareness project.org/wpcontent/uploads/2016/07/analysis_herberg_062816.pdf
9. IMF-WEO, (2015). International Monetary Fund, World Economic Outlook, "Database", (Online: Web) Accessed on 19th Oct. 2016 URL: https://www.imf.org/external/pubs/ft/weo/2015/02/weodata/index.aspx
10. IONS (Indian Ocean Naval Symposium) (2018). "About IONS", [Online: web] Accessed 6 November 2017 URL: http://www.ions.global/
11. Jakobson, Linda and Rory Medcalf (2015). "The Perception Gap: Reading China's Maritime Objectives in Indo-Pacific Asia," *The Lowy Institute*, 23rd June 2015 URL: http://www.lowyinstitute.org/publications/reading-chinasmaritime-objectives-Indo-Pacific-asia-perception-gap#_ednref68
12. Kaplan, Robert (2014). China's Unfolding Indian Ocean Strategy - Analysis, *Centre for New American Security.* [Online: web] Accessed 11th August 2017 URL: http://www.cnas.org/content/china%E2%80%99s-unfoldingindian-ocean-strategy-%E2%80%93analysis#.U6R8WZTVheB
13. Khurana, Gurpreet Singh (2016). "First China-India Maritime Dialogue: Beyond 'Icebreaking'", *Centre for International Maritime Security,* [Online: web] Accessed 15th December 2016 URL: http://cimsec.org/first-chinaindia-maritime-dialogue-beyond-icebreaking/23990
14. Nalpathamkalam, Abhilash Roy (2012). "Cooperation Without Trust: India-China Relations Today", *Heinrich Böll Sifting*, 11th October 2012 URL: https://in.boell.org/2012/10/11/cooperation-without-trust-india-chinarela tions-today
15. Nath, Kamal (2005). "India, China Economic Ties Poised to Grow", *Statement at the World Economic Forum,* Davos, Switzerland, 27 January 2005 (Online: Web) Accessed on 19 Oct. 2016 URL: http://pib.nic.in/newsite/erelcontent.aspx?relid=6761
16. Outlook (2005). "Beyond Bhai Bhai", *Outlook India*, 11th April 2005, [Online: web] Accessed 29 July 2016 URL: https://www.outlookindia.com/website/story/beyond-bhaibhai/227029.

17. Sinha, Neha (2017). "China's First Overseas Military Base in Djibouti", *Vivekananda International Foundation*, [Online: web] Accessed 12th October 2017 URL: http://www.vifindia.org/article/2017/august/24/china-s-firstover seas-military-base-in-djibouti
18. Singh, Abhijit (2016). "Why India's South China Sea Stand Matters", *Institute for Defence Studies and Analyses,* New Delhi, 19th August 2016 URL: https://idsa.in/idsacomments/why-india-south-china-sea-standmatters_asingh_190816
19. Singh, Abhijit (2015). "Decoding China's Military Strategy White Paper: Assessing the Maritime Implications", *Institute for Defence Studies and Analysis,* New Delhi, 2nd June 2015, [Online: web] Accessed 14th March 2017

URL

1. http://news.xinhuanet.com/english/china/2015- 05/26/c_134271001_2.htm
2. Singh, A.K. (2017). "Unpacking China's White Paper on Maritime Cooperation under BRI", *Institute for Defence Studies and Analyses*, New Delhi, 28 June 2017 URL: https://idsa.in/issuebrief/chinas-white-paper-on-maritimecooperation-under-bri_aksingh_280617
3. Waldo, Mohamed Abshir (2009). "The Two Piracies in Somalia: Why the World Ignores the Other?" *Somali Press Review*, [Online: web] Accessed 4th April 2016 URL: https://issuu.com/abelgalois/docs/somalias_twin_sea_piracies

Policy Paper/Issue Briefs/Working Paper

1. Ameri, Michele and M. Shewchuk (2007). "Maritime Security and Safety", *United Nations Institute for Training and Research,* Division for Ocean Affairs and the Law of the Sea, *Briefing,* October 17.
2. Bateman, Sam *et al.* (2011). *ASEAN and The Indian Ocean: The Key Maritime Links*, Singapore: S. Rajaratnam School of International Studies, Nanyang Technological University (Policy Paper*).*
3. Feldt, L.P. Roell and Thiele, R. (2013). "Maritime Security-Perspectives for a Comprehensive Approach*", Institute for Strategic, Political, Security and Economic Consultancy (ISPSW),* Berlin, Germany, Issue No. 222.
4. Hangzo, Pau Khan Khup (2011). "Non-Traditional Security Challenges in the Indian Ocean Region", in Sam Bateman, Jane Chan, and Euan Graham (eds.), *ASEAN and the Indian Ocean*, RISI Policy Paper.
5. Hatcher, J. (2013). "China's Growing Indian Ocean Maritime Interests: Sowing the Seed of Conflict", *Australia, Sea Power Centre.*
6. Rubel, R.C. (2012). "Navies and Economic Prosperity—the New Logic of Sea Power", *Corbett Working Paper*, London: King's College.

Conference/Seminar Paper

1. Ghosh, P.K. (2004). "Maritime Security Challenges in South Asia and the Indian Ocean: Response Strategies", Paper prepared for the Center for Strategic and International Studies—American-Pacific Sea Lanes Security Institute Conference on Maritime Security in Asia, Honolulu, Hawaii, January 18–20.
2. Mohan, C. Raja (2013). "China's rise, America's pivot, and India's Asian ambiguity", India 2012: a symposium on the year that was, URL: http://www.indiaseminar.com/2013/641/641_c_raja_mohan.htm